# OCCAM'S
# NIGHTMARE

ISBN 978-1-304-03018-4

# For Mum

**(look, Mum, I finally finished something!)**

# CONTENTS

# INTRODUCTION

*Doggett: "You're familiar with the principle of Occam's razor?"*
*Scully: "Yeah. You take every possible explanation and you choose the*
*simplest one. Agent Mulder used to refer to it as 'Occam's principle of*
*limited imagination'."*

*The X Files*
*8X04 "Patience"*

It's June of 2012 and I'm sitting in a hired lecture theatre with what I can best describe to be a UFO cult.

David Wilcock, handsome, 39 years old (though he looks ten years younger), perfect teeth, hair like David Spade, is a self-proclaimed journalist, researcher of ancient civilisations, and expert on "consciousness science," and he's standing here, archetypically American with the flair of a motivational speaker, educating us about the secret extraterrestrial organisation that rules the world.

For tens of thousands of years, a species of intergalactic humanoid immigrants has walked among us in secret, interbred with humanity to sustain a dynasty of shadow government over human beings, known to us as the Illuminati. Their activities are nefarious. Despite the opinions of some misinformed people (misinformed deliberately, it seems, by the elite) these Illuminati are *not* Annunaki reptiles from the Pleiades constellation, but rather the cone-headed beings who at one time populated Atlantis. Their constant warring meant that ultimately they were nuked (or allowed to be nuked) by the council of beings who form the intergalactic federation and uphold the laws of the universe.

We shouldn't call them "aliens," Wilcock tells us. That's a prejudicial term made up by Hollywood. He prefers to call them "ETs."

You're probably wondering how I got here. I mean, I wasn't always curious about the intergalactic federation and its politics – originally, I was only interested in human politics, which is why, in September 2011, I began following with some curiosity the "Occupy Wall Street" movement. What was it? It was a sudden worldwide upsurge of youthful disillusionment about... something. The media was always confused. It was a protest about nothing, or about everything, their noted and deliberate refusal to state a goal or mission or list of demands frequently cited by the media as evidence that they didn't know what they were protesting about. According to Occupy, they didn't need an excuse to be angry. They just wanted to get mad, mad at the establishment, mad at the super-rich, mad at the culture of greed that led the world along the rocky path through one unnecessary economic crash after another. By not establishing goals, the Occupy movement gave a message of refusal to "work within the system." By not adhering to a political ideology, they were able to gather numbers, to get support from any political ideology that felt the world should be somehow different to the way it is (which is, let's face it, pretty much all of them, almost by definition.)

But although the Occupy movement didn't share any one political ideology – socialists, anarchists, libertarians, hippies, even some hard-right nationalists joined the fray – they did find, oddly enough, some common ground. They all thought, to some degree, that the world is run by a group of people who have become unaccountable. They just disagreed about who those people are. And although they fought for a large variety of different causes, some were a little stranger than others. Case in point: One of the Occupiers, actually a founding member of my local chapter of the group and an administrator of the Facebook page, said through the course of regular conversation something about Obama having lived on Mars for a time.

Now, I didn't know if it was supposed to be some kind of metaphor, the really complicated kind usually reserved for writers of political cartoons, but it was definitely "Mars" that he'd said. Specifically, that Obama had been recruited by the CIA back in the 80s to work at a Mars base that he accessed via a "jump room." This, I thought, was a strange cause for Occupy Wall Street to adopt – economic reform, corporate transparency, and openness about Obama's interstellar past.

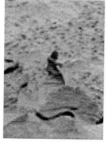 Curious, I Googled for references to Obama on Mars, to figure out what that could possibly mean. Maybe it was some kind of inside joke. What I found very quickly was a man's name – Andrew Basiago. Basiago is a lawyer of apparently high standing in Vancouver, Washington state. Sometime around 2008 or earlier, he adopted an unusual hobby – analysing and poring over terrain photographs sent back from the Spirit rover on Mars. One image I came across was one I'd seen before. I actually

remember a series of light-hearted news reports about the so-called "person on Mars," a rock formation captured on film by the rover that looks kind of like a little guy sitting there with his arm pointing out. Mainstream society tends to see this kind of thing as a curiosity, a funny coincidence, like seeing Jesus's face in an Oreo. But seeing that picture, the little gremlin guy bathed in shadow and pointing to nothing in particular, seems to have done something strange to Andrew Basiago's mind.

Sometime in 2008, Basiago started writing academic papers and submitting them to the National Geographic Society, who sadly declined to publish any of them. The papers, the first of which is titled *The Discovery of Life on Mars*, is a detailed catalogue of all the life forms, statues and buildings that Basiago has found in the Spirit pictures. And what's interesting isn't that Basiago was seeing shapes in the soil and mistaking them for something organic, like the "person" and the famous face in Cydonia. He was actually looking at a completely empty plot of Martian real estate and talking about all the animals he saw there. He was imagining it.

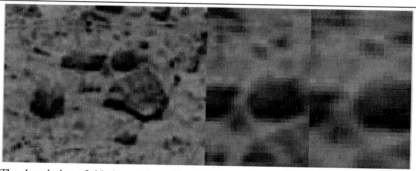

The description of this image from *The Discovery of Life on Mars*: "The humanoid in The Rock Enclosure on Tsiolkovski Ridge is surrounded by other anomalous beings. To his right on the hillside, bald humanoids in blue clothing are sitting on the hillside (left). Up the hill, other beings are standing behind a large rock shaped into the face of a rabbit, gerbil or similar small animal (right). Other humanoid beings can be seen standing in apertures in the soil among statues of huge heads (bottom)."[1]

---

[1] Basiago, Andrew D. (2008). *The Discovery of Life on Mars*. Mars Anomaly Research Society. This is probably the only academic reference that this paper will ever attract. It should be noted that the "Mars Anomaly Research Society" that I'm formally attributing at the publisher of this document boasts a membership of one – Andrew Basiago, founder, president and sole contributor. If you're at all interested in reading it, as of 2012 it was still available at Basiago's website, along with all his other "academic" contributions, at http://www.projectmars.net/

Despite this, word found its way to the internet UFO community where people started passing it around and commenting that they could see all the bald blue aliens and gerbil face statues in the sand too. The reasoning seems to be the appeal to Mr Basiago's authority – he's a respected lawyer, he has two university degrees (neither of which have anything to do with alien-spotting in grainy photographs), and he seems really confident and sure about what he's saying. If he sees aliens, then consarn it, there are aliens. But the most important proof of the truth of what he's discovered is National Geographic's refusal to acknowledge it. *What are they trying to cover up?*

Having all these people embrace Basiago's ideas has only served to expand them to ever weirder territories. In 2009, Basiago began to claim that, as a nine year old, he had been involved with something he calls "Project Pegasus" which is a time-space bridge of some kind invented by Nikola Tesla that the United States has owned since the 70s. For some reason, the US government was shooting kids through these time portals willy-nilly as though they'd never read Bradbury's *Sound of Thunder* or even seen that Simpsons episode based on it. Basiago claims to have met Jesus, to have been involved in the CIA's psychic remote viewing experiments, and to have visited the USA's base on Mars. And another member of Project Pegasus at this time was of course a young Barack Obama.

By this point I was completely transfixed by Basiago's rapidly intensifying descent into fantasy and the way that people were willing to believe it no matter how far his spaceship floated away from this rational dimension. And now I had rational people, average people with average jobs and average social lives, at a protest halfway across the world from Basiago, citing Obama's secret involvement with the Pegasus Project from his base on Mars as evidence that the United States has a corrupt political system.

But there's more to this story – remembering this fellow's specific terminology, "jump room," I was led to a website maintained by one David Wilcock. The words "jump room" come up in an interview that Wilcock is having with a couple of other weirdos in which he's talking about the same kind of stuff Basiago was pulling out, though Wilcock doesn't have the thousand-mile-stare of a lunatic when he speaks about it. It occurred to me that Basiago hadn't just made everything up. This stuff about Mars bases and time travel and UFOs, it didn't just spring fully formed in Basiago's imagination.

Basiago had been listening to Wilcock. And although what Wilcock was saying was still nuts, it was a little closer to sanity than what Basiago had been spouting. That stuff about Obama was pure Basiago, so Basiago actually took someone else's theory, added to it, made it crazier, and released it back into the wild. It's like insanity follows the laws of Darwinian evolution.

There was a point in the Wilcock interview that serves, I think, as a great introduction to this book. While Wilcock was talking about secret Mars bases, Martian artifacts, terraforming the planet, teleportation, memory wipes and artificial realities, someone else in the interview suddenly said aloud what I was with some amusement beginning to realise.

It was the plot of *Total Recall*.

Somewhere behind this string of Chinese whispers of a conspiracy theory some guy was feeding me at Occupy Wall Street, some guy who wanted to lobby the government to reveal it knows the secret of time travel because a lawyer from Washington says he met Obama on Mars after listening to David Wilcock discuss jump rooms on UFOs, somewhere back behind all the extra details that have been tacked on at every point in this chain like a katamari ball of crazy, at the beginning there lies the real truth behind it all. And the truth in this case was that someone saw *Total Recall* and mistook it for a documentary. That's it. Whether they really believed it or just found inspiration from it to weave an elaborate fantasy, the conspiracy theory that perhaps thousands believe actually began as a Schwarzenegger movie.

David Wilcock smiled and acknowledged, yes, it was exactly the plot of *Total Recall*, down to the memory wipe chair and, probably, the woman with three breasts. So you have to conclude that he took all this from a movie, right? Don't be so sure.

Wilcock says that it proves everything he says is true, because they went and made a movie about it.[2]

---

[2] From *Jumproom to Mars: A new conversation with David Wilcock*, viewed on YouTube at http://tinyurl.com/ctu2n7n
Wilcock: "Daniel pointed out to me something that is sort of snuck in to Total Recall that you don't really notice if you're not paying attention. But at the end of the movie— obviously if you've seen it you know that there's an alien system that they find there, Schwarzenegger himself actually puts his hand on this thing that fires off, some kind of gigantic technology that puts these heat rods into the ice cap, in the southern and northern pole, I would imagine, melting the ice back into atmosphere which in turn basically makes

And that's what brought me ultimately here, to this small room in the Brisbane Convention Centre, listening to the jump room guy discuss beings who, for PC reasons, we really should be calling ETs rather than aliens. It was kind of titillating to actually get to meet the man who started me on this journey of discovery. Since I began work on this book I'd hoped to be able to get into one of David Icke's lectures, Icke being one of the most prominent of the eccentrics I was researching, but I'd narrowly missed the boat on Icke's 2012 Australian tour, which he alluded would probably be his last due to the deteriorating health condition that his obsession with alternative medicine was supposed to be curing. So when I'd heard that Californian psychic Wilcock was coming to Australia, I decided to settle.

I'd heard about Wilcock numerous times throughout my investigations into fringe pseudoscientific culture, but he really came onto my radar again when I stumbled upon a truly bizarre radio interview that he gave in which he begins by crying uncontrollably in the fakest way imaginable. The Illuminati, he sobbed, had been sending him death threats. According to his tormentors, if he got away with mere torture, he would be lucky. The only way that he could avoid his fate was if lots and lots of people read his latest article about alien conspiracies so that it could rack up thousands of hits. That was their ultimatum – a bizarre one to be sure, but Wilcock swore that he was merely the messenger. What followed was 90 minutes of some of the most bizarre conspiracy fantasy I've ever heard, including a call-in from an anonymous Illuminati whistleblower with the worst attempt at an Irish accent I've ever heard, who purported to be calling direct from an orbiting spaceship.[3]

---

the air on Mars breathable so that it's like a colonisable place. What you see at the end of the movie is that there's a… a mountain, where the atmosphere blows out of the top, and it's *exactly* the shape of a pyramid. And they never talk about it, it just kind of happens." The circular reasoning at work here is that Wilcock, having discovered that his "source" into the government's Mars colony project, Daniel, has basically fed him the plot to *Total Recall*, decides that *Total Recall* must be based on a true story rather than the other way around. After that, Wilcock then takes elements from *Total Recall* to use as evidence about things that are truly happening in the world. The line of reasoning is summed up thus: Daniel sees a movie about Mars colonies → Daniel comes to believe there are Mars colonies → Wilcock believes Daniel → Wilcock then sees the movie → Wilcock, already believing in Mars colonies, comes to believe the movie reflects reality → Being that the movie is true, everything in the movie must be true, i.e. the existence of pyramids on Mars and, presumably, three-breasted prostitutes.
Later in this interview, they also discuss how *2001: A Space Odyssey* is a true story.

[3] http://tinyurl.com/cgsavw7

About 70 bucks would have earned me a ticket for Wilcock's six hour conference. Pay twice that, and I would get an additional hour of Q&A, a group photograph and a gift bag. What the hell – in for a penny, in for a pound. The "gift bag," as it turned out, contained a copy of Wilcock's book (New York Times bestseller, it insists), the latest issue of the alternative *Veritas* magazine that hosted the event, and a piece of paper somewhat hastily headlined "DAVILD WILCOCK SURVEY."

There was, as I expected, absolutely no photography or recording permitted at the event. As much as I would have liked to sneak a digital recorder in for my own notation, I admit that I was a little nervous around these people. One look at the various middle-to-late-aged hippies standing in line (including one granny with an eyepatch who looked like a retired Bond villain) conformed to my expectations. I would need to take care, here. I wouldn't want to look too bored or too amused, I'd have to avoid speaking to anyone in depth, and I would need to ensure I applauded when appropriate. This wasn't just an awkward party where I wind up speaking to the lone conspiracy theorist – I was in their hive. It was I who was different. And these people were highly paranoid by nature. If they suspected I wasn't there for the right reasons, they wouldn't just shun me. They would think I was a paid enemy agent. Wilcock had been receiving death threats, after all.

The bizarreness of what I'd gotten myself into really hit home when the evening's host introduced his guest as "one of the world's most published authors on quantum physics." It was soon to become very clear that these people had a very different concept to the one I had about both "quantum physics" and "publication."

David Wilcock is his own hero. While Icke finds strength in his humility, Wilcock is notorious among his detractors for his egomania. In his youth, he idolised the famous psychic Edgar Cayce, and now he claims to literally be Cayce, reincarnated. Not just that, but his past lives include Pythagoras, King David, and the Atlantean ambassador to an alien race called "Ra-Ta." He never mentions his awkward 60 years as a trucker named Brett. In every seminar, he finds time to explain how he knows he's the reincarnation of Cayce – it's the astounding facial similarity, you see. Never mind the fact that there's no facial similarity whatsoever. Edgar Cayce, for example, didn't have a towering fivehead.

After introductions, Wilcock takes to the stage like a rock star, to the momentous applause of his 200-or so local fans. I try to look impressed, but I've been allocated the most uncomfortable chair known to affordable function seating, and beside me on both sides are two unreasonably portly gentlemen, one of whom is farting *constantly* (I couldn't say which). My recurring neck cramp is taking serious issue with the seating arrangement, and it feels like some small elven creature is sitting on my shoulder and jamming a cattle brand into my shoulderblade whenever I droop into the wrong posture. This is how I'm going to be spending the entire day, with very few, very short breaks (Wilcock insists that he needs every minute he's got – what he's telling us today is the abridged version of a lecture that usually takes 16 hours).

## Occam's Nightmare

In the beginning of the 14th century a Franciscan friar known as William of Occam came up with a logical principle, or at least the principle is attributed to him, which became known as "Occam's razor." The principle, in its technical form, is "entities should not be multiplied beyond necessity." Entities, in this case, refer to elements or complexities within an explanation. You may have heard it phrased in popular culture as something more like "the simplest explanation is usually the correct one," but that's not a very good way of putting it because most explanations for things are pretty damn complicated. It's better to say something like "the simplest explanation that matches all the known facts." Once you prove a theory wrong by showing how it's not possible, then you can move up the ladder to the next, more complicated explanation.

**Entia non sunt multiplicanda praeter necessitatem.**

**Entities should not be multiplied beyond necessity.**

*William of Occam*

Let's imagine something that needs explaining. Let's say, raining frogs. One day, the clouds open up, and it just rains frogs for an hour. Everyone is scratching their heads wondering how it happened, because frog rain isn't something you see every day.

Terry thinks that frogs can fly. Terry isn't very bright and always had trouble with the 'animal facts' portion of primary school, forgetting what a cow says and erroneously categorising a giraffe as a "barnyard animal." But really, we can't fault Terry for his ignorance, because that really is the simplest explanation. Back in the ancient days, before we even knew anything about frogs, some cave people witnessing frog rain would probably rightly conclude that frogs could fly.

But frogs *can't* fly, and we know this after having examined frogs for quite some time. It's not even plausible that the frogs have been keeping their flying ability a secret from us for all this time so that they could spring it on us now. Frogs are physiologically incapable of flight, so based on what we know about the universe, we can debunk Terry's theory and start looking for more exotic explanations.

Kevin thinks that the frogs may have been caught in some kind of tumultuous wind phenomenon, like a tornado or something. This is a pretty good theory, because based on what we know about tornados and frogs, we know it's possible. Until anyone can rule out the idea that the frogs were sucked up and dumped by the wind, that's what everyone decides to go with.

Note though that we had to first *debunk* Terry's theory to arrive at Kevin's. If, for example, you looked up and saw a flock of birds overhead, it's unlikely that you'll assume they were thrown up there by a tornado. The simplest explanation for the birds really is that they are just flying. It's *possible* that they were caught in a tornado, but there's no reason to assume that. Realising that something is merely possible is no reason to believe it, because it's *possible* that you're just a brain in a jar in Frankenstein's laboratory and you're imagining your entire life. It's *possible* that your garden is infested by leprechauns and that Kevin Bacon sits outside your window and watches you sleep. Believing that everything that's possible is true is a great way to spend the rest of your life in a mental institution.

But there's someone else in this group of people getting bombarded by frogs, and he doesn't agree with Kevin. Steve thinks that the frogs were abducted by a UFO, and were later dumped from the ionosphere for unknown, possibly nefarious reasons.

This is a more complicated explanation by far. And Steve's problem is that he didn't debunk the tornado theory in order to arrive at it. He just flat-out asserted that aliens did it and that was that. Kevin thinks this is completely wack. But out of respect for Steve's feelings (because Steve is his brother in law and he promised his sister he'd be nice) he points out that Steve's theory raises more questions than it answers. He's already proposed an entire alien civilisation in order to explain some frogs falling out of the sky. But a more immediate question is that if the frogs are being dumped by a UFO, then why can't they see the UFO?

Ah, Steve replies, that's because the UFO is invisible.

So now we have *invisible* UFOs. What happened? Kevin offered Steve some evidence for why his theory is more complicated than necessary, but instead of reaching for a simpler explanation, Kevin just made his more complicated. He's going the wrong way.

Kevin goes further to ask about why, if UFOs are going around dumping frogs everywhere, we don't know about it already. Steve explains that the government is covering up the existence of frog-dumping aliens. So now we have invisible UFOs *and* a widespread government conspiracy, and all of this is necessary, Steve thinks, to explain raining frogs. Furthermore, he'll keep adding to this theory, making it ever more complicated, every time someone points out part of the UFO story that doesn't make sense.

This kind of mentality is disturbingly common, because you would think that, if it looks like a duck, walks like a duck and quacks like a duck, sure, sometimes it's an experimental Japanese android, but most of the time it's a duck. The point is, you certainly can't *assume* it's an android just because that's a fringe possibility. Even if you hear on the news that Japanese scientists are working on a lifelike duck android that will be indistinguishable from the real thing, and then the next morning you go down to the local pond and you see a duck, there's no reason to say "well, must be one of them fancy new robots." Not until you've eliminated the much more likely possibility that it's a duck by hitting it with a golf club.

But Occam's razor tends to work against our natural inclinations as human beings. For whatever reason, we actually seem predisposed to coming up with elaborate explanations for mundane things. When people saw the sun for the first time as a species, our first instinct was to create some story about the sun god Ra travelling across the sky with a flaming chariot, and to explain how this was possible we had to go further and talk about an entire race of deities who lived together on Mount Olympus, and to explain that we had to come up with the idea of Valhalla... Look, I know I'm mixing up my cultural understandings in a way that would be hilarious if it weren't so racist, but the point is that we as human beings have a tendency to come up with needlessly complicated explanations for things. For some people, this makes us see the world like one big Dan Brown novel, in which every event in the world is actually the result of an interconnected, sprawling, elaborate plot by a shadowy secret society with nefarious intentions.

Occam's razor therefore has an opposite, and I like to call it "Dan Brown's hammer." If Occam's razor is all about shaving away unnecessary complexities from an explanation, then Dan Brown's hammer is about nailing a whole bunch of new ones onto it.

What's important to understand, I think, is that people who are inclined toward this inverted system of logic are, indeed, using a system. If you were to walk through the looking-glass and into a world where everything is backward, like Bizarro World, then this is the logic that everyone there would use – they *embrace* fallacies rather than avoid them, and they *avoid* what we think of as standard logic as if it's fallacy. And this is what makes a conspiracy theorist or a believer in alternative medicine or alternative science impossible to argue with. It's not that the debate is deadlocked – their entire framework of logic is *literally incompatible* with ours. It's like trying to argue with a foreigner but neither of you speaks the other's language. And it's because they believe that our entire system of science is based on fallacy that they tend to reject it wholesale. It's in this way that different, seemingly unconnected beliefs tend to be linked together. For example, people who believe that homeopathy works tend also to believe in Atlantis, that vaccines cause autism, that contrails are really a secret aerosol spraying operation, and that Barack Obama was not born in the United States. These beliefs are not connected except in the sense that they are all the opposite of what the establishment says is true.

There is a derogatory catch-all term that describes all of the strange beliefs in this book – we call it "woo." Whosoever coined this term is uncertain, but people who spend their time arguing against woo for fun or profit call themselves the "skeptic" community. There's a misconception among true believers that skeptics are simply closed-minded people who ignore the paranormal through a kind of stubborn pride or a lack of imagination, and conspiracy theorists chide skeptics for "failing" to be skeptical of what the establishment says (read: failing to believe the truth is always 180 degrees from what science claims). The truth is that skeptics aren't rejecting certain beliefs through a religious fervor for the five senses and a brainwashed adherence to the scientific establishment. Scientists have spent an enormous amount of time investigating these things. They just can't find anything. And they keep trying.

During the 20th century, for example, scientists spent a great deal of time trying to prove the existence of psychic phenomena. The so called "Stargate Project" (not the one MacGyver worked for in his latter years) investigated psychics and remote viewers right up to 1995, when they stopped after decades of frustration at not being able to find anything. Believers in psychic phenomena think that their experience and intuition bolster its validity and that the skeptics are blind and simply towing the party line. But the thousands of genuine, earnest investigations into the matter have all shown that psychically inspired knowledge is accurate about as often as random guesses are accurate. Sometimes, psychics perform a little better than random guesses. Sometimes, they even perform a little worse. As *Mumford, et al*. point out in their research paper on remote viewing,[4] the fact that psychics perform no better than random chance doesn't actually prove that they're not psychic. It does prove, however, that actually being psychic would be an *astonishingly* useless skill.

Now, religion is an interesting thing. I'm not going to be talking about religion in this book because I think it's kind of beyond my scope, not only for such a short and light-hearted book, but for my own understanding. But I should mention religion however briefly, because I can foresee the argument that a lot of my friends usually throw at me when I talk about this kind of stuff in company: Shapeshifting reptiles, alien conspiracies, spooky physics, sure it's pretty nuts, but *it's no crazier than what Christians believe.*

That's a valid point, and most skeptic sources that attack this kind of reasoning do so based on a fundamentally atheist point of reference – that the problem of people believing in things like the Illuminati is just a microcosm of a greater problem of people believing in God. Attack one aspect, and you have to attack the whole thing. I think that's true to a point. But I think that there are concepts within philosophy and theology that, while not "beyond the scope" of science per se, are really asking different kinds of questions to those which science is asking. There's nothing wrong with *believing* in your own moral, emotional, existential framework. These are questions that,

---

4 Mumford, Michael D.; Rose, Andrew M.; Goslin, David A. (1995). An Evaluation of Remote Viewing: Research and Applications. *American Institutes for Research Report.* September 29.

while possibly just as objectively real, science can't really answer for you, and not through any failing or shortcoming of science.

The science writer Stephen Jay Gould popularised the concept of "non-overlapping magisteria." By this he means that there are domains of inquiry that don't necessarily overlap or compete with one another. There are of course times when religion (or, at least, its followers) does try to use science's own tools to compete with it – like the whole debacle of "creationism" being taught as a scientific confirmation of the truth of religion and the untruth of evolution somehow by extension, which led to some pretty memorably forehead-slapping examples of religion forgetting its place within its own magisterium.

Generally speaking, I'm only interested in tackling those worldviews that overlap with the magisterium of science – and get it wrong. Whether there's a higher intelligence, whatever that might mean, or a human soul, is beyond my interest here, in so far as we're going to be investigating the allegation that the Queen is a shapeshifting, blood-drinking Satanic lizard from another dimension.

So, what can we know about the origin of this strange, upside-down logic? There are only three reasons why a person might claim something that is wrong: Either that person is knowingly lying, or else they are unintentionally misinformed, or else they are in some way mentally ill and so incapable of discerning truth from fiction (or of even knowing the difference, in some cases.)[5] As such, the collective lake of beliefs that woo-proponents subscribe to derive from three sources – insane people, con artists, and legitimately poor thinkers. It is in some cases very, very difficult to differentiate between the three.

As far as I can manage, I'm going to avoid making fun of mentally ill people here, because it's a cheap shot and there's no point to it. There is a popular quote whose author is lost to the sands of time, which says something like "You can't rationalise someone out of a position that they didn't rationalise themselves into." The problem is that many of the strange ideas that our culture takes seriously have been

---

[5] It was the theologian and novelist C.S. Lewis who proposed what has come to be known as "Lewis' trilemma," or the "Lunatic, liar or lord" argument for discerning Jesus' divinity. Richard Dawkins in *The God Delusion* pointed out the neglected fourth possibility – that Jesus may have been honestly mistaken.

unknowingly posited by crazy people who plugged their delusions into the system.

How many conspiracy theorists who think the government is after them are legitimately insane? While researching for this book, I studied many, many crazy ideas that tend to interlock with one another. One phenomenon in particular is what's known to its theorists as "gang-stalking." This is the belief that the government or some other shadow power either recruits civilians or agents disguised as civilians to harass ordinary people. It's a secret project with unknown goals. The gang-stalking support community uses the term "targeted individual" or "TI" for someone who is a victim of this harassment, which is often permanent throughout the individual's life. The harassment usually takes the form of apparently ordinary people doing *seemingly* ordinary things, like sitting near you on the bus, or standing on a balcony within sight of your house, or taking the garbage out at the same time as you. But they are actually doing these things to harass you and very, very slowly drive you insane. That's the gang-stalking conspiracy in a nutshell.

What I soon realised, though, is that it's also textbook paranoid schizophrenia. The website *Medical News Today* defines it thus:

> **Paranoid schizophrenia** is a schizophrenia subtype in which the patient has false beliefs (delusions) that somebody or some people are plotting against them or members of their family. People with paranoid schizophrenia, as with most subtypes may also have auditory hallucinations - they hear things that are not real. The individual may also have delusions of personal grandeur - a false belief that they are much greater and more powerful and influential than they really are.
>
> An individual with paranoid schizophrenia may spend an extraordinary amount of time thinking about ways to protect themselves from their persecutors.[6]

So what appears to be a community dedicated to a conspiracy theory is actually a group of unwell people exhibiting the same symptoms and gravitating toward one another, developing a theory for their shared

---

[6] Nordqvist, Christian. (2010). What is Paranoid Schizophrenia? What Causes Paranoid Schizophrenia? *Medical News Today.*
http://www.medicalnewstoday.com/articles/192621.php

delusion. But because they all think their delusion is real, their theory reflects that. It's kind of the downside of the internet age – rather than having any hope of realising that they are alone in their beliefs and that they need help, they Google their symptoms and find forums full of people backing up their story and insisting it's real.

Another variation on this phenomenon is the so-called "Morgellons disease." Huge in the conspiracy culture, especially among those who believe the government is poisoning us to death, Morgellons sufferers believe they're ravaged by a mysterious skin condition that causes itching, bizarre lesions, and typically, the emergence of strange, coloured fibres from under their scabs. The condition became so predominant that scientists launched investigations into it, assuming that there might be something to it. But, in the end, all they concluded was that the condition is delusional parasitosis – a belief in parasites that aren't there. People with this condition obsessively scratch themselves, creating their own rashes and lesions, and it's coupled with a compulsion to collect hairs and clothing fibres from their bodies and around the home, believing that they're excreting them from their own bodies. They just found their own name for it once they consulted Dr Google about it.

But the gang-stalking and Morgellons communities have been adopted by the conspiracy community at large, not because the conspiracy community are experiencing these delusions, but because shit, why not. So the conspiracists get more fresh evidence and material for their ill-derived beliefs, while the sufferers of delusion start using the language of the conspiracy community (New World Order, chemtrails, etc.) and find an even larger community to feed off. It's a symbiotic relationship of really unhealthy thinking.

Most of the people who believe in the ideas in this book have arrived at them, I believe, from bad logic, and by drawing from earlier sources of bad logic and stapling worse logic onto them. But mental illness does contribute to the mythology, and so do con artists who are out to make a quick buck off the gullibility of others. How can we tell the difference? We can't, really. Not without marching them all into a psychologist's office and having them individually assessed, and I don't think taxpayers are going to shell out for that. Some ideological leaders in conspiracy culture, particularly those who draw on the New Age and Theosophy, like David Icke, claim to draw their information from psychic revelations – voices in their head. In my opinion, the world of psychics consists much more greatly of con artists than it does of people who genuinely believe they're psychic (those who use magician's tricks like cold reading to prove their psychic "powers" *must* be using them consciously, after all. There are no magicians who genuinely believe they're cutting a woman in half.) Then again, many New Agers get their psychic revelations from a spirit guide named "LSD." Or maybe they really are in contact with the spirits – we can't prove it either way, but we can seek to investigate the veracity of the claims that these ghosts, real or otherwise, are making.

The purpose of this book is to explore, as best as I'm able to piece it together, the genealogy of the components of what has come to be an entire culture of rejecting standard logic, from the beginning of the 20th century (sometimes a little earlier) through to now. We can clearly see how different authors and thinkers are inspired by earlier ones, not in spite of but *because of* the fact that those authors rejected or inverted logic to come to their ideas.

# SECTION ONE:
# WEIRD HISTORIES

*"I am disillusioned enough to know that no man's opinion on any
subject is worth a damn unless backed up with enough genuine
information to make him really know what he's talking about."*

*H.P. Lovecraft*

The Illuminati, David Wilcock explains, the secret rulers of the world
who want to enslave you to their own insidious agenda, are not shape-
shifting alien reptiles. I find it amusing that Wilcock mocks David Icke,
possibly the world's most notorious conspiracy theorist, for believing
in such nonsense. He explains that this is a silly thing to believe,
because it's clear to anyone who has looked at the evidence that the
Illuminati are the cone-headed alien humanoids who were once the
colonists of Atlantis.

Many thousands of years ago, Wilcock explains, the aliens
opened the Earth up for immigration. This is unusual, he says, because
ordinarily, aliens aren't allowed to interfere with other planets. "The
universe has rules," he says. But for reasons that even Wilcock doesn't
seem to know, the planet was at one time open to colonisation by
whatever alien species wanted to come here. Predominantly, these were
the cone-headed beings, who lived on Atlantis (which Wilcock seems
to believe is Antarctica), and the Annunaki reptiles, who came to
Sumer to mine gold. The reptilians and the Atlanteans had a great
battle, and in the end, the alien law-makers who watched over this (a
very Biblical kind of story) had to nuke the world to destroy them all.
Once again, the borders were closed, although aliens still walk among
us. Wilcock shows us a picture of Sumerian statues depicting the
reptilians. "Note," he says, "that they are wearing Masonic aprons."
The audience *oooohs* and nods.

Actually, the image doesn't depict anything that looks remotely
like a Masonic apron, but I'm willing to bet that nobody in the audience
knows what a Masonic apron looks like anyway.

The discussion turns to pyramids, now. A key element of
Wilcock's thesis is the question of how so many different cultures

separated by space and time could have built such identical standing structures with no contact between them. A full half hour of the lecture is dedicated to a slideshow presentation of pyramids – Wilcock is obsessed with them. But this display has the opposite effect on me than to convince me – looking at all these images, I actually realise for the first time how *remarkably different* all the various pyramids are from each other. From the pyramids in Giza to the ones of Mesoamerica and others scattered variously around Europe, there's very little to indicate any crossover of architectural style. It's almost as though there was no connection at all.

Various "identical" pyramids from around the world that pyramid aficionados want us to believe are proof that ancient cultures all ripped off each other's designs – or else they were all built by the same aliens. Personally, I didn't realise there were so many possible variations on the "triangle" design. Clockwise from top left: Pyramid of the Magician, Mexico; The Great Pyramid, Egypt; Temple of the Inscriptions, Mexico; Cathedral of San Salvador, Spain; Pyramid of Cestius, Rome; Monk's Mound, Illinois, USA; Caral pyramid, Peru.

But Wilcock's pyramid fetish doesn't stop with the traditional pyramids. The PowerPoint presentation now starts bringing up pictures of ordinary mountains. "Pyramids," Wilcock indicates. I can only see hills. Giant, natural-looking mounds of dirt in Bosnia, he refers to as the "largest pyramids on Earth." A clay hill in North America – pyramid. He then brings up the admittedly amazing "chocolate hills" in the Philippines, natural conical formations of limestone that dot the islands. Apparently, the Philippine government has been trying to build a hotel in the area in order to attract tourism to the hills, but they haven't been able to drum up enough funding.

"Think about it," Wilcock says, "If the Philippine government can't even get it together to build a single hotel, then *how could they have built all these pyramids?*"

## I'm Not Saying it Was Aliens, But…

When I was a young boy, I was fascinated by books in my Grandmother's cabinet. I think they mainly came as gifts from Reader's Digest subscriptions and would never have seen the light of day if I hadn't learned how to turn the key in the cabinet, which I did after getting bored of vandalising it. There were books about architectural mysteries and great feats of human endurance in the distant past, about unexplained ancient technologies, and the historical basis of myth and legend. I'm not sure how much I sincerely believed, but there were theories I at least found plausible, like that a technologically advanced civilisation on Atlantis might have blown itself up with a nuclear bomb or something well before the time of Plato, or that the famous explosion in Tunguska may have been caused by a micro black hole passing through the Earth. I think that it was just the wonder of a science fiction novel playing itself out in the distant past that enchanted me.

Most of these theories were, in some way, linked to the writings of a guy named Erich von Däniken, a Swiss writer who is considered the father of the so-called "ancient astronauts" hypothesis.

Every time you hear somebody talking about how Stonehenge was built by aliens, or how there are UFOs pictured in medieval paintings, or pyramids can be found on Mars, they're following in the tradition of von Däniken, whose books, most famously *Chariots of the Gods?* (1968), put forward the idea that ancient mankind was visited thousands of years ago by colonial aliens, who were possibly after resources or just curious about our biology, and they built all those mysterious ancient structures all over the place, like the pyramids and the Easter Island statues and all that. Von Däniken's evidence for all this was based on the many architectural mysteries we were still digging up circa the 1960s. Certain maps that seem to represent the Earth as seen from space, giant drawings in the ground that could plausibly have been used to direct spacecraft, and of course the mystery of how the hell people over 4000 years ago could have moved rocks heavier than semitrailers.

And this is a good question, right? We're told again and again about just how incredibly impressive these old feats of engineering were. How could a bunch of druids and cave-people have moved a bunch of ridiculously massive rocks all the way out from distant quarries to build their structures in the middle of nowhere? Von Däniken goes to great lengths to point out just how ludicrous the task of building the Great Pyramid must have been. Even hundreds of thousands of workmen working day by day and hour by hour to push 2.5 million multiple-ton blocks from the quarry to the construction site, and then *uphill* to the top of the pyramid, would take, by von Däniken's calculations, *664 years*. And that's assuming they were able to lay ten blocks per day, an estimate that von Däniken considers already extraordinarily conservative. How could they possibly have done all of that without cranes, trucks and bulldozers?

For that matter, how did anyone ever travel more than a few miles away from home before we invented steam trains? Was it UFOs? *Did we hitch-hike on UFOs?*

Von Däniken's fallacy is confusing the forward march of technology with a growth in intelligence and ingenuity. Whenever we see some depiction of cavemen slobbering and dragging their knuckles on the ground, we're making the mistake of presuming they were somehow less intelligent than we are today. That's not true at all – we're the same species, and Grogg from Cave 14 had just as much a capacity for knowledge as we do today. Pick him up in a time machine, bring him back to the modern day and put him in school, and he'd grow up the same as the rest of us. Or, at the very least, he'd join a gang and terrorise old people. But he'd do it with *street* smarts.

What they didn't have was tens of thousands of years' worth of accumulated knowledge. So they couldn't build bulldozers. However, if you sent a bulldozer back in time and parked it in their backyard, they probably could have operated it, after a bit of trial and error.

These days, it's inconceivable to us that we could build something like Stonehenge without the help of bulldozers and cranes. But that's because we've been conditioned to the existence of bulldozers and cranes. If you were dropped in a field with a bunch of big rocks, and you were told to build a monument without the help of any kind of modern technology, you might be surprised with what you can come up with.

A retired Michigan carpenter named Wally Wallington (yes, that is someone's real name) put himself in just this situation, for no real reason but shits and giggles. The task he set himself was to build a replica of Stonehenge using only techniques that would have been available 4000 years ago. He didn't even allow himself the use of metal tools – only wood and stone. And he succeeded. *By himself.*

Wallington is currently selling the secrets of his technique at theforgottentechnology.com, but if that sets off your scam alarms, there are videos on the internet showing him accomplishing many of the key tasks.[7] And it's shockingly easy. It all comes down to basic physics and a little bit of inventiveness.

Von Däniken and many others make the mistake of assuming (because they presume ancient people were also retarded) that the people of ancient Egypt, Britain, Easter Island and wherever else has huge monoliths would have tried to move them simply by pushing and lifting, what von Däniken calls the "heave-ho" method. That, rather than think outside the box and try something new, they would have just tried to drag a six-ton square hunk of rock across the bare dirt until they got sick of it and gave up. Von Däniken, to reiterate, calculated that hundreds of thousands of workmen would take 664 years to build the Great Pyramid of Giza. Wally Wallington did the same calculation using his own method, and as he reports on his website, he can do it in 25 years with 520 people.

Game Wallington.

Remember that in order to make a complicated explanation plausible, you have to defeat the simpler explanation. Von Däniken *thinks* that he did that by pointing out the impossibility of building vast structures with stone age technology, but what he forgot to account for is human ingenuity. Of course, von Däniken makes a point of painting ancient people as bemused five-year-olds. His theory, that the religions of times past were actually in worship of aliens, is based on the notion

---

[7] http://tinyurl.com/8lc79ww

that ancient people mistook vastly technologically superior entities as gods, for hundreds of years. Maybe that's possible, but even supposing aliens would be for some reason motivated to convince the locals they were gods, by proving that human beings *could* have built these megastructures, we have removed the necessity of bringing aliens into this story at all. Aliens are no longer needed to explain anything, and by ascribing motives to the aliens once they're here (like trying to paint themselves out of history by pretending to be gods) you're just adding complications to the story in order to protect the alien narrative.

Within the community of real scientists who didn't scoop their credentials out of the bottom of a box of *Cap'n Crunch*, archaeological theories that deal with science-fiction concepts like aliens, ancient technologies and hidden knowledge in the guise of mythology are generally listed under the umbrella of "pseudoarchaeology." Regular archaeology is all about digging up artifacts from the remote past and speculating on the lifestyle of the people who lived in these places. You can usually spot pseudoarchaeology because, in true Dan Brown style, it begins with the speculation—usually fantastic speculation, like aliens—and then manipulates the current evidence so that it fits that speculation. Usually this means cherry-picking the evidence that would support such an idea, and disregarding that which would oppose it.

There's a reason why pseudoarchaeology so closely reminds us of science fiction. In fact, ancient alien contact didn't find its origins in obscure academia at all, but in popular science fiction. It's entirely plausible that all of today's hoopla about ancient visitors can be blamed on H.G. Wells, who kick-started the early 20th century's alien craze with his Martian invasion novel *The War of the Worlds*.

Inspired by Wells and his contemporaries, two then-obscure science fiction authors rose to prominence within the genre with tales about ancient aliens who granted the earliest humans their technology in exchange for their rule over us as gods. These authors, recognisable to most of us today, were H.P. Lovecraft and L. Ron Hubbard. Lovecraft and Hubbard wound up leaving two very different legacies – Lovecraft became one of the most important foundations for the modern horror genre, upon whose shoulders stand Stephen King, Robert Bloch, Whitley Streiber (who, perhaps not incidentally, became an important figure in shaping modern ufology), filmmakers John Carpenter and Guillermo del Toro, and various other artists who used their inspiration by Lovecraft's work to design the contemporary horrorscape, notably H.R. Geiger, the designer for the *Alien* movies.

Hubbard, on the other hand, became the foundation for Scientology, upon whose shoulders stands Tom Cruise.

There's no smoking-gun evidence that Erich von Däniken was a fan of Lovecraft and Hubbard, but the similarities can't be denied. All three authors produced work that was, thematically, virtually identical. The key difference is how they presented their work to the public. Lovecraft claimed his work to be pure fiction, Hubbard made his into a kind of religion, and von Däniken presented his as science. And it's worth noting that, while von Däniken never admitted to inspiration by Lovecraft directly, he *did* admit a significant inspiration by French authors Jacques Bergier and Louis Pauwels, who were huge fans of and correspondents with, you guessed it, H.P. Lovecraft.[8]

It's never a good thing when, as a scientist, you can ultimately trace your sources to the imagination of a fiction writer. But that's where the ancient astronauts theory owes practically its entire origin. Worse, Lovecraft would have hated this legacy so much that it's a good thing he's dead, lest he attempt suicide. Hubbard, the notorious egomaniac, not so much. Nevertheless, Lovecraft's work sold poorly in his own time and the value of his work was only recognised after his death. Von Däniken, by taking an almost identical concept and putting it instead in the "non-fiction" section, became a phenomenally popular author immediately, allowing him to write many sequels, which was a good thing for him because it gave him something to do while he was in prison for embezzlement. (Oh, by the way, he went to prison for embezzlement.)

Thanks to von Däniken's wild idea, ancient alien visitation became a huge phenomenon to the chagrin of legitimate archaeologists who were able to tell right away that the books were packed with errors. *Chariots* was to its time what *Fifty Shades of Grey* was to 2012. Go into a bookstore today, and half of the books on the shelf have covers tinted black, pictures of whips or chains or stilettos on them, and titles containing a number and a colour. After *Chariots* was published, the covers all had aliens and pyramids on them and titles ending with "…of the Gods." Dozens of authors spilled out of the woodwork to write books that explained ancient structures and mythologies as having been of alien origin. Of course, if you investigate the credentials of the

---

[8] Colavito, Jason. (2011). *The Secret History of Ancient Astronauts: Ancient Astronauts and the Cthulhu Mythos in Fiction and Fact.* http://www.jasoncolavito.com/secret-history-of-ancient-astronauts.html

top names in ancient astronaut theory, you come up with some interesting revelations:

- **Erich von Däniken:** has no education in any scientific, archaeological, or anthropological field. Though he did work previously as an hotelier, during which time he was convicted of embezzlement and, it is said, diagnosed by court order as a pathological liar. Since then, he's been caught on around forty thousand separate occasions falsifying evidence and plagiarising other authors. Occasionally, he even admits it.
- **Giorgio A. Tsoukalos:** the face of History Channel series *Ancient Aliens*, director of the Ancient Alien Society. Has never published or authored anything, and has no education in any scientific, archaeological, or anthropological field. Though he may hold a bachelor's degree in sports information communication.
- **Zechariah Sitchin:** the now deceased author of a popular series of books on ancient aliens in Sumer. Had no education in any scientific, archaeological, or anthropological field, though he did pick up a degree in economics.
- **Robert Temple:** author of *The Sirius Mystery*, has a degree in Oriental studies and Sanskrit. I suppose that's anthropology, though his hypothesis about frog people from Sirius came from African tribes who don't speak Sanskrit.
- **Graham Hancock:** author of *Fingerprints of the Gods* and *The Mars Mystery*, has a degree in sociology, worked as a journalist.
- **David Wilcock:** former fat kid.
- **David Hatcher Childress:** who dropped out of an archaeology degree after one year, and thus has more relevant education than every other expert in the field combined.

Though a lot of people got caught up in the craze of interpreting ancient history as having involved alien visitation, *none* of them have the educational background required for, well, interpreting ancient history. Often enough, they have no education in any kind of science, and make some bafflingly outrageous leaps in the name of either wishful thinking or simply selling books. And in the end, there's no claim I know of made by von Däniken or any of his descendent authors that hasn't a more likely explanation that doesn't have anything to do with aliens. It says a lot that creationists probably have even more convincing evidence against evolution than anyone has of aliens visiting Earth at any time in the planet's history.

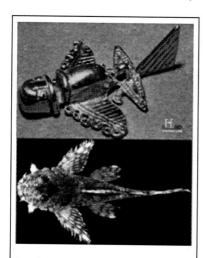

Ancient astronaut theorists like to go on about how this ancient figurine could only be a model of a spaceship or flying machine. It certainly couldn't be modelled after this fish that it looks exactly like.

Today, ancient astronaut theories are a prominent theme in modern science fiction – and while not so many people "believe" in them in the same way as they once did, we nevertheless have a distinct fascination with them. The filmmaker Roland Emmerich relies on them heavily, particularly in the film *Stargate* and the television series of the same name. It was a foundation for *The X-Files*, and has been hinted at in almost every prominent sci-fi series from *Doctor Who* to *Star Trek*. In an interesting example of creative circularity, 2012's prequel to the Lovecraft-inspired *Alien* was an exploration of the von Däniken style of ancient alien mythos, as bluntly stated in its title, *Prometheus*, the mythological figure who was punished for stealing technology from the gods. Critical consensus is that it was fairly disappointing. But fiction is the only realm in which ancient astronauts have any place. As cool as it sounds that there are cities out there built in measureless eons behind history by the vast, loathsome shapes that seeped down from the dark stars, the mundane reality just involves a bunch of really determined people and a lot of hard work.

## The Fred Flintstone Theory of Atlantis

A significant amount of pseudoarchaeology derives from a reluctance to write off any of the stories of ancient people – no matter how fantastic – as fictional. I can't go as far as to say it's racism per se, but there's a more benign albeit similar form of bigotry that writes off ancient peoples as grunting simpletons. Just like we assume they couldn't have had the ingenuity to build something as impressive as the pyramids, so too do we figure that they were incapable of such literary

25

devices as metaphor, satire and fantasy. Anything we find scrawled on a cave or scribbled on parchment from that long ago must be a variation of something these people actually saw. Thus images of humanoids descending from heaven inside orbs, for example, serve as proof of aliens visiting Earth rather than some Palaeolithic flight of fancy. One wonders what our descendants, ten thousand years from now, would try to prove by studying *Harry Potter*.

One of the most enduring pseudoarchaeological myths, so embedded within our culture that I wouldn't blame you for having thought it was true, is the legend of Atlantis. People are always talking about Atlantis as though it's a real thing, this ancient island with its advanced culture that sank into the ocean. We don't discuss it in terms of *whether* it existed, but rather *where* it is and *why* it sank. Because, you know, islands don't usually do that. Or ever.

Every now and then, news headlines will report that somebody or other has made a discovery that might finally reveal the location of Atlantis. Back in 2009, the internet exploded with news articles about the discovery of what could possibly be Atlantis, uncovered by *Google Earth*. A fuzzy image of what appeared to be a rectangular grid of dark lines on the bottom of the seabed, too straight to be natural, showed up on the satellite-generated map. Speculation in the media about the

**Contents** [hide]

The contents page for Wikipedia's article on the location of Atlantis provides a conservative number of possibilities.

possible explanations for such a phenomenon ranged from "probably Atlantis" to "definitely Atlantis." But while thousands of laypeople and journalists, and even some curious archaeologists, pored over the images in fascination, Google employees and those literate in computer imaging tried to get the message across that, while they were right in pointing out that it wasn't natural, the reality was that the image was what's known as a "graphical artifact." A slight error in stitching together multiple satellite images – a computer glitch. Conspiracy theorists continue to assert that Google is covering something up.

In recent decades, Atlantis has been "found" so many times, in so many places, that we've just about run out of places for Atlantis to not be. The age of exploration is pretty much over – we've scoured the Earth for its lost cities, and as technology advances, we've just about found everything there is to see on the ocean floor as well. So where is it? We have to consider the evidence, right? The ancients were discussing *something* when they were going on about Atlantis.

Well, let's consider who these ancients were that we're using as compasses to the location of the real, geological Atlantis. The first recorded mention of such a place came from Plato, the great Greek philosopher. Since then, the legend of Atlantis has cropped up in quite a few texts by... people writing about Plato. Which makes Plato our only primary source. Nobody else has ever offered their take on the story, nobody has ever recorded what they know about Atlantis who didn't get the story from Plato first, except maybe some psychics like Edgar Cayce. But using psychics to independently confirm the existence of Atlantis is like using fairies to independently confirm the existence of leprechauns.

Remember, all we need to build a convincing case about the existence of Atlantis is the independent testimony of two human beings. Somewhere across the sands of time, over thousands of years of written history, we need to find two people who have heard of this advanced, hugely influential society who, as the story goes, created a mighty and cruel empire across the civilised world before it was vanquished. It should be as easy as finding two people who have heard of Rome. But somehow, Plato is the only person who thought the existence of such an incredible civilisation was interesting enough to write down. So, given that, how reliable is Plato?

The fact is, Plato was not a historian. He wasn't an anthropologist or a social scientist. He was, in fact, a very accomplished novelist. What he wrote was exclusively fiction – granted, it was exceptionally meaningful fiction, but in the same way that George Orwell was meaningful. There was an enormous amount of social commentary pumped into every paragraph of *Animal Farm*, but nobody argues that the socialist revolution of Manor Farm by pigs, chickens and cows is a real historical event.

Plato was an allegorical storyteller. He wrote about human nature through imagined parties thrown by the prominent philosophers of the time. In simplest terms, it was like philosopher crossover fanfiction. Many of the characters that Plato used in his stories really existed, but Plato was much less interested in historical accuracy than he was in making a point. He never wrote anything just for the sake of recording what happened. On the contrary, he wasn't opposed to making some crap up in order to reveal something important about ourselves.

So the evidence *for* Atlantis consists of an allegorical story written by – and *only* by – a known fiction writer who lived several thousand years after the events he's recording and never seriously suggested were true, and the testimony of some psychics.

There's also the fact that, over time, we've pretty much scoured the Atlantic Ocean for any evidence, however small, that there was ever an island out there. Of course, there's always the possibility, as many have suggested, that Atlantis wasn't where Plato said it was. But once we advance that theory, we're entering dangerous territory – we're questioning the only source we have for an event about the details of that event. Once we start arguing that Plato was partly or mostly wrong about Atlantis, we're most of the way to arguing that it was entirely fabricated. This is where we begin to invent excuses to verify something that we've already decided to believe is true. To debunk Plato about Atlantis is to leave us with *no* reliable witnesses. It's like me telling you that I was abducted by fairies, and even after admitting I was mistaken, you still believe in fairies because of my account.

It has been suggested that Plato may have gleaned inspiration from the Minoan civilisation on the island of Thera in the Mediterranean, which indeed perished by a volcanic eruption. But this fact, right or wrong, is irrelevant – we don't need Thera to explain the story of Atlantis, because the notion that Plato just made it all up is as reasonable as any other explanation. In fact, nobody until recently believed that the Atlantis story was factual. In other words, Plato wrote his story as fiction and nobody at the time thought otherwise. They would likely look at you with the same bemused expression as someone today would if you asked whether Hogwarts is real.

If you think about it, the Platonic myth that the island fell into the ocean is actually similar to a device that writers use today. Compare it to *Lord of the Rings* – Tolkien deliberately wrote this as a kind of creation myth. Middle-Earth is based on our world and presented as *history* (though not a history that is supposed to be taken seriously). In order to make this work, Tolkien had to explain why the modern world doesn't have a bunch of elves and dwarves running around, so he designs a fate for these races and donates Earth to the human beings. Even though it's fiction and meant to be taken as fiction, Tolkien was constrained to setting up history to play out the way that it really did, in the end. Likewise, if Plato writes a historical story set in our world and he creates a huge island in the Atlantic where none currently exists, he has to destroy that island in the end. The point of Plato's story was not the destruction of Atlantis, which he reduces to a mere footnote, but the political allegory he was making. And everyone in antiquity knew exactly what he was doing. As classicist Alan Cameron puts it:

> It is a basic misunderstanding of Plato's purpose, which was undoubtedly political allegory. Antediluvian Athens and Atlantis both represent different aspects of the historical Athens: antediluvian Athens the sturdy, virtuous farmers of the days before the Persian Wars; Atlantis the corrupt, imperialist seapower that developed out of the Delian League. For further details it will be enough for our present needs to refer to the brilliant essay of P. Vidal-Naquet. In order to save the phenomena, clearly Plato's myth had to explain why there was no longer any such huge island on the far side of the straits of Gibraltar. The catastrophe was merely a device to achieve this end, a detail rather than the essence of the story. Contemporaries familiar with both Plato's ideas and his ways of expressing them would (of course) have realized this. That is why no contemporary was tempted to believe in the historical reality of Atlantis. It would be another two generations before such a misunderstanding was possible.[9]

As I mentioned, Plato was not a historian. But there were historians living before and after Plato, great historians, like Herodotus, author of the first ever scientifically produced history book. He wrote about the Battle of Thermopylae and reckoned that the great king Xerxes was the greatest threat that Athens had ever known. And, as another kick in the

---

[9] Cameron, Alan. (1983). Crantor and Posidonius on Atlantis. *The Classical Quarterly*. 33(1) pp. 81-91

pants for the true believers, Herodotus had never heard of Atlantis. Supposedly one of the most influential and cataclysmic series of events for ancient Greece, the empire of Atlantis, its invasion of Athens, and its subsequent tragic destruction, just didn't fit anywhere into Herodotus' comprehensive historical narrative. Almost like it didn't happen at all.

So here we're forced to take one man's word against another. One man, an actual historian of the time, who rigorously researched a comprehensive history of the wars and geography of the Mediterranean world, against another, who was not a historian, didn't pretend to be, didn't even intend to be, and whose business was fiction, writing thousands of years after the fact and nevertheless claiming that his myth was hearsay, the ancient equivalent of "it happened to a friend of a friend of mine." Whose version do we accept? Many people still say Plato, but not for any reason derived from logic.

Of course, we're just debunking the Platonic version of the Atlantis story. The modern version is something more complicated, the result of people tacking more and more details onto it over time, with absolutely nothing to back it up. Plato's Atlantis was the villain in his story, the mighty naval empire that went up against Athens and was defeated by its own hubris. These days, depending on who you ask, people see Atlantis as some utopian civilisation, often with super-advanced technology.

Acting as a companion to the ancients-were-idiots misunderstanding, many pseudoarchaeologists such as David Hatcher Childress and Zecharia Sitchin believe that nuclear warfare took place in distant prehistory. Von Däniken believes this too, though his conclusion is that aliens did it. Childress believes the Atlanteans did it. Sitchin, as far as I can tell, believes Atlanteans did it but the Atlanteans were aliens.

Nuclear warfare makes a pretty good explanation for how Atlantis could have been wiped out in the absence of any evidence of natural disaster. But again, only if you're taking Dan Brown's hammer to the situation. If we can't find any evidence of earthquakes or volcanos or comet impacts or whatever is supposed to account for the fall of Atlantis, then we're supposed to agree this puts the story of Atlantis into question. But others, who come at it with the opinion that the story of Atlantis is unquestionable for some reason, need to hammer more outlandish theories onto it, like that it must have been nuclear war that wiped out Atlantis, and for that to be true, there must have been some advanced civilisation on Earth at that time, so that's what happened.

In late 2011, producer Foster Gamble put together a documentary called *Thrive* that was popular particularly among the Occupy movement. On the face of it, it looked like and was promoted as your typical new age "fight the system" rallying cry, but to actually sit down and watch it, the film takes about five minutes to get to the real point of the story – ancient astronauts gave us incredible technologies and something about the New World Order suppressing UFO knowledge.[10]

According to *Thrive*, ancient alien-inspired civilisations knew the secret to free energy and they inscribed it in hieroglyphs all over the world. Most people who put forward the "ancient advanced civilisation" hypothesis refer to some variation of this – ancient steampunk computers found fossilised in stone, recipes for anti-gravity devices scrawled onto walls, UFOs depicted in cave paintings, advanced mathematical theorems they couldn't possibly have known encoded onto clay pots via someone systematically throwing his own feces at it. These things are used as evidence that some super advanced civilisation, equal or more advanced than our own, existed in antiquity.

But there's something really weird with this picture, isn't there?

As a thought exercise, try to imagine how difficult it would be to hide the existence of our modern civilisation from future people living a few thousand years from now. Let's presume that the alarmists are right and that in a few years we blow ourselves up in a spectacularly arrogant world war, bust humanity back to the caves, rewind the calendar and start again. What are the chances that the new human civilisation, just entering their industrial revolution in the year, say, 6000 AD, would be unable to locate any trace of us?

I mean, there would be people who insist we existed, that they had computers and aeroplanes all the way back in the 20th century, but those who make that claim would have no hard evidence and would be ignored as pseudoscientists by the intellectual consensus. After centuries of academic and scientific investigation into their planet's

---

[10] Personally, whenever activists or university campuses advertise one of these films with new-agey titles like *Thrive* or *Zeitgeist* or *What The Bleep*, I like to count down the minutes before someone in the film mentions aliens.

past, digging far into the earth to investigate its geological and demographic history, they would find no significant evidence whatsoever of an advanced human civilisation existing in 2012. In fact, they would find dinosaur fossils, but they would never find New York. And understand, we didn't actively try to hide our existence from the future – we just accidentally died one day.

Does that sound implausible? It's the very claim that people like David Hatcher Childress are making, except *not quite*: He dips into ancient artifacts, art and literature to produce what he claims is evidence of ancient advanced technology. In his book *Technology of the Gods*, he goes on about Bible passages that seem to describe space travel, evidence of robots in Hellenistic Greece, primitive statuettes that look like aircraft, and postulates that the pyramids of Egypt are actually a power plant complex, and that the Egyptians had a full electric power grid (which is, of course, how they built all that fantastic stuff. They had access to power drills and bulldozers after all.)

The funny thing about all this is that this world of robots and lasers and satellites that supposedly existed in the distant past is still set upon the backdrop of *the Bronze Age*. When Childress is describing what he thinks is a passage about Plato talking about a robot, he is describing barefoot, toga-wearing Plato, walking out of his stone hut to fetch water from the town well, and also there's a robot. When Childress is raving about the pyramid power plant of Egypt, he is describing a crude pile of rocks slapped together in the most basic of geometric shapes that was nevertheless capable of achieving fusion reactions and distributing it across Egypt, probably, via an interconnected network of electric eels tied head-to-tail.  And the instructions for using it are represented by little drawings of birds and crocodiles and little people doing that Egyptian emu pose, painted onto a slab of rock from earthen pigments someone had to literally spit onto the wall.

In other words, these people had electricity, but they didn't have steel. They had space travel, but they didn't have the printing press. They had robots, but they didn't have pants. This was a scientifically modern society, but exactly as it's portrayed in *The Flintstones*. And that's how people like Childress can get away with suggesting that some super-advanced society used to exist in antiquity but we can't find any hard evidence of it – they built their rockets out of wood and their computers looked like ordinary rocks, so we've simply mistaken them for a primitive society.

But all of this is built upon the need to explain how Atlantis can be real despite the mountains of evidence that it is not. So why the need to hold onto Atlantis so fervently? Like the ancient astronauts stuff, Atlantis was once thought necessary to explain things that it is no longer necessary to explain. When I mentioned that nobody in Plato's time took the Atlantis story seriously, this was true right up to 1882, when a mostly forgotten fable from one of Plato's lesser known manuscripts became the subject of a book by a Minnesota congressman and amateur classicist Ignatius Donnelly, *Atlantis: The Antediluvian World*. For Donnelly, Atlantis provided a much needed explanation for where humankind came from as well as observed similarities between ancient civilisations in terms of architecture and mythology. In Donnelly's own words, what he sought to prove was:

> 1. That there once existed in the Atlantic Ocean, opposite the mouth of the Mediterranean Sea, a large island, which was the remnant of an Atlantic continent, and known to the ancient world as Atlantis.

> 2. That the description of this island given by Plato is not, as has been long supposed, fable, but veritable history.

> 3. That Atlantis was the region where man first rose from a state of barbarism to civilization.

> 4. That it became, in the course of ages, a populous and mighty nation, from whose overflowings the shores of the Gulf of Mexico, the Mississippi River, the Amazon, the Pacific coast of South America, the Mediterranean, the west coast of Europe and Africa, the Baltic, the Black Sea, and the Caspian were populated by civilized nations.

> 5. That it was the true Antediluvian world; the Garden of Eden; the Gardens of the Hesperides; the Elysian Fields; the Gardens of Alcinous; the Mesomphalos; the Olympos; the Asgard of the traditions of the ancient nations; representing a universal memory of a great land, where early mankind dwelt for ages in peace and happiness.

> 6. That the gods and goddesses of the ancient Greeks, the Phœnicians, the Hindoos, and the Scandinavians were simply the kings, queens, and heroes of Atlantis; and the acts attributed to them in mythology are a confused recollection of real historical events.

7. That the mythology of Egypt and Peru represented the original religion of Atlantis, which was sun-worship.

8. That the oldest colony formed by the Atlanteans was probably in Egypt, whose civilization was a reproduction of that of the Atlantic island.

9. That the implements of the "Bronze Age" of Europe were derived from Atlantis. The Atlanteans were also the first manufacturers of iron.

10. That the Phœnician alphabet, parent of all the European alphabets, was derived from an Atlantis alphabet, which was also conveyed from Atlantis to the Mayas of Central America.

11. That Atlantis was the original seat of the Aryan or Indo-European family of nations, as well as of the Semitic peoples, and possibly also of the Turanian races.

12. That Atlantis perished in a terrible convulsion of nature, in which the whole island sunk into the ocean, with nearly all its inhabitants.

13. That a few persons escaped in ships and on rafts, and, carried to the nations east and west the tidings of the appalling catastrophe, which has survived to our own time in the Flood and Deluge legends of the different nations of the old and new worlds.

If these propositions can be proved, they will solve many problems which now perplex mankind; they will confirm in many respects the statements in the opening chapters of Genesis; they will widen the area of human history; they will explain the remarkable resemblances which exist between the ancient civilizations found upon the opposite shores of the Atlantic Ocean, in the old and new worlds; and they will aid us to rehabilitate the fathers of our civilization, our blood, and our fundamental ideas-the men who lived, loved, and labored ages before the Aryans descended upon India, or the Phœnician had settled in Syria, or the Goth had reached the shores of the Baltic.

In other words, Donnelly thought it was necessary to find an explanation for where all these civilised people came from, how cities and language and technology appeared all over the world where there were only tribes before, and where ancient people got their mythology about enlightened races of gods. According to Donnelly, the Atlantis story ties these threads up neatly.

The truth is, we don't need some single enlightened group of people to travel the world educating savages in order to explain the spread of civilisation. There's a common misconception that human beings can't create civilisation on their own, they need to be taught the technology. Different civilisations appearing to spring up independently is something we think needs to be explained. But civilisation appears out of necessity. People create technology to solve some kind of problem that they have. The people of ancient times had absolutely no use for robots and lasers. Some civilisations don't need anything more complicated than spears, but if nature pressures them, they invent. We don't need an Atlantis any more than we need to find the actual cave that Plato was talking about in his cave analogy.

The depressing truth about the Atlantis legend in its modern incarnation is that white people were puzzled about how brown people could have learned how to build things without any white people to teach them. So rather than ask themselves whether they were just being really racist, they invented a forgotten white civilisation that simply must have existed to educate the savages. It's really rather impressive how much nonsense comes about from a need for more efficient racism.

## Esoteric Geology

Not since the time of Plato and Aristotle has science seriously postulated that we're significantly wrong about the shape of the Earth, but as is usually the case with cult sciences, mountains of scientific evidence aren't as convincing as myths, speculations and the hearsay of a few very unique individuals.

It was around the 1880s when people became titillated by the idea that the world might actually be flat after all, after an author known only as "Parallax," later revealed as the pseudonym of an eccentric English inventor named Samuel Rowbotham, wrote a book called *Zetetic Astronomy: Earth is Not a Globe*. For some years, Rowbotham made a meager living lecturing on his ideas despite the fact that he was never actually able to win a debate about it. In true form for the pseudoscientist, he avoided ever actually engaging in argument about his ideas (one story has him abruptly ending a lecture after someone asked him why boats dip below the horizon before their sails. Though one could just as easily have asked, you know, why there was a horizon at all. As flat planes have no horizon, then I should be able to see Europe from my backyard in the same way as I can see the moon.)

Rather than the form of the globe that we know today, Rowbotham's alternative model was that of a circular disc, with the North Pole in the centre, and what we think of as the "south pole" is really a giant wall of ice that surrounds the perimeter. The sun, rather than orbiting the planet, travels in a circular path around the middle, and instead of a ball of fire, it's a spotlight that shines directly down, explaining why it doesn't just light up the whole disc at the same time.

Of course, to accept this model, you have to ignore the existence of horizons, the arc of the sun, eclipses, seasons, the movement of the constellations, the inaccuracy of flat maps, seismology, the tides, and the fact that people had been regularly sailing west out of America and crashing into the eastern side of China somehow for around 400 years. But this was a small sacrifice for

Parallax, whose model was practically entirely based on the fact that whenever he tested the surface of a body of water, it turned out to be pretty level, a fact that he demonstrated again and again and again.

Rather than measure his ideas against the scientific consensus, Rowbotham shrugged away the scientific consensus as a vast conspiracy. It's a tactic that will become nauseatingly familiar to us as we go on to describe the rise of conspiratorial paranoia in the next section. Rather than meet his opponents in level discourse and participate in experiments, he charged admission for lectures where he'd talk at his fans about his level water observations.

Eventually, detractors so enraged him that he agreed to an experiment to test the curvature of the ocean. The idea was simply to stand at the beach at Cornwall and observe a distant lighthouse through a telescope. Rowbotham's opponents calculated that the lighthouse was far enough over the horizon that only the lantern on top should be visible over the water. This calculation was wrong – in actual fact, *less* of the lighthouse was visible than scientists had predicted, because they failed to account for the refractive index of the air (its ability to bend the visible light). To the layman, this seemed to prove the earth was even curvier than science thought, but Parallax had a trick up his sleeve – he declared victory on the basis that his opponents had been wrong. Never mind that they were wrong against his favour, they were still wrong.

This is a fine early example of the woo-artist's tendency to operate on upside-down logical principles. It's common, when faced with greater debunking evidence, to try to poke holes in the science and identify slight inaccuracies, because proving that science doesn't know everything is a lot easier than proving you know more than science.

It's a tactic that works, though. Even though the results of the experiment seemed to show more curvature than expected, the inaccuracy of the scientists shattered the idea that science is infallible, which is the claim that opponents to science mistakenly believe science is trying to make. With science humbled, the illusion is that nobody really knows what they're talking about, and so anyone's theory is as good as any other. And so the orb theory, which should have been even more debunked than expected, paradoxically *lost* credibility, and the disc theory prospered.

The Flat Earth Society still exists, and lists a membership of around 400 people as of 2012. In a way, it is the final frontier for cult science. Even the most prominent of the alternative science and conspiracy theory proponents dismiss the flat earth, and in fact, they use it *against* mainstream science, often referring to those who don't accept their evidence about ancient aliens or who believe in lone gunmen as "flat earthers." Even the fringe thinks that they're taking their scientific denialism too far.

There is another earth shape theory, however, that is more popular among alternative science proponents than the flat earth. Though it does seem strange that it's *more* popular, considering it's even less intuitive. It's the *hollow* earth theory. Hollow earthers admit that the planet is a sphere, but they believe that it is shaped like a ping-pong ball – a hollow shell. They say that the crust of the earth is all there is to it, that there's an opening at each pole and that you can walk right around the lip and onto the underside. Some theorists believe that there is an "inner sun" at the core of the earth that provides light for the denizens of the inner earth. Naturally, you'd think the inner sun would just crash right into the sides of the planet, but hollow earth believers have a number of ways to Dan Brown's hammer this problem into submission, most of which involve commanding the laws of science like a fez-wearing circus monkey.

As crazy as the idea sounds, the hollow earth theory owes its origin to a number of often unrelated sources, both mythological and scientific, throughout history. A number of scientific theories have seriously been put forward throughout history that the planet might be hollow, though these were usually legitimate models that were needed to explain certain anomalies with how the planet worked. Real science used Occam's razor to dismiss hollow earth theories in favour of the more likely model of a solid crust above a liquid mantle, but it took some time to settle on it. Edmond Halley, after whom the comet is named, thought that the earth might be hollow and contain several concentric spheres. Leonhard Euler, too, another of history's greatest mathematicians, also proposed a hollow earth model.

But then, many religions and cultural myths make reference to some kind of underworld. Most familiar, probably, is the Judaeo-Christian concept of Hell. But the ancient Greeks had their underworld, as did the Celts, the Indians, the Norse and the Native Americans. So intertwined with our culture is the idea of a mysterious underworld filled with fantastic creatures that this particular trope survived right up to the science fiction era, where authors like Jules Verne and H. P. Lovecraft made devices out of them.

At the height of pulp science fiction's popularity, one magazine, *Amazing Stories*, began to publish stories by an author

39

named Richard Sharpe Shaver. They were the usual kind of fare about adventuring into the hollow earth and meeting fantastic creatures inside. The difference between Shaver and Jules Verne, however, is that Shaver insisted that he wasn't making stuff up. The stories that he told were dictated to him, he claimed, by the actual inhabitants of the hollow earth. These adventures, though fictionalised for the sake of publication, were real.

Now, there are two things that are probably important to mention here. First, Richard Shaver believed that the hollow earth people were speaking to him through the welding equipment he used as part of his job as a mechanic for the Ford Motor Company. Second, he spent parts of his life, on and off, inside of a mental institution. There is an outside possibility that the guy may have been a little nutty. Still, hollow earth theories wound up together with centuries of mythology about underworlds, and intermingled with the already existing Atlantis mythology. Atlantis and the hollow earth became part of the same tradition of pseudoarchaeology, and those who subscribed to the alternative geological and anthropological theories espoused by Richard Shaver's welding equipment started asserting that the residents of Atlantis ultimately wound up in the caverns of the inner earth after their nonexistent continent exploded.

Modern adherents to the hollow earth theory rely heavily upon the myth that the famous polar explorer Admiral Richard Byrd discovered the entrance to the inner earth at the North Pole during one of his expeditions. This belief is bolstered by two things – The first, a quote by Byrd, reported in a number of newspapers in February 1947, where he said: "I'd like to see that land beyond the pole." It's a sad sign when your alternative theory about something so well established as the shape of the world relies upon nine-and-a-half words quoted out of context almost 70 years ago by a man probably not quite famous enough for most of us to have learned his name in school. But that's what people do to bolster the evidence for their weird beliefs, coincidentally the same thing that people do to gather ammunition against the political candidate they don't like – they mine for quotes until they find something said off the cuff that perhaps wasn't as carefully worded as it could have been. Sure, technically speaking, there's no land "beyond" the poles, because once you get there, you're just coming back from the other direction. But I'd sooner make the assumption that Byrd was speaking with a poetic flourish than that he was making some specific reference to a giant mystery hole to an upside-down netherworld that only he knew about.

The second piece of evidence marched out for Byrd's knowledge of the hollow earth is a purported "secret diary" of Byrd's actual adventure in the underworld. The diary came to light around 1995 when a man named "Harley Byrd," who variously claims to be either the grandson or the nephew of the Admiral, found it among Byrd's possessions. The diary, available through Amazon and reprinted on various hollow earth websites, is dated the 19th of February, 1947, right after his "beyond the pole" quote, and details his flight over the Arctic toward the North Pole. Instead of an icy wasteland, he unexpectedly finds himself in a green valley populated by mammoths. As the flight continues, he comes upon a shimmering city, whereupon strange, tall, Germanic-looking beings approach in strange aircraft, take psychic control of his plane, and engage him in a lengthy philosophical conversation about the dangers of nuclear war.[11]

There are several dozen reasons for us to suspect that none of this actually happened. But, no matter what your thoughts are regarding mammoths and inner-earth aliens, the diary reveals itself to be counterfeit in one more verifiable way – although it documents Byrd's adventure to the North Pole in February of 1947, basic research shows us that Admiral Byrd was, at this exact time, assisting the US Navy to establish a research base... at the *South* Pole. Whoever decided to mock up this fictitious journey accidentally placed Byrd on exactly the opposite side of the Earth to where he actually was at the time, indicating that it's either a fake, or Byrd was much, much more lost than he realised.

Another last-ditch effort to bolster the hollow earth theory is the claim that the scientific evidence proves that the planet cannot be solid. As repeated ad nauseum by hollow earth proponents, the physics of planet formation are such that all planets must be created hollow. At least, according to the very limited grasp of physics that these people adhere to. David Icke explains the concept thus:

> The very spin of the planet creates centrifugal force which throws matter to the outside, very much like a spin dryer in which the clothes spin around a hole in the centre. When the planet was in its molten form, spinning into existence before it

[11] If you're curious but you don't want to shell out cash money for Byrd's ridiculously fake secret diary, it's reprinted online at www.admiralbyrddiary.com. The writers of the site appear to have some wacky beliefs of their own, but at least they don't believe the diary is genuine.

cooled, how could it possibly remain solid to the core? It's against all logic and laws of force.[12]

Of course, David, that sounds about right, scientists are forgetting about centrifugal force. Presumably, that's also why everyone keeps getting flung off the surface of the earth all the time – just like clothes in a spin dryer.

Atlantis, the hollow earth and other esoteric geological concepts are important to history in ways that most people don't realise – namely, the part these ideas played in shaping the Holocaust. That does sound like a fairly out of the blue accusation, but all this talk of superior white civilisations coming out of the west to educate the ignorant can never go anywhere good.

In 1911, a German secret society called the Thule Society was started by one Walter Nauhaus from Berlin. The Latin word "Thule" was the name given in ancient times to a land on the edge of the known world, which was most likely Scandinavia in reality, but after Ignatius Donnelly revived the legend of Atlantis, European occultists began to conflate Atlantis with Thule, the ancient home of a superior white race. To become a member of the Thule Society, you had to sign a declaration that you were Aryan, a pure descendent of the Atlanteans, and neither you nor your wife were polluted by Jewish or coloured blood. One of the symbols they adopted was the swastika, the hooked cross, an Indian Vedic symbol. In the 19th century, German scholars believed a now disproven theory that the Indians were descended from an influx of Aryan people some 3,500 years ago, and so the Thule Society chose the swastika to symbolise this migration, as they figured they knew exactly where all these white people came from – Plato's great sunken continent.

The Thule Society was prominent in Germany by 1919, and as they were kind of racist, they wound up becoming associated with and supporting a lot of right-wing workers groups. Adolf Hitler was never a member, but the Society's membership nevertheless read like a who's who of prominent Nazis like Heinrich Himmler, Rudolph Hess, and Dietrich Eckart, to whom *Mein Kampf* was dedicated. Though Hitler himself was never documented to have any occult leanings (his horrid racism was rooted in more secular conspiracy theories, as I'll explain later) the Nazi party, which sprang at least partially from the offshoots of the Thule Society (and adopted their swastika logo), was nonetheless

---

[12] The Biggest Secret, p. 251

packed with people with bizarre mystic ideas. Though anti-Semitism came to Europe with many diverse justifications, it can't be discounted that one of them was a belief that white people came from Plato's sunken continent and marched into Europe via India and, as some believed, the hollow centre of the earth, and then something something so let's kill Jews.

The connection between Nazis and the hollow earth theory comes up again and again, and the degree to which the actual Nazis may have believed in a hollow earth is largely speculative as a lot of the claims come from "historians" who are occasionally Nazis and believe in a hollow earth themselves. One such source is Ernst Zundel, a prominent holocaust denier who believes that the Nazis fled to the hollow earth through the entrance in Antarctica, and go about their time nowerdays buzzing us in UFOs, which are really Nazi antigravity devices. Sounds legit.

Even today, people are coming up with new ways to argue that the shape of the earth is not what they say it is, because all is apparently lost if we allow that scientists are right about even the most fundamental of concepts. Another esoteric theory that has some traction at the moment is the "expanding earth." Like the hollow earth, it's a theory that was once seriously proposed by non-crazy people – before we knew about plate tectonics, we knew we needed to explain why the world's continents all fit together like a jigsaw puzzle. Today we know that it's because they slide around on the liquid mantle like pucks on a hockey rink, but at one time it was considered that the planet was actually growing – if you take away all the oceans, the earth's continents all lock together in a solid ball of land half as large.

The expanding earth was first seriously proposed by the eminent Australian geologist Samuel Warren Carey. At the time, it was the only way that geologists could explain the movement of the continents – imagine the continents arranged on the surface of a balloon so that they all lock together, and then blowing up the balloon so that they gradually break away from each other separated by the balloon's naked surface, which represents the ocean. Of course, what this model leaves unexplained is how the planet could be gaining mass, seemingly from the inside. The balloon model is fine and dandy until you realise that God isn't standing in front of the Earth blowing air into it. But the expanding earth, or "expansion tectonics," was certainly a promising hypothesis that would have solved this puzzle if only we could figure out how the world could be physically growing.

We never did figure that out, though, considering it would contradict one of the most fundamental scientific laws, which is that mass doesn't just appear out of nowhere and stick around. Luckily, we soon discovered an alternative explanation that doesn't require us to throw the laws of physics in the bin. In the 1960s, an intensive study of the ocean floor located deep seams that stretched around the surface of the globe, giant cracks that open into the very molten core of the planet. The most important discovery about these ridges was that the ocean floor is younger the closer you get to them. What this means is that the planet's core is constantly barfing up new solid ground. Magma that erupts from these volcanic fissures, cooled by the ocean, creates new rock that pushes the old rock away from it. You can imagine this as though the continents are each riding on an escalator – as the ground emerges from one side, it is forced back down into the molten core on the other side. Understandably, the act of mighty continents driving vast swaths of land back into the centre of the earth with blunt trauma is a pretty forceful and energetic process, so you would expect that the ground would occasionally rupture and shake and a bunch of stuff would fall over. That's how the brilliant theory of plate tectonics explained both continental drift *and* earthquakes in one fell swoop.

Still, although plate tectonics fits so neatly as an explanation for geological activity and doesn't create any major new questions, there are still people who adhere to the expanding earth hypothesis because... well, it's hard to say. I would presume that it's simply because plate tectonics is the model that is accepted by the scientific community, and there is a kind of person who would declare it false on that basis alone. Perhaps the foremost proponent of the expanding earth idea today is Dr James Maxlow, an Australian geologist who works for the mining industry and, on the side, valiantly upholds the expanding earth theory against the naysayers who comprise the entirety of his profession. Historically as well as today, the biggest question facing expanding earth theorists is where the extra mass comes from. In answer to this question, Maxlow reveals in his 2005 seminar in Brisbane: "Unfortunately, human nature decrees that we must understand the cause of things before we understand the physical side of things, or want to comprehend the physical side of things."[13] In other words, who cares what the mechanism is? The important thing is that it really, really looks like the planet is expanding.

---

[13] http://tinyurl.com/bw9t453

I beg to disagree with Dr Maxlow here. I think the mechanism is important, because if it's true, we have to rewrite physics back to around the turn of the first millennium. And that's a serious problem for the theory, considering that plate tectonics has no such problem, and in fact no major problems. Those who doubt plate tectonics, along with adherents to most other exotic scientific explanations, appeal almost exclusively to a "yeah right" appeal. In this case, "yeah right, oceanic crust is constantly being pushed underground by the movement of the plates. Pull the other one, mate." But it never ceases to amaze that those who find plate subduction hard to swallow, for some reason, prefer to subscribe to a theory that requires a magical mass factory at the centre of the planet that sucks new matter, I suppose, out of another dimension. Maxlow can protest all he wants that the mechanism isn't as important as the observation, but let's formulate our scientific theories around rules of the universe that we know to be real, rather than appeal to exotic new physics to fulfill a fervent desire for the world to be some kind of Terry Pratchett novel.

## The 2012 Phenomenon (And Don't You All Feel Stupid Now)

NASA's astrobiology website recently launched a feature called "Ask an Astrobiologist."[14] True to the name, the public is invited to submit questions to astrobiologist David Morrison, all those hard-pressing astrobiology questions of which I can't think of a single one right now.

This, perhaps, turned out to be a mistake. Since switching on this feature, Morrison reports he has received almost 1000 questions about the coming of something called "Nibiru." The bombardment is so heavy that NASA has had to go to increasingly desperate measures to convince the public, even to the extent of getting Morrison to release a video statement, that there is no such thing as Nibiru. Still, the questions keep coming.

Let's back up a moment. In 1999, the year the prominent conspiracy theorist Prince insisted that he'd party the hardest, a crisis began to sweep the population and the media. It was referred to colloquially as the "Millennium bug," or "Y2K." The problem was this: Scientists and engineers set up all of our computers and electronics with internal clocks that used only the last two digits of the year to keep track of time. These computers being the products of the 20th century, nobody took the time to consider what would happen when the

---

[14] http://astrobiology.nasa.gov/ask-an-astrobiologist/

numbers stopped counting up. Toward the end of the 90s, people suddenly realised that the date was going to click over to "00" on the dawn of the millennium. This would confuse them and, it was reasonably assumed, all our electronics would get confused and stop working or maybe start killing people or something.

Movies and television specials were made to capitalise on the fear of the coming Y2K problem. At a special United Nations conference, delegates from 120 countries met to discuss contingency plans for the crisis. Billions of dollars were spent attempting to upgrade computers to fix the bug before it manifested. As the new year approached, everyone grit their teeth... and then, nothing. The year 2000 came and went. There were a few minor, temporary glitches in places as far off as Hong Kong that caused to lasting ill effects (the impact on Australia was felt as two bus ticket machines broke down), and the world otherwise went about its routine.

The aftermath of a doomsday scare is something strange to behold – it's strange for its silence. Waking up, perhaps, to a period of relief, people just go about their business. January 1st brings with it a few late night jokes from Leno, and then the issue is never mentioned again. Despite the omnipresence of the Y2K crisis I remember from my childhood, there is precious little information about it on the internet today. Everyone just moved on.

But it didn't go away, not really. Prognosticators of the Y2k scare, like David Wilcock, merely pulled or revamped their websites to focus on a new date for the apocalypse – December 31, 2012. Since you're reading this in 2013 or later, unless you're a time-traveler, we can reasonably assume that nothing happened, and the 2012 thing is remembered, like the Millennium Bug, as an amusing and overblown hysteria that we're already beginning to forget.

Let me take you back a few months. According to the popular theories, one of three things would happen on December 21, 2012:

One, the world would be completely or mostly destroyed for any one of a myriad reasons. So you're dead, and your loved ones won't remember you to mourn your passing.

Two, human civilisation would undergo some kind of spiritual or evolutionary Renaissance. We would all ascend to some higher ethereal plane and obtain some kind of universal wisdom the likes of which no philosopher save for Plato in his most lucid fever dreams could have ever predicted, at which point we would presumably have no more need for books that describe the world in a way that our miserable reptile brains can comprehend.

So if you are reading this, we can probably assume that the third scenario is true: Nothing happened. The world looks pretty much the same as it did before. We're still going to war for stupid reasons, politicians are still arguing about how to stave off environmental catastrophe, people are still watching reality TV, Hollywood is still remaking movies they really should leave alone, and kids are still disrespectful to their parents.

If we're dead, or we've all ascended to the astral plane, either way I'm in the comfortable position of not having to admit I was wrong. So let's assume we're all alive and still human and leap right into talking about how everyone was wrong about the slightly embarrassing fad of human history that was the 2012 phenomenon.

The story begins way back in the medieval period at the height of the Mayan civilisation in what is now Mexico. Unaware of the ongoing Dark Ages in faraway Europe, the Mayans were perhaps the most powerful and influential civilisation in Middle America until their collapse, a story you already know if you've seen Mel Gibson's *Apocalypto*, a story which was followed up by an even more depressing Spanish conquest. But along with their many innovations, the Mayans had a bit of an obsession with calendars. They had different calendars for different purposes, but the important one is what we call the *Long Count*. It's kind of like our calendar – they picked a year to begin, and counted up from there. (Their "year one" was 3114 BC). Unlike our calendar, however, theirs also had an end date. Any guesses what that is?

To be clear, the Mayan calendar doesn't end on December 21, 2012 for any special reason associated with that date. That's simply where they ran out of numbers. It's kind of the same deal as the Y2K bug – remember when they were afraid of the year 2000 because computers only kept track of the last two digits of the year and so they were going to roll back to zero and we thought this would confuse them and send them into a murderous robot uprising or something? In a similar way, 2012 is when the Mayan Long Count calendar rolls back to zero. And, like Y2K, people think for some reason that this means the end of civilisation as we know it.

Here's a bit of trivia for you. Have you ever wondered why we have 10 digits in our counting system? It's not entirely arbitrary. It's simply because we have ten fingers. Early humans used their fingers to count, and so they could represent up to ten things just by holding up their hands, which is probably as many things as anyone really needed to count back in the Stone Age. When we invented writing, we just used the same system, replacing fingers with ten symbols. When we get past 9, we just roll over to zero again, but we put a 1 at the beginning so we know we're still counting – 10.

The Mayans were a little different – they had 20 digits, probably because they used their toes as well. There were apparently a lot of things to count in ancient Mexico. The Mayan way of counting was the same as ours except that the digits rolled over when they reached 20.

The Mayan Long Count calendar was just a line of numbers that they used to denote the date, the same as how we can denote a date numerically like this: 21-12-2012.

A Mayan date looked like this: 0.0.0.0.1. That was the day the Mayans set for the beginning of the world, which we believe is August 11, 3114 BC for whatever reason. But instead of just recording the day, the month, and the year, like we do, the Mayans recorded the day, the month, the year, plus a 20 year block called a *katun*, and a 20 katun block called a *baktun*, which is a pretty cumbersome way of doing things (imagine if every time you wrote the date you had to note the day, the month, the year, the decade, and the century.)

A Mayan year had 18 months of 20 days, to fit their estimate that there were 360 days in a year, which is close enough to forgive them five measly days. For reasons we're not sure about, their highest count, the baktun, only seems to go up to 13. Everything else was counted in factors of 20, and 18 for the month.

So whereas our calendar, known as the

"Shoot, I ran out of room."
"Don't worry, 5000 years is long enough. We won't need this thing anymore after we invent the Blackberry."

Gregorian calendar, repeats every 365 days (364 in a leap year), the Mayan calendar never repeated for thousands of years, which is probably longer than they thought they would survive anyway (and they were right!)

But just like the odometer in a really old car, that first digit does eventually need to roll over. And through the mists of time, centuries after the Mayan civilisation collapsed, their ridiculously, unnecessarily long calendar kept ticking over, until it gets to 13.19.19.17.19. That happens on December 21, 2012. *And then, night falls.*

In 1966, the celebrated archaeologist Michael D. Coe was probably the first person to hypothesise that the end of the Mayan Long Count corresponded with some kind of apocalypse. Now, it's important to note that this is just a whimsical theory, because *the Mayans themselves never said that.* There is no evidence that the Mayans believed *anything* about 13.19.19.17.19 except that they didn't figure they needed a sixth column to tack another few millennia onto their calendar, and if they did, they had thousands of years to prepare for it.

But let's say there really was some forgotten doomsday mythology associated with the end of the Mayan calendar, which is possible. It's important to note that Coe wasn't suggesting that the world would *actually end* with the Mayan Long Count, just that the Mayans may have *believed* that. If you were afraid of what might happen at the end of 2012, I would ask, when did you convert to the Mayan religion? It doesn't make much sense to believe the world is going to end in 2012 if you don't also believe in the prophesised return of the feathered serpent god Quetzocoatl. It's the same as believing that the end of the world would come after three years of winter, at which time the god-wolf Skoll devours the sun, like the Vikings believed.

Because the Mayans never said anything about 2012 themselves, the date was wide open for new-agers to say anything they like about it. After Michael Coe dropped the baton on the 2012 date, it was picked up by popular new-agers such as José Argüelles, whose Central America-ish name probably lent a lot of credibility to his ability to tap into the spiritual heart of the Mayan civilisation, despite the fact that he was from Minnesota and his real name was Joe. The new age community has reached fever pitch about the date's possible implications, what John Hoopes describes as a "bubble" in New

Ageism.[15] Proponents of freaky deaky metaphysics have made a lot of money selling to the public whatever nonsense they made up about 2012 on any particular morning and on any particular drug.

Roughly, we can sort the pseudoscientific bastard children of Mayan interpretation into two camps (though they're not mutually exclusive). There are the New Agers, like Argüelles, who believe in ill-defined and vague-by-design concepts such as spiritual ascension and global awakening and universal consciousness fields and things like that. Then there are those who subscribe to what we call *catastrophism*. As the name implies, this is the fetishistic concept of our planet and solar system having been shaped and designed by incomprehensibly huge, catastrophic disasters. It's commonly adhered to by the kind of people who line up overnight for every Roland Emmerich movie.

Probably the most popular founding father of modern catastrophism was the Russian psychiatrist Immanuel Velikovsky, who used his extensive knowledge in the field of psychiatry to develop a new astronomical theory for the creation of the solar system. In typical pseudoarchaeologist style, he formulated his theory based on the myths and legends of ancient people, reinterpreting their mythologies as literal facts. In his case, rather than trying to find aliens in the pages of ancient lore, he saw descriptions of what he believed to be astronomical catastrophe, and postulated, for example, that the planet Venus was originally a comet that flew into the solar system, bounced off the other planets like billiard balls, ramming them into new orbits, and then passed perilously close to the Earth, where it triggered worldwide natural disasters – earthquakes, volcanos, and tidal waves. Of course, this would have been what sank Atlantis, because you can't believe one nonsense theory about ancient history without believing them all, apparently.

The 2012 phenomenon picked up other pseudoarchaeological concepts as it rolled along, like rolling a hotdog along a dusty hallway, except that the dust is made of bullshit, and also the hotdog is made of bullshit. Catastrophism is no different, and it eventually boarded the 2012 train, notably with John Major Jenkins and other authors who speculated that 2012 would bring the Earth into some kind of syzygy or celestial alignment, most commonly with the equator of the Milky Way, or more recently, with Sagittarius A*, an excitingly huge and scary black hole at the centre of our galaxy. This is predicted by

---

[15] Hoopes, John W. (2011). A critical history of 2012 mythology. *"Oxford IX" International Symposium on Archaeoastronomy Proceedings IAU Symposium No. 278*

catastrophists to trigger a whole heap of Earth disasters such as the aforementioned holy trinity of earthquakes, volcanos, and tidal waves, but also more exotic disasters such as pole reversals, crustal displacements, and the sudden appearance of a bunch of little black holes that will whiz around our solar system making for a bad day for everyone involved. Absolutely none of this is based on science.

Speaking of Roland Emmerich, it's worth noting that the director probably has the dubious honour of having done more than anyone else to plant the terror of 2012 catastrophism in the public consciousness, having made the somewhat socially irresponsible, and definitely lazy, decision to use the pre-established 2012 mythology as the promotion for the 2009 disaster action film aptly named *2012*. Though the film itself doesn't really involve Mayan prophecy or indeed any of the disaster scenarios related to 2012 culture (Emmerich preferred to make up his own nonsense about neutrinos from the sun mutating and microwaving the Earth from the inside out, or something), it did come with its own promotional base built-in. Most films that take advantage of viral advertising need to cough up a lot of money to create the artificial mythology that they'll use as a basis for their promotion, but Emmerich simply had to attach the words "Google 2012" to his teaser trailers and posters, and the greater public introduced themselves to the pre-established world of 2012 catastrophism. Of course, unlike Emmerich's film, the catastrophist tradition didn't consider itself to be fiction. Emmerich's film is credited as being based, in part, on the work of the very deadly serious pseudoarchaeologist Graham Hancock. And so, like deliberately detonating a smallpox bomb in the heart of a major city, Emmerich exposed the general population to the 2012 panic in the name of selling a movie. Very soon, NASA started getting those panicky emails about Nibiru.

Just what in the universe is Nibiru? This is the point at which pseudoarchaeology reaches its pinnacle of absurdity. Take the bowl of ignorance that Erich von Däniken produced, filter it through the drug-addled minds of some New Agers and, to be sure, a few genuinely mentally ill people, then add a little positive reinforcement from pop culture, and what you get is a baffling nigh-hysterical implosion of critical thinking that leads scientists wondering just where it went wrong. Well, here's what happened:

After von Däniken and his disciples came Zecharia Sitchin, and if the pseudoarchaeology family can already be considered eccentric, Sitchin was even by those standards the mildly embarrassing crazy uncle. His studies focused on the mythology of the people of Sumer, modern Iraq. Like the other theorists of his discipline, Sitchin took a highly literal approach to ancient mythology, believing that stories about creatures coming down from the sky are literal historical accounts of exactly that. But Sitchin went beyond the question-oriented work of people like von Däniken and proposed answers to mysteries like who these aliens were, where they came from and what they wanted.

According to Sitchin, the Sumerian legends tell the story of beings who came from "the twelfth planet." Being that the Sumerians classified the sun and the moon as planets (ten and eleven), the twelfth planet must be some as yet undiscovered planet orbiting beyond Pluto. The planet orbits in an elliptical path around the sun that takes it close to Earth every 3600 years, at which time the alien inhabitants, called *Annunaki*, hop off and cause shenanigans in our world. The last time they were here, the Annunaki came to mine gold, but because they were too lazy to work the mines themselves, they genetically altered some hominids they found here in order to create human beings for slave labour. And that is how our species came to be. We are the half-alien bastard children of gold miners from Planet X.

What Sitchin offered here was something that von Däniken could not – a definitive mythology. Various proponents of the ancient astronauts hypothesis have traditionally taken a "what if" approach to their findings. "Surely ancient people couldn't have built such incredible monuments. *What if* aliens did it?" It's up to us to speculate what motives these beings might possibly have had, where they came from and what they had to teach us. Sitchin, however, offers closure for these questions, and that is a very attractive thing for those who are allured by this Star-Trekkish interpretation of prehistory. What Sitchin has done, essentially, is what the ancients did when they tried to explain the movement of the sun as gods carrying it across the sky in chariots, or to explain drought by suggesting the goddess of the rain had been kidnapped from Midgard by the frost giants. He's created a mythology that puts closure to complex investigation. And what puts his explanation above the mundane scientific version of events is that Sitchin's story is *freaking awesome!*

As always, the Chinese whispers continued as Sitchin's version of the story was expanded upon by other amateur researchers bedazzled by the idea of ancient alien contact, which at this point looked less like von Däniken's idle musing about pyramids and more like the grand mythology of *The X Files*. Although Sitchin's mythology is closely associated with the 2012 phenomenon, the man himself never made that connection – Sitchin's Nibiru isn't scheduled to make an appearance until 2900, which gives us almost another millennium before we have to worry about gold mining aliens getting all up in our faces. There are probably a few authors who meddled with Sitchin enough to bring it into alignment with the 2012 phenomenon, but it went through two notable transformations in the first decade of the 21st century:

First, Turkish pseudoarchaeologist Burak Eldem, in his book *2012: Rendezvous With Marduk*, retconned Sitchin's proposed 3600 year orbit for Nibiru in order to suggest that the planet's next return to our part of the neighbourhood will occur in 2012, which is more about messing around with research to make it fit a pre-decided hypothesis than it is about finding an actual pattern.

Also notable is the influence of Nancy Lieder. Rather than another pseudoarchaeologist applying bad logic to ancient scripture, Lieder offers another perspective to this rapidly growing snowball of crazy. An average woman who has the good luck to actually be in telepathic contact with alien beings, Lieder's contribution to von Däniken's and Sitchin's legacy is very probably inspired more by some form of mental illness than any scientific inquiry. However, at this point, it's difficult to separate simple poor logic from genuine mental illness. We've Dan-Brown-Hammered this story to the point of no sane return.

Nancy Lieder became something of an internet celebrity in the mid-1990s when she started assaulting newsgroups with the warnings being beamed into her head from aliens from Zeta Reticuli. Initially, she warned that the comet Hale-Bopp (the same one that was central to the Heaven's Gate suicide cult tragedy) didn't exist, and was in fact a hoax designed to distract us from the existence of the rapidly approaching Planet Nibiru. Back then, she claimed that Nibiru was to pass close to Earth in 2003, but when that never happened, the Zetas told her that the mysterious planet was hiding behind the sun.

Rather than anyone trying to find Ms Lieder some much needed help, people started to get on board with her theories as presented on her website *ZetaTalk*. An amalgamation of various ancient astronaut theories, as well as themes from popular ufology and Illuminati conspiracy theories I'll be discussing in section 2, Lieder became a kind of Pied Piper for both known and undiagnosed schizophrenics who can be found spouting variations of her theory all over the internet. That is, in a way, the downside to the anarchic, user-generated nature of the world wide web – those who are already swayed by the faux-academic theories of otherwise sane individuals like Sitchin can have a difficult time distinguishing simple bad science from literal mental delusion. As a result, thousands of people wind up concerned about the Nibiru Armageddon, unaware that what they're reading is a veritable Frankenstein's Monster of bad logic, pseudoscience, misinterpretation, and mental illness.

Lieder's claims about telepathic contact with aliens need no debunking in and of themselves. But it is worth mentioning that Lieder, as far as prophets go, isn't exactly Nostradamus material. The predictions communicated to her from Zeta Reticuli have boasted a 100% failure rate, from Nibiru's arrival in 2003, to earthquakes and cataclysms that never came to pass. Lieder's alien friends are accurate less often than a magic 8-ball.

"Nibiru" now has a front-and-centre position in the culture of 2012 catastrophism. Having drifted, rogue-planet-like, away from its origin as an explanation for pyramid-building aliens, Nibiru drunkenly hooked up with Velikovskian theory to produce a cultural fear that this wandering planet was going to mosey on into our solar system soon and, like Velikovsky's malicious Venus, its proximity would cause earthquakes and tidal waves and polar reversals and, according to some wackjobs, turn the moon upside-down. As the relevant date approaches, catastrophism is permeated into and diluted by our popular culture by disaster artists and filmmakers like Roland Emmerich, who find it slots perfectly into a cultural fetish for doomsday scenarios. More recently, Lars von Trier released his end-of-the-world film *Melancholia*, which, although it doesn't reference Nibiru or Sitchin, is almost certainly inspired by the culture surrounding Nibiru – the film takes place in the final days before Earth collides with and is destroyed by a giant rogue planet, which, as Nancy Lieder predicted, was hiding behind the sun this whole time.

It is possible, though, to cut the Nibiru theory off at its roots. It's not just the case that it won't get here soon after 2012 (by now, it would be the biggest and brightest object in the sky besides the sun and the moon), but we can prove that Nibiru doesn't—cannot, in fact—even exist.

In my seventh year of primary school, 1996 or thereabouts, I remember a project was given to the class for each of us to choose a planet of the solar system to research and present as a poster. As I was drawn to spooky stuff even back then, I naturally chose Pluto, the cold and dead outermost planet named after the Greek god who ruled the underworld. With my mother's help, I made a bleak looking poster with two black Styrofoam balls stuck to it representing Pluto and its moon Charon, the ferryman who transports souls across the river Styx.

My own kids could never repeat such a project today, and not just because, in the 16 years since then, Pluto has been found to actually have four moons. More importantly than that, astronomers made an astounding and game-changing discovery in 2005 that forever altered the way we think about our planetary neighbourhood. It was a rocky object orbiting the very outer reaches of our solar system, and it was slightly bigger than Pluto.

The headlines immediately declared the object, now known as Eris, to be the tenth planet in the solar system. But behind the scenes, the discovery was stirring a wave of controversy within the astronomical community. Namely, with all the thousands of meteors, asteroids and comets whizzing around our cosmic backyard, how exactly does one define a planet?

In 2006, the International Astronomical Union came to a decision that made headlines worldwide – after a re-evaluation of the definition of planets, Eris and Pluto, as well as any other object that failed to meet the new criteria, were hereby demoted in status to "dwarf planets," reducing the number of planets in our solar system to eight, with Neptune being the most distant.

What does this have to do with Nibiru? If Zecharia Sitchin interpreted the Sumerian texts correctly, then the Annunaki aliens inhabit the "twelfth planet" (remember this includes the sun and moon, making it the tenth planet by our definition). This made sense as an undiscovered planet beyond Pluto, when Sitchin wrote it, but given our current knowledge, the notion of a "tenth" planet is much more complicated. Sitchin suggests that the knowledge of the number of planets in our solar system was given to the Sumerians by advanced aliens, but what definition were *they* using? Surely they knew, as we have come to know in the past couple of decades, that there are actually *dozens* of "planets" in our solar system. We recognise eight, but only through a fairly arbitrary categorisation that, to keep tradition more or less intact, accepts Mercury as a planet but denies Eris. Do the Annunaki, through some coincidence, use the same definition that we do now? Do they use the definition we used prior to 2006? Or do they use another definition? The idea of a tenth planet would have made sense to Sitchin at a time when there were nine planets and possibly another to be discovered, but given what we know today, for a tenth planet to exist, there must be at least two new objects at least the size of

Earth beyond Neptune (at this point unlikely) or else the Annunaki are living on Eris, or Pluto, or even Neptune or Uranus depending on your definition, and none of those places would be very comfortable. To be sure, none of these objects are coming near Earth, as Sitchin predicted, any time soon.

But let's say there's some way we can work out the semantic problem. No matter where Nibiru rates within the number of planets in the solar system, it's still impossible by the very laws of physics for a planet to behave the way Sitchin says this one does.

Let's look at the basic details of Sitchin's Nibiru – a large planet that orbits around the sun, and comes close to Earth once every 3600 years. Basic physics tells us that for such an object to travel from the outer solar system to the inner solar system within its orbit, Nibiru must be on an elliptical orbit – not a circle, but on an oval-shaped path that takes it through the orbits of the other planets, like Halley's Comet. From the two details we know about Nibiru—the length of its orbit and the distance it comes from the Earth, it's possible to calculate the shape of its orbit around the sun. According to an orbital calculator available online (at janus.astro.umd.edu) the orbit of a planet that comes within close proximity of the Earth once every 3600 years would be so elliptical that it's nearly a straight line. Like throwing a ball straight up in the air. At its furthest point, the gravitational force pulling it back toward the sun would be so weak that a meteor impact could knock it right out of the solar system like a billiard ball that gets cued right off the table and into someone's beer glass. In fact, if it comes within shouting distance from any of the big planets like Saturn or Jupiter (as it's sure to do, ducking constantly across their orbits) then the gravitational perturbations would drag it into some other orbit, or fling it out into space, or crash it into something, or throw it into the sun. In short, the ancients shouldn't have worried about seeing Nibiru again in 3600 years, because it can't possibly have survived that long.

It's a novel theory that Sitchin came up with, the alien visitors from the twelfth planet, but he failed to check the physics to see if it made any sense, and unfortunately for his very exciting narrative, the existence of Nibiru, on the path he described, with the length of orbit that he described, is scientifically impossible. The only way that it could work would be if Nibiru has the kind of magic powers that Nancy Lieder ascribes to it, with the ability to speed up and slow down and do a U-turn or stand perfectly still behind the sun if it's feeling shy.

But let's pretend through some miracle of physics that this planet has managed to survive in its fragile orbit for all this time, or that there's some other fact Sitchin was missing or got wrong that makes it possible. The most important fact about Nibiru, actually the foundation of the entire theory, is that aliens live there. You know, the actual ancient astronauts. Without the aliens, there's no reason to believe in Nibiru at all. So what Sitchin is actually asking us to believe is that there's a planet somewhere out beyond Pluto that is teeming with advanced life forms who UFO themselves over here whenever they're in the neighbourhood.

Let's think about that for a moment. Astrobiologists generally think that life is fairly rare in the universe because Earth lies within what they call the "Goldilocks zone," a narrow band of distance away from the sun where it's not too hot and not too cold for biological life to exist without freezing or bursting into flames. Scientists think that there may be very simple life on Mars or perhaps one of the moons of Jupiter, but they certainly don't think there's anything living on Mercury or Saturn.

Now think about Pluto, so far out that it's always night and the sun looks like nothing more than an unusually bright star in the sky. The temperature on Pluto is between -218 to -240 degrees Celsius (-400 to -360 degrees F). At its coldest, it is cold enough to freeze nitrogen. For context, you've probably seen scientists or teachers doing cool stuff with liquid nitrogen, dipping different objects like bananas in there and showing them freeze solid immediately. The surface temperature on Pluto is cold enough to freeze *that stuff*. In winter on Pluto, it actually *snows nitrogen*. You could make a snowman out of Pluto's atmosphere if not for the fact that you would already be very, very dead.

Nibiru, according to Sitchin, is much further out than that. And it has people? At that distance it's just about the least likely place in the universe for life to exist. You would just as soon find people walking about on the surface of the sun. And you might argue that aliens as advanced as the Annunaki would obviously have some kind of really good air conditioning technology, but they had to evolve for billions of years at the full mercy of the elements before they were able to invent it.

Now, I like to think I'm creative enough to come up with a few scenarios in which life could exist on Nibiru. Maybe already advanced aliens travelled from a more habitable part of the galaxy to settle there (although I don't know why they would choose the least habitable planet in the solar system to colonise when Mars is just sitting there). I've seen some people suggest that Nibiru is somehow naturally centrally heated. But there's that hammer again. Arguing further at this point is just an effort to support the Nibiru hypothesis, which would make sense if we *saw* Nibiru and its aliens and then had to explain how that is possible. But that's not the case – ancient astronaut theorists see certain phenomena on Earth and then invent hypotheses to explain *that*. Nibiru is a hypothesis to explain a phenomenon, it is *not* a phenomenon itself that needs an explanation. All it needs is to be falsified or not. And it is falsified. Like the theory that the sun orbits the Earth, it is proven wrong. To come up with creative theories to defend it is to defend something you have already decided to believe is true. And why? My first question for anyone who believes in Nibiru and its aliens is what exactly facilitates that belief? What led you to believe that, and why continue to believe it in the face of contrary evidence? Besides the fact that it would be *really cool?*

Finally, there are those who would be swayed by the photographic "evidence" of Nibiru that clogs up the internet. Do a simple search and you'll find thousands of blurry dots in the sky that people declare to be Nibiru(!!!), though no two look alike and the thing seems to approach and recede and change shape and colour depending on who is looking at it. And apparently it has the power to vanish completely, as well, because otherwise you should be able to see it right now. As I mentioned, if it was due to enter Earth's orbit close to 2012, it would be about as obvious as the moon right now. The damn thing would light up the night sky. There are people who argue that the government or somebody is covering it up by blacking out telescope images, but you wouldn't need a telescope to see Nibiru at the moment. It would be so visible to the naked eye that you could pretty much see the Annunaki on the surface, shaking their fists at you and whispering "Soon, Earthling, soon."

But still, there are those images. What else could they possibly be? Besides stars, or galaxies, or nova, or Venus, or planes, or lens flares? If you knew for sure that it was none of those things (because you are a professional astronomer) then sure, maybe be open to the possibility that it's this impossible planet that has the ability to turn invisible whenever it feels like it. Otherwise, relax. You can believe in ghosts before you believe in Nibiru. You can even believe in aliens… just not from Nibiru. With all due respect to the late Mr Sitchin, this myth is, as they say, thoroughly busted.

But *what about the gosh darn Sumerians?* What were they talking about if Nibiru wasn't really there? They knew *something*, right? Well, it's true that the ancient Sumerians did go on about something they called Nibiru, but Sitchin was mistaken about what that was. So even if you believe that the Sumerians trump our scientists in terms of who knows more about what's in our solar system, the fact is that even the *Sumerians* didn't think there was a big planet out beyond Pluto with aliens on it.

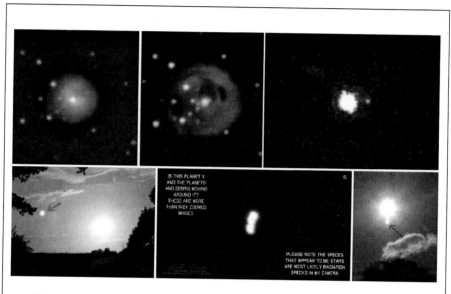

**Various photographs of stars, nebulae, galaxies and lens flares that amateur astronomers on the internet have concluded are probably Nibiru. Probably.**

Michael S. Heiser, Professor of ancient Semitic languages at the University of Wisconsin-Madison, did some independent research to follow up on Sitchin's translations and figure out just what the Sumerians were talking about when they mentioned Nibiru. The results were a little inconclusive – Heiser found that the Sumerians occasionally referred to Nibiru as the name of a god, but it was also the name they gave to Jupiter. Once they seem to get confused and refer to Mercury as "Nibiru." Sometimes they even say it in reference to one of the fixed stars. So even the Sumerians couldn't seem to settle on one thing for Nibiru to be – practically the only thing they never associate it with is some new planet out beyond Pluto.[16] Everything that they call Nibiru is a known object that you can see right now. So not only is the

---

[16] Heiser, Michael S. (2005). The Myth of a Sumerian 12th Planet. http://www.michaelsheiser.com/nibiru.pdf

existence of Nibiru impossible, but nobody has ever actually claimed it exists in the first place. Except Zecharia Sitchin, of course.

Human beings have an odd inclination toward doomsday scenarios. It's probably a manifestation of the fact that our lives are couched within the defined boundaries of beginning and end. We are born, and we die. So too must the greater scope of our human society have a birth and a death. As such, most cultures around the world have a creation story, and most have an end times story. Most of them are really fanciful. The Bible of course has its tale of the great serpent who will do battle with the Archangel Michael while the four horsemen travel the globe spreading famine and disease, and ultimately, Christ returns to raise the dead and subject them to final judgment. The Vikings had their Ragnarok, where the wolf god Skroll devours the sun and the serpent Jormungand wages war on humanity. Secular society hasn't destroyed our fantasies of apocalypse, it just called for new, more sci-fi versions of the tale, like zombie apocalypses, alien invasions, and the coming of Nibiru.

Even now, end of the world fetishists are moving the goalposts for the next date of Armageddon. Not long after 2012 passed, Pope Benedict XVI became the first pope of modern times to abdicate his throne, and the news started to report on a curious emerging belief pointing to an ancient Catholic prophecy that states that the 266th pope would preside over the end of the world. Benedict XVI was pope number 265. We'll wait with bated breath to see if the prophets are right this time.

# SECTION TWO:
# SOME DARE CALL IT CONSPIRACY

*"Man is a credulous animal, and must believe something; in the absence of good grounds for belief, he will be satisfied with bad ones."*

*Bertrand Russell*

We're halfway through the lecture when Wilcock begins his discussion of, as he says it with a mock-ominous tone, the "dreaded Illuminati." They are aliens. But they're not necessarily the ones we think they are. I find it amusing that, at this point, Wilcock mercilessly ridicules the ideas of David Icke, that the Illuminati are shape-shifting reptilian monsters. The reptilians, the Sumerian Annunaki, do exist, but they are not the Illuminati.

After summarising all the famous figures who he has been in past lives (and telling us how embarrassing it is, but insisting that it is what it is), he gives us a sermon that essentially amounts to him being the saviour of mankind. He stops short of proclaiming himself the son of the godhead, but his claims are downright messianic. His personal research into the secret powers that control the world is the most important of its kind ever undertaken, and for his efforts, he has almost single-handedly brought down the Illuminati. His fans, living their whole adult lives in some cases under the spectre of the great ancient evil, are incredibly overjoyed to hear this. Imagine a Christian minister standing before his congregation and announcing that he personally killed Satan – and them believing him. That's similar to the applause Wilcock is getting right now.

Wilcock's Illuminati narrative is unique. He doesn't have the same hopeless, bleak outlook of the likes of Alex Jones (in fact, he mocks Jones a few times and does a pretty spot-on vocal impression). He's an optimistic conspiracist. He paints a fairly sad and pathetic impression of the Evil Organisation, that it's kind of small and desperate after the barrage of public awareness that Wilcock and his friends have dealt to it. According to Wilcock, there's a second Illuminati, a good one, based in China, called the "Dragon Family." He weaves some kind of story about how the Illuminati and the Dragon

Family have been engaged in a millennia-old battle for world dominance, and they keep stealing each other's gold or something. I couldn't really get a firm grip on his *Game of Thrones* style tale of political intrigue, not with my back complaining to me about the fat guy's elbow lodged in my ribs, but it's not a version I've heard before. If anything, it's refreshing that he's applied a little imagination to the same old story. Apparently, due mainly to Wilcock's efforts to expose the truth, the heads of the Illuminati are going to be arrested in the coming weeks.

The establishment, of course, is going to fall along with it. But we'll be fine without the financial systems, as long as we remain spiritual. "The American dollar only has around six weeks left," he says, according to his sources, "The Euro, not much longer."

Then he adds, "Please don't put that on the internet."

## New World Order

It's a classic go-to plotline for any writer who needs a canned villain motivation: Evil rich guy wants to take over the world. Or if not one man, then a shadowy secret agency like KAOS, SPECTRE or Cobra Command. But what if this secret, evil organisation actually exists? What if a cabal of cackling Saturday morning cartoon villains really has infiltrated every level of every government in the world, and pulls the puppet strings behind every major event in a kind of Goldberg machine-styled plot toward consolidated power, unrestrained evil, and the slavery of the entire human race? This is the honest belief of thousands of people who think the New World Order is upon us. And there are no Super Friends to save us from it.

In 1999, journalist Jon Ronson began work on a project of personal interest – he wanted to see the world through the eyes of individuals who had been labeled, in one way or another, dangerous extremists. Having apparently a bigger set of berries than I could ever imagine carrying, Ronson went about this by actually spending time and hanging out with said extremists, including Islamic jihadist Omar Bakri, the survivors of Ruby Ridge, the Weaver family, Ku Klux Klan leader Thom Robb, and conspiracy theorist David Icke. As he describes in his book about the experience, *Them: Adventures With Extremists*, he learned a fascinating fact about these diverse figures that nobody had really realised before; so fascinating, in fact, that it became the new thesis of the book. It turned out that all of the extremists he spoke to and studied—Islamic fundamentalists, rural American gun nuts, white supremacists, Irish protestant militants, radio pundits, and others—all shared one singular belief that underwrote much of their extremist ideology: They all believed that the world was being run by a secret society, an evil organisation behind the scenes of politics, the secret rulers of the world, and they called themselves the New World Order. This single, specific belief was so prevalent among the ideologies that Ronson studied, even the ones that competed with each other, that Ronson wondered whether it might actually be true.

The New World Order, or secret government, is a concept that grew out of the Cold War paranoia of the mid-1900s. But really, it's just another name for a concept that has always existed in our minds. To the west, communism was a genuinely terrifying thing. Contrary to the capitalistic democracy everyone was used to, communism with its big-government ideals looked like some kind of monolithic, unfeeling, robot dystopia, kind of like Skynet but with more Kalinka dancing. This gave rise to McCarthyism, the fear of communist infiltration in our government, our media and our entertainment, with the express purpose of turning the nation communist from the inside out.

Since the fall of the Berlin Wall, McCarthyist paranoia remains. It's like a residue of the Cold War just stuck to us, and though we're not afraid of communism anymore, we're afraid of *something*. We still think we've been infiltrated, we still think something monolithic and evil is wresting control of our lives invisibly from behind an iron curtain. Any day now, the New World Order is going to move into the final phase of their plan, and then they will seize control, collapse all borders into a one world nation, enforce Satanism and exterminate billions in death camps. Any day now. It's been "any day now" for the past three or so decades.

Back in the 90s, George Bush Snr made the mistake of adopting "new world order" as a kind of buzz term. For him, it referred to the world that was emerging after the Cold War ended, a world no longer ruled by two competing superpowers threatening each other with nukes. Bush was trying to express America's new policy of working with other world governments and talking things out, to replace its previous policy of paranoid isolationism that didn't work out very well for it. In 1991, Bush made a speech saying "we have before us the opportunity to forge, for ourselves and for future generations, a new world order. A world where the rule of law, not the law of the jungle, governs the conduct of nations. When we are successful, and we will be, we have a real chance at this new world order, an order in which a credible United Nations can use its peacekeeping role to fulfill the promise and vision of the UN's founders." What Bush almost certainly didn't realise was that this phrase was a dog whistle for conspiracy theorists who thought he was talking about the secret evil government that he momentarily forgot to not tell us about. The popularity of the phrase exploded and to this day the internet uses Bush's quote as proof positive that the NWO is about to take over, even though it's now 20 years since he said it.

Most of the topics I'm covering in this section fall under the umbrella of what is usually called "conspiracy theory." Conspiracy theories assert that certain events are orchestrated by powerful groups of people for reasons hidden to the general public. Frequently, they claim that either innocuous, natural or apparently straightforward events are actually cover-up operations or flat-out forgeries (like the moon landing or an earthquake), or that events that really are the result of a conspiracy (like 9/11 or a company failure due to corruption) were perpetrated by a different group for reasons that are not revealed to the world at large.

Because the New World Order is the shadow villain behind everything else, it is less a conspiracy theory and more like a motherboard that conspiracy theories plug into. It provides a convenient go-to answer for the most important question that conspiracy theorists face – which is, "why?" It provides instant motive. All conspiracies can claim to be another cog in the mysterious plan of the secret government, the nature of which we know not. Why kill JFK? NWO. Why bring down the World Trade Centre? NWO. Why fake the moon landing? NWO. Why give everyone a disease and pretend you're inoculating us against a different disease? NWO. Because the NWO is evil. That's all.

Belief in a secret government is almost written into our DNA. It's merely an extension of our distrust of the Other. We already think that powerful people are greedy, evil, and acting in their own self-interest even if that means grinding the common people up in the machine that makes their money. It's not too much of a stretch to think of ourselves as pawns in a plot by powerful people to obtain more power and more money. Isn't that just what consumerism is *by definition*?

As Jon Ronson discovered, every extremist ideology has a "them." Every extremist is, in a sense, a conspiracy theorist. Extremists from anywhere on the political spectrum tend to think of themselves as being part of a minority fighting an uphill battle. And all of them think that their ideological enemy—*Them*—is somehow in control, or might

64

take control any day now. For the liberals and socialists, it's the neoconservatives; for the atheists, it's the Christian right; for the Muslims and white supremacists, it's the Jews; for the neoconservatives, it's the socialists and Muslims; for the Christian right, it's the atheists and Satanists; for the libertarians, it's the globalists; for the Zionist Jews, it's the white supremacists.

One of the most amusing things about this phenomenon is that often groups whose ideologies directly contradict each other are assumed to be in league by the groups who oppose them both, because more than one group of people who all oppose each other is a difficult concept for people to grasp. Hard-line Christian neocons, for example, hold the belief that the secret cabal is composed of Muslims, communists, and liberal atheists, as if those are three groups who wouldn't immediately murder each other if they were all placed in the same room for an hour.

Michael Barkun, perhaps the world's leading secular authority on the New World Order web of beliefs, identifies three important failures of logic that are intrinsic to all of them:[17] First, *there is no such thing as coincidence*. The NWO theorist lives in a world almost theistically designed, in that the NWO is an agency not dissimilar to God. Like living inside a movie, where every object in every scene has been placed deliberately and with purpose. It's not a case, therefore, of seeing triangles and trying to figure out which ones might have been planted by the NWO, because you can guarantee that every single one was.

Barkun's second characteristic is that *nothing is as it seems*, or as Agent Mulder often translated it, "Trust No-One." The NWO controls all media and world events, to the extent that there's no sub-power-structure operating independently beneath it. There are no genuine political conflicts, no genuine terrorist attacks, no genuine lone gunmen. *Everything is a conspiracy*. While a NWO believer might admit it's technically possible for an independent psycho to shoot the president tomorrow, it has never happened before, because all historical assassinations, you will be told, were planned by the NWO. At least, if you ask them to think of one that wasn't, they won't be able to.

Third, and most importantly, *everything is connected*. A conspiracy theorist will often feed you the straw-man argument that

---

[17] Barkun, Michael. (2006). *A Culture of Conspiracy: Apocalyptic Visions in Contemporary America*. University of California Press. pp. 3-4.

*you're* the one who is crazy for suggesting conspiracies don't exist, because the dictionary definition of a "conspiracy" is merely "two or more people planning a crime in secret," so what you're really doing in dismissing conspiracy theories is denying that bank robberies ever happen. But in reality, the NWO theorist is the one who doesn't believe in conspiracies. They believe only in The Conspiracy. All the little conspiracies that take place in the world day by day are really part of the Master Conspiracy that works toward one single, indivisible goal – the One World Government.

The conspiracy theorist has an iron-clad defense against having to criticise his or her worldview. For the conspiracy theorist, any argument contrary to their belief is actually part of the conspiracy. The conspiracy community refers to these contrary arguments as "disinfo," and often suspects their proponents to be either knowing agents of the conspiracy or brainwashed by it. Conspiracy theory actually has a lot in common with religious thinking – proponents actually believe that logical argument and scientific analysis are tools of the conspiracy, that making an argument that you can't counter is a tactic that the conspirators use to hide the truth. It's much the same as when a young-earth creationist argues that analysis of the geological record or of dinosaur bones is a tactic inspired by the devil to convince you that the earth is old. In both cases, the conclusion is presupposed on faith – unlike scientific reasoning, where the conclusion is derived from the reliability of the evidence, for a conspiracy theory, the reliability of the evidence is judged by how well it aligns with the conclusion.

The conspiracy theory, in this way, is actually immune from evolving or reflecting upon itself. Given the faith-based nature of conspiracy theory, I know that I cannot sway dyed-in-the-wool conspiracy theorists with anything I say here. It's not simply because my arguments won't be strong enough, it's because my arguments *can't* be strong enough. For the conspiracy theorist, any argument denying the conspiracy is wrong *by definition*. Any conspiracy theorist who reads this far (which is itself unlikely) has already declared me a shill, a paid agent of the shadowy forces who secretly control the world, and this book will be seen as part of the brainwashing program. Instead, I hope I can provide some insight into the nature of conspiracy theory and provide some alternative logic for those who might be dabbling with it and considering heading down the road to nonsensetown.

## Back, and to the Left

At 12:30 in the afternoon of November 22, 1963, the then President of the United States, John Fitzgerald Kennedy, was shot and killed in Dallas, Texas, in his open-top sedan as it drove past crowds of horrified witnesses. An unhinged and disgruntled communist multiple-defector named Lee Harvey Oswald was soon arrested for the crime, but before he could go to trial, Oswald was in turn assassinated by a nightclub owner named Jack Ruby, on the stairs of the Dallas police headquarters as he was about to be transferred to the county jail. Before *he* could be convicted, Ruby was then assassinated by lung cancer in the same hospital where both Kennedy and Oswald had been pronounced dead not too long ago. And so everything was wrapped up in a neat little package that reeked more of a government cover-up than anything since a "weather balloon" crashed in Roswell. With everyone involved in the whole mess dead, the government ran an investigation that swiftly concluded that Oswald, Ruby and cancer had all acted alone and everyone should stop talking about it immediately.

The JFK assassination has been called the "mother of all conspiracy theories." The academic David Burchell describes the theory as the model for every conspiracy theory ever since.[18] Researchers pored over the evidence for years, scrutinising every frame of the Zapruder Film, the minute of amateur footage taken of the assassination. A survey taken in 1994 to explore the prevalence of conspiracy belief revealed that 69% of respondents thought that some kind of conspiracy was involved. Only 14% believed that Oswald did it, and 17% weren't sure.[19] This put it head and shoulders above all other conspiracy theories of the time in terms of how widely it was believed. Of course, this may have something to do with the recent release of Oliver Stone's (somewhat intellectually insulting) movie *JFK*, which brought Kennedy conspiracism out of the closet by validating it in a Hollywood blockbuster (mirroring, in a sense, the way Emmerich's *2012* and *Stargate* would play a hand in validating pseudoarchaeology.) Stone's film painted the JFK conspiracy as truth, right up until the cinematically brilliant courtroom climax, in which Kevin Costner recreates the seemingly implausible events on the day of the assassination, concluding with what has been cited time and again

---

[18] In an interview with ABC Radio National, 28 November 2011. Available at: http://tinyurl.com/cuknfts

[19] Goertzel, Ted. (1994). Belief in Conspiracy Theories. *Political Psychology*. 15 pp. 733-744.

as the knockdown argument – Kennedy, shot as we are told in the back of the head, doesn't pitch his head forward, but instead back, and to the left. Back, and to the left. Back, and to the left. Back, and to the left.

There is one important thing that stands out about the theory that JFK's assassination was some kind of conspiracy – in a way, it's plausible. At least, it's not completely implausible. The circumstances surrounding the murder *are* kind of strange. There are valid suspicions that some of the people who could have been involved may have had a motive. I'm not saying that it's true, but it's easy to see how it might be tempting to believe. JFK is like the gateway drug of conspiracy theories – once you're hooked on that, it's tempting to experiment with the harder stuff.

But it's necessary to point out that the quality of the investigation into Kennedy's death is not the reason that conspiracy theories emerged to question whether Oswald was responsible. Polls in fact show that those who believed Oswald had been framed already believed it immediately after the assassination took place.[20] They would have believed it no matter what the investigation concluded. Let's face it, when the people who conducted the investigation are the same people who you're accusing of committing the conspiracy, then what does it matter what the investigation actually says? If there are problems in the final report, this is proof of a conspiracy, but of course, if there are no problems in the final report, this is also proof of a conspiracy, because it means the conspirators are *that good*. When the conclusion is foregone, then the conclusion is exactly as bulletproof as Kennedy's skull wasn't.

For many years after the assassination, the Kennedy conspiracy theory was a huge topic in pop culture. But it wasn't the conspiracy theory that was being ridiculed. The conspiracy theorists had latched onto a fact that most conspiracy theories ultimately rely on – the official explanation is unlikely. Few people who try to recreate the exact circumstances behind the assassination are able to pull it off. There are too many variables to be able to stage a perfect re-enactment. It was a difficult shot to make. And so the ridicule that the "lone gunman" story has faced has always been based on the absurdity of that story. *That* guy shot *that* target from *that* angle? *Ha!*

---

[20] Aaronovich, David. (2009). *Voodoo Histories.* Jonathan Cape: London. p.120.

When you think about it, that light post is probably the assassin.

But what people don't understand is the difference between *objective* absurdity and *relative* absurdity. Occam's razor tells us that evaluating the objective absurdity of an event is pointless. You have to provide an explanation that is relatively *less* absurd. Nobody has been able to do that. Alternatives to the official story are not based on the known facts, but on hypothetical scenarios that would seem to have required fewer variables. The most common claim, that the real assassin was a second gunman on the grassy knoll, is based on the idea that a shooter on the grassy knoll would hypothetically have had an easier time hitting Kennedy than a shooter in the book depository. So what? It would have been easier still for Kennedy's wife Jacqueline to shoot him from three inches away. Does that mean she did it? What conspiracy theorists assert—that it's absurd that Oswald managed to deliberately hit Kennedy in the way that he did—relies wholly on the skill of Oswald relative to the ease of the shot, and completely fails to take chance into account.

According to the research I did on Wikipedia a few seconds ago, there have been over 25 known assassination attempts made on sitting US presidents in the nation's history. Of those, four have been successful – Abraham Lincoln, James Garfield, William McKinley, and John Kennedy. Theodore Roosevelt and Ronald Reagan were also shot, but survived. Still others were the targets of attacks that instead killed someone else. These are only the ones we know about – the number of times that someone showed up at a rally with a gun, or who misfired, or who sat in a book depository and simply missed, might be three or four times higher. People are trying to kill presidents all the damn time. When you take this into account, the chance that four out of maybe a hundred people managed to kill a president through chance alone is actually downright *likely*. Depending on how many assassination attempts have actually been made, this statistic might even be unusually low. It may be more likely that there's a conspiracy that *keeps* presidents from being assassinated.

There is a glitch in the human brain that tends to tell us that any likelihood less than 100% is equal to zero. This is why conspiracy theorists tend to see everything that happens in the world as being part of a deliberate agency, hence the all-powerful nature of the New World Order. It's a strong submission to a kind of fatalism. If we conflate, as the conspiracy theorist does, the unlikely with the impossible, then we're left with two kinds of event – events that didn't happen, and events that were certain to happen through meticulous, omniscient planning. So the conspiracy theorist doesn't have to put forward an explanation that's more likely based on the facts that we know – they merely have to state, as they always do, that Oswald shooting Kennedy's moving target from that awkward angle was unlikely. The leap is made that it was therefore impossible. Since the assassination did in fact occur, a conspiracy must have been involved, and what *really* happened on that day, though it's many times more complicated than a lucky shot by Oswald, is the most plausible *conspiracy* theory.

The Kennedy assassination is probably the most widely held conspiracy theory of all time, even though it falls for all the same fallacies that any other conspiracy theory does. I would argue that there is a political component to this. The public perception is that the conspiracy theory is a distinctively right-wing phenomenon. Whether it's a conservative conspiracy theory (such as that Barack Obama was born in Kenya) or a libertarian theory (such as that the government orchestrated 9/11), they all seem to come from the right wing of politics. Conspiracy theories posited by the left seem more likely by sheer virtue of the fact that we already see right-wingers as cackling supervillains sitting on a chair made of skulls in a shadowy castle in Transylvania.

Compare, for example, the near universal acceptance of the Kennedy assassination conspiracy theory against another from the same era – a theory that surrounds an event which was many times more unlikely than Oswald shooting Kennedy, but is nevertheless notorious for how universally ridiculed it is. That is the event that saw, with the technology of the 1960s, three men fired into space, who then not only landed safely on the surface of the moon, but actually walked around on it, then got back into their craft, travelled all the way back to Earth, and survived for another 50 years.

If the JFK assassination is the father of the conspiracy theory, then the moon landing is the father of the tinfoil hat-wearing conspiracy wackjob. But why do we consider the former more plausible than the latter? The proponents of both go about their methods in pretty much identical ways. They obsess over the likelihood of the scenario (forgetting the hundreds of failed assassinations in one case and the 10 failed Apollo missions in the other); they pore over photographs, looking for the most minute detail that might indicate something is amiss; they analyse the political motives of the people involved and consider the *motive* to commit a conspiracy to be *proof* of a conspiracy. But the most notable difference, I think, is that one conspiracy, if true, would have been committed against Kennedy, while the other would have to be committed *by* Kennedy.

I think it's safe to say that the moon landing is largely considered to be a Kennedy accomplishment, even though the Apollo program was begun by Eisenhower and the landing accomplished by Nixon. Kennedy was the definitive Cold War president, and the moon landing the most iconic Cold War victory. It was Kennedy who made the iconic "not because it's easy but because it's hard" Apollo speech, and Kennedy and his administration who would have needed to plan such a conspiracy. Importantly, the *proponents* of conspiracy theories, those who manufacture them, believe in both the moon hoax and the assassination conspiracy. They're too far down the rabbit hole to discriminate. But in terms of the passive acceptance of conspiracy

Look very closely at this unaltered image from the Apollo mission, and you may be able to see a 1942 Buick Series 80.

theories by the general public, it's easy to see the role that politics plays. The assassination of JFK is considered one of America's greatest tragedies, while the moon landing is considered one of its greatest accomplishments. Blaming some deeply evil conspiracy for the death of one of the most beloved presidents is par for the course, but attributing the moon landing to those same people is like punching America right in the dick.

Like with JFK, the moon landing conspiracists didn't waste any time before asserting that the landings were hoaxed. A guy named Bill Kaysing was first to publish on the subject, and his assertions are the familiar ones to anyone who has amused themselves with this particular conspiracy – the technology of the time just wasn't advanced enough, there would have been too much radiation on the moon for the astronauts to survive the trip, the blast craters didn't look like they should, et cetera. All based on a conflict between what a layman living before the space age expected to see on the moon and what he actually saw.

Ironically, pushers of the moon hoax assert that the landing was filmed on a sound stage on Earth primarily because what they saw on the moon tapes *doesn't* look like it was filmed on Earth. Moon conspiracists fall victim to the idea that conditions on the moon are identical to those on Earth simply because they don't grasp that the moon environment is exotic. A common argument, for example, is that pictures taken of the base of the lunar module don't look like any dust was thrown up by the landing thrusters. If it landed on Earth, they argue, dust would have been blasted all over the place in distinct craters, and thrown up on top of the module's feet. This is true—it can be demonstrated, if you like—but demonstrating this on Earth is pointless. The patterns that are made when you blast dust around on Earth are due to the presence of air. Conspiracists have difficulty grasping what it looks like when you blow dust in the absence of an atmosphere, but we have an easy way of finding out – turns out that it looks exactly like the photographs at the base of the lunar module.

Although the arguments for the moon landing conspiracy are no more or less ridiculous than those for the JFK conspiracy, we can see the difference between what happens in the public perception when you accuse an American hero of a conspiracy and when you accuse an American villain. In 2002, conspiracy theorist Bart Sibrel had a notorious run-in with Buzz Aldrin – after viciously harassing the astronaut for several minutes, Aldrin punched Sibrel right in the face, an event that bumped Aldrin's reputation even higher than the kudos he'd already earned for walking on the moon. I imagine it might be seen a little differently if Nixon had punched someone for accusing him of the Kennedy murder. In conspiracy theory, as with all things, context matters.


## Satanic Panic

Contemporary proponents of the New World Order conspiracy theory can be roughly compartmentalised into two factions – many are deeply religious, usually subjects of a particular school of Christian belief which is awesomely named "premillennial dispensationalism," a phrase that I sometimes like to say aloud in an empty room. This is the belief in a particular literal narrative of the End Times, in which a single man, the Antichrist, is going to unite the entire world and become the dictator of Earth shortly before Jesus returns and punches him out. It's the storyline of *The Omen*, basically. Premillennialism merged easily with secret government conspiracism, and now many Christians use the terminology of New World Order conspiracy theory in their own narrative of what is happening in the world in the lead up to the rapture.

Then there are the atheistic or secular faction, who focus mainly upon politics and what they see as a political or racial conspiracy by powerful and rich individuals, often banking dynasties. Alex Jones is one of the most prominent figures in this style of conspiracism. Often, these individuals will see religion not as the path to the truth, but as another tool of the system, a sham belief that has been used throughout history as the elite's primary means of population control.

Nevertheless, both factions of conspiracism, bizarrely, are united by a single almost universal agreement that largely keeps them from opposing one another – those responsible are all Satanists. The religious factions believe that the elite figures behind the New World Order are actually practicing witchcraft and deriving their power and wealth from Satan, while secularists like Alex Jones often clarify that the elite merely *believe* they are deriving their power from Satan. Just as there are, among the population of a secular nation, those who don't participate in any one religion but nevertheless believe in the possible existence of magic, psychic power, ghosts and other spooky phenomena, so too is conspiracy culture full of people who may not necessarily believe in Jesus or the narrative of the Christian End Times, but nevertheless fear that David Rockefeller and the Baron Rothschild are actually, genuinely deriving magic powers by sacrificing children to a 40 foot owl demon named Molech.

Secular society's passive belief in demonology is a fascinating thing. That percentage of folk who never or rarely attempt to communicate with benevolent supernatural entities still generally think it's a *really bad idea* to light candles, whip out an Ouija board, and try to talk to something that identifies itself as "Belphegor, Duke of Lies." A CBS poll conducted in 2009 revealed that two thirds of Americans believe in the devil, and nearly as many suspect that demons can actually possess people.[21] There is a strange discrepancy between a nonreligious individual's reluctance to trust any part of their lives to the generosity of angels and their fear that there are still evil beings that can come after you if you chant certain phrases in Latin. It's why supernatural horror movies still have a wider audience than shows like *Touched by an Angel*, and why heavy metal still sells better than Christian rock.

Here's an interesting fact about Satanism: It doesn't exist. Or else it's so rare that for all intents and purposes it doesn't exist. When you think about it, that makes a lot of sense – people who believe in an omniscient, omnibenevolent deity aren't going to sell their soul to His less powerful antagonist for the temporary ability to fly or perform really cool magic tricks or whatever, with the understanding that they'll spend eternity in Hell for it. It's kind of oxymoronic to truly believe that Satan can grant you powers while not also believing that God is going to kick your ass for it. One belief kind of relies on the other being true.

Confusion arises from the fact that there is actually a religion called Satanism that was invented in the 60s by an eccentric Chicago musician named Anton LaVey. It has its own church and holy scripture and everything. The fact is that this "Church of Satan" is nothing more than what happens when atheists decide they want to be really edgy and scare Christian folk with their shaved heads and occult jewellery. If you actually delve into the tenets of LaVeyan Satanism, you discover that they not only do not believe in an entity named Satan, but

If it helps make Anton LaVey seem less frightening, here he is wearing a ridiculous devil horns hoodie.

---

[21] http://www.cbsnews.com/2100-215_162-8407.html

that they actively disbelieve in him and all supernatural concepts. Coincidentally, LaVey cribbed much of his philosophy, again, from our friend H.P. Lovecraft, seeing the universe as vast, indifferent, and atheistic. Satanists, who claim to worship the self, built their religion almost entirely around the work of Ayn Rand, with a Lovecraft cosmology, and just enough tongue-in-cheek fake occultism to make Christians quiver and make life harder for those of us who are trying to prove that there never was any devil worship in the world. Those who believe otherwise can easily point to Anton LaVey and plug their ears when you try to explain that he never actually seriously worshipped any devils. LaVeyan Satanism is basically the Marilyn Manson of religions – as long as Oprah's viewers believe that you're as evil as your make-up suggests you are, then you sell a lot more records to goths.

The result is that an immense number of people believe in Satanism passively enough to fear it, but nobody believes in it strongly enough to practice it. There is no evidence that the honest, serious worship of Satan or devils has ever taken place by anybody. You'd be forgiven for not realising this, because it's such a trope in modern culture that anyone would think devil worshippers are as common and mainstream as scientologists. Certainly, both premillennialist and secular conspiracy theorists believe that there is a vast, organised underground Satanist network, and that they look exactly like pop culture and metal album covers tell you they do – red, hooded robes, inverted pentagrams around their necks, reading creepy Latin phrases from a skin-bound tome, and sacrificing children upon a black altar to any of a pantheon of demon characters from medieval Christian apocrypha, in exchange for powers that would appear mildly entertaining to David Blaine's fanbase.

In the 1980s, fear about the commonality of and national threat posed by Satanists exploded into one of the most expensive and farcical criminal trials in American history, in which a serious court of law was faced with the task of deciding whether preschool teacher Ray Buckey actually was Satan-worshipping neo-witch who obtained the ability to fly by regularly molesting children. The McMartin preschool trial ultimately cost $15 million to prosecute, destroyed the lives of everyone that the state was accusing of devil worship, and led to such insane incidents as the actual demolition of the preschool building in search of secret chambers, dark altars or horned gods. In the end, nobody was convicted of anything, and rational observers shook their heads and made comparisons to the Salem witch trials.

It's uncertain whether the McMartin trial would have gained such momentum if it was just a guy being accused of witchcraft. Society takes child molestation accusations more seriously than anything else, and the initial accusation was entirely that. It was only later that the accuser, parent Judy Johnson, who later turned out to be a paranoid schizophrenic, started adding to the molestation story claims that Buckey and his colleagues were sacrificing animals, flying around the room, and participating in ritual Satanism in between roll call and nap time. These bizarre claims were taken seriously by a society which was incidentally (but perhaps not coincidentally) falling into a hysteria now commonly known as the "Satanic panic."

The Satanic panic is a good example of how a short-lived burst of hysteria can tear through a society like a viral epidemic. It partly owes its origin to the bestselling book *Michelle Remembers* by Canadian psychologist Lawrence Pazder. In the book, Pazder describes his treatment of a patient, Michelle Smith. In very much the same way as alien abduction panics come about, Pazder used the dubious technique of hypnosis to unlock Smith's repressed memories about ritual Satanic abuse at the hands of her parents while she was a child.

Just about the worst result that you can get from going to a psychologist is that the psychologist begins to believe your delusions. That's like trying to put out a small fire by accidentally throwing a bucket of petrol onto it. Of course, this is exactly what Pazder did. Possibly it's because he'd fallen in love with her (he soon left his wife to marry Smith), but the important thing is that we now had *two* people running around screaming about widespread devil worship, and one of them had a bunch of college credentials.

From there, the allegations of Satanic ritual abuse spiralled out of control, with parents and psychologists all over the world looking for warning signs of devil cults tampering with children. The sad result is that a lot of genuine child abuse cases were confused and polluted by the distraction of Satanic ritual abuse. While psychologists should have been investigating the less occult aspects of child abuse, they were more interested in figuring out how much of it was being committed by Baphomet, the horned prince of the underworld. In comparison, a drunk Dad didn't seem like such a big deal. After the McMartin case, lawsuits about suspected Satanic cults operating around children began to stack up all over the world, and despite no evidence having ever been found, the reality of Satanic ritual abuse, for a short and embarrassing time, was considered a serious emerging phenomenon in professional child psychology. Criminal investigators saw Satanic symbols everywhere (often mistaking any symbol they didn't immediately understand as an occult reference) and suddenly the cults were all around us, many of them operating through that evil sounding music that kids were listening to.

It doesn't take much for one anecdote to spawn a full-blown moral panic. You can compare the Satanic panic with a whole bunch of hysterical episodes that turned out either to be overblown or never to have existed to begin with. These panics are often exacerbated by mainstream media coverage. In the fall of 1998, a group of ten youths in New York City thought it would be funny to go around randomly sticking people with pins, but the media reported suspicions that the prickings may have been from HIV-infected syringes.[22] A short panic erupted in New York about a secret cabal of people who were randomly infecting people with AIDS, sticking them in night clubs and hiding syringes within cinema seats. As a result, patronage of night clubs and cinemas plummeted. In the end, the truth was revealed, no syringes were ever used and there was certainly no AIDS threat, but rumours persist to this day that shady individuals are still wandering around infecting people with HIV. In actual fact, only a handful of people have ever been accused of threatening somebody with a syringe, and there is only one occasion in history when someone has been deliberately infected in this way – a prison guard in a Sydney gaol in 1990.

Satanic panic entered mainstream conspiracy culture when conspiracists started connecting Satanic abuse "repressed memories" such as those of Michelle Smith with what they already suspected was happening with government projects such as MKULTRA. Evil government plots turned into evil *Satanic* plots. Combine that with suspicions that all these rich and powerful bankers were up to something no good within the walls of their secret mens clubs, and Satanic ritual became cemented as an integral part of what conspiracists believe the secret shadow government is up to. This is even though the very existence of Satanic ritual abuse has been entirely discredited – because "discredited" is not in the conspiracy theorist's dictionary (in its place, someone has awkwardly pasted the definition of the word "proven.")

As I'll discuss shortly, society has a way of becoming extremely morally suspicious of the motives of any subculture or group

---

[22] Wolff, Craig. (1989). 10 Teen-Age Girls Held in Upper Broadway Pinprick Attacks. *The New York Times*, November 4. http://tinyurl.com/8lvduwu

that acts secretly or in a way that people don't understand. The Jews are frequently the target of accusations of evildoing, mainly simply because they have their own rituals and celebrations that the public aren't invited to. A popular anti-Semitic panic that originated during the middle ages, known as the "blood libel," asserted that Jews ritualistically drink blood and sacrifice babies as part of their religious practice. Because if a bunch of foreign people are holding a party and they're not taking the minutes, the immediate and most reasonable assumption is apparently that they're eating a baby in there.

Just about every secret society in history has been charged with Satanism at some point in history, and to the career conspiracy theorist, they all still are. The Freemasons, the Yale Skull and Bones society, the annual meeting of business moguls known as the Bilderberg Group, and an old rich guy's piss-up in the woods called the Bohemian Club are the groups most often cited as Satanic cults by conspiracists. As if they didn't have enough secret clubs to accuse of Satanism, conspiracists also dig into history to find ones that don't exist anymore, like the Illuminati, to drag into the modern day and then call Satanists.

## The Riddler and Adam Weishaupt

Generally the believers in these evil cabal theories like to find a suitably evil quasi-Latin sounding word from history to link back to, and *the Illuminati* is the hands-down favourite. The Illuminati is actually a group that really existed in the 1700s... for about twelve years. A short-lived political group of freethinkers and philosophers in Bavaria, started by a guy named Adam Weishaupt, the Illuminati quickly grew in size and was then almost immediately dissolved after the King of Bavaria freaked out and illegalised it.

The reigning theory among Illuminati theorists is that the group merely moved underground and has spent the past two centuries infiltrating governments and powerful corporations with the goal of world domination in mind. The Illuminati is usually referred to synonymously with the Freemasons because they were similar in nature and, after conflating them for so long, people don't understand the difference.

The founding father of the NWO/Illuminati conspiracy theory was John Robison, a mathematician and philosopher in 1700s Scotland, who was the first person to panic about Masons and Illuminatis and published a tract called *Proofs of a Conspiracy*, which is held in high regard by conspiracy theorists today thanks to a political group who at some point found a copy in a dusty warehouse and discovered that it answered all their questions about who was really running the world. It didn't matter that there is no evidence of anyone on Earth calling themselves "Illuminati" after 1789.

So who can we blame for the modern hysteria about secret Illuminati control? One political group, minted in the forge of Cold War paranoia, plays an important role in the development of conspiracy culture during the 20th century. They were the original Tea Party, and they were (and allegedly still are) the John Birch Society.

The radical conservative group started as a loud and hysterical anti-communist activist group in 1958. They coined the term "New World Order" as a term with negative implications (until then it had mostly been considered an optimistic term) and connected it with the Illuminati after digging up and republishing Robison's work. The JBS hated communists arguably more than McCarthy did. They hated communists more than cats hate dogs. And for them, there wasn't just a risk of America falling under Soviet control – the Soviet Illuminati already ruled over America, via the banking system and the United Nations, which they saw (and most NWO theorists still see) as the headquarters of the World Government, a kind of Dracula's Castle where Illuminatis gather presumably on giant, black thrones and cackle over their latest accomplishments before eating some babies.

In a controversy that mirrors charges against Barack Obama today, the JBS accused President Eisenhower of being a communist plant, and always relentlessly campaigned to get the USA to withdraw its United Nations membership. Their fears were the same as many NWO fears nowerdays, that first there would be a police state, then borders would dissolve, then nations would cede sovereignty to the UN and we would find out who is to be the first President of Earth, probably one of the damn Rockefellers or perhaps Jeb Bush.

Much of what the internet has to say about the Illuminati/Masonic conspiracy involves spotting secret codes and symbols. Code-spotting is a favoured pastime of the NWO conspiracy theorist, because those damn Illuminatis leave them *everywhere*. Somewhat ill-advisably for an organisation trying desperately to remain a secret, the Illuminati behaves kind of like Batman's foe *The Riddler*, in that they can't seem to resist leaving clues about themselves on every surface. The most commonly claimed Illuminati symbol is the pyramid with the eye on top ("the all-seeing eye") that appears on the American dollar bill. Conspiracy theorists go on to claim all triangles are signs of the Illuminati, because triangles (besides being the simplest geometric shape in the universe) are reminiscent of this pyramid.

By the same token, the eye symbol is also a sign of the Illuminati. So in any media logo or album cover or movie poster or celebrity photograph, if you see an eye, or something that kind of looks like an eye, or a triangle of any description, then you've just been punked by the Illuminati.

Consider these observations from Vigilant Citizen, a website dedicated to spotting Illuminati symbology within popular culture. The following is an analysis of the persona of pop star Lady Gaga[23]:

> Gaga is a term that immediately refers to absent mindedness. Here are some synonyms taken from a thesaurus:
>
> - Given to lighthearted silliness: empty-headed, featherbrained, flighty, frivolous, frothy, giddy, harebrained, lighthearted, scatterbrained, silly. *Slang* birdbrained, dizzy.
>
> - Afflicted with or exhibiting irrationality and mental unsoundness: brainsick, crazy, daft, demented, disordered, distraught, dotty, insane, lunatic, mad, maniac, maniacal, mentally ill, moonstruck, off, touched, unbalanced, unsound, wrong.
>
> "Gaga" is probably the easiest word to say in the English language, as it is often the first sound emitted by babies trying to imitate speech. So her name basically says: I'm a lady and I'm empty-headed. This empty head can filled with any crap

---

[23] Lady Gaga, The Illuminati Puppet. *The Vigilant Citizen*.
http://vigilantcitizen.com/musicbusiness/lady-gaga-the-illuminati-puppet/

you want. Imitate me young people. This state of mind is achieved after successful mind control.

Her name is also said to be inspired by Queen's song "Radio Gaga". The video of this song contains many scenes of the 1927 movie Metropolis. As seen in my article on Beyonce/Sasha Fierce, the motion picture tells the story of a woman from the working class that was chosen by the elite to give life to a robot, through a mix of science and Black magic.

The article continues with an analysis of the music video for Lady Gaga's *Paparazzi*:

Lady is in a bedroom with her boyfriend and they're "getting it on." Notice the Masonic checkerboard pattern on the wall and a ram's head, representing Baphomet. He takes her outside on the balcony (which also features a checkerboard pattern). After noticing cameras taking pictures, the guy starts acting strangely and things get violent. He finally pushes Lady off the balcony.

While falling down, the background becomes a swirling pattern, typically associated with hypnotism. Lady Gaga falls down rather stylishly, hinting the fact that this descent is not physical. It represents the "trauma" victims of mind control have to go through in order to be "rebuilt from scratch".

Lady Gaga then enters a mansion in a wheel chair and gradually takes off her clothes.

She slowly starts walking, with the help of crutches, representing her reeducation by the occult elite (she is inside a mansion). She is dressed like a robot, hinting Maria from the movie Metropolis, as seen above. Another scene shows her dancing in a half white/half black wedding dress. This signifies her (forced) association with the "dark Brotherhood". Her transformation is then complete.

We then see her next to the boyfriend that pushed her off the balcony.

She is wearing Mickey Mouse clothes, hinting once again Monarch programming. She is behaving in a very robotic way, as if her thoughts and actions were controlled by someone else. Gaga then proceeds to poison the guy and smiles very weirdly about it. The fact that she murdered her boyfriend refers to the level "Delta" of the Monarch project, which is also known as the "killer" programming.

After carrying out her murderous mission, Lady Gaga is more popular than ever and reaps the rewards of being an Illuminati slave.

For comparison, here is Lady Gaga's own analysis of her song and the accompanying music video:

> The song is about a few different things – it's about my struggles, do I want fame or do I want love? It's also about wooing the paparazzi to fall in love with me. It's about the media whoring, if you will, watching ersatzes make fools of themselves to their station. It's a love song for the cameras, but it's also a love song about fame or love – can you have both, or can you only have one?[24]

There's no mention here of the Illuminati, a "Dark Brotherhood," or mind control. Illuminati believers will say that this is a cover, a lie manufactured to cover the truth. But you have to ask yourself, why would Lady Gaga go to the trouble of creating a pop song that is explicitly about Illuminati mind control and the New World Order scheme, present it to the world, and then totally deny it with a cover story? It's not like she released the song accidentally. Why do it at all?

Seekers of Illuminati symbology seem to see themselves as detectives who seek out clues in the world to uncover this secret agenda. But criminals who engage in conspiracy don't deliberately leave clues lying around for the good guys to find them. They're not comic book villains. Actual detectives look for clues that were left lying around accidentally.

Now, it's true that there are certain archetypes of criminal who will knowingly leave clues for detectives to find. They are usually the kind of criminals who wind up better known by media nicknames. The Zodiac killer sent coded messages to the media. The Beltway Sniper left Tarot cards. The Son of Sam left letters. Jack the Ripper sent a half-eaten kidney in the mail to boast about his crimes. But these individuals are loners with pathological mental conditions, they are playing games with the authorities to see how far they can push it without getting caught. Conspirators, on the other hand, are trying as hard as they can

---

[24] Interview with Lady Gaga.
http://dancemusic.about.com/od/artistshomepages/a/LadyGagaInt.htm

*not* to get caught. If the Illuminati exists, then it has an *enormous* motive to not get caught, and the best way to not get caught is to refrain from explicitly broadcasting to the world what you're up to. If you're looking for evidence of the Illuminati, then you should be looking for evidence that they've left lying around inadvertently (a difficult task, if they're as powerful as they say.) Instead, people look for signs that the Illuminati has *deliberately released and then covered up*, as though they're a bunch of Zodiac killers getting off on sending out coded messages and then running away giggling.

So what's more likely? That Lady Gaga went to the trouble of writing a song about the Illuminati and then made a cover story in a desperate effort to cover up the existence of the Illuminati? Or that the Illuminati symbolism in her song is just a bad interpretation?

The human brain is actually programmed to see patterns in the world. A huge part of our lived experience is based on seeing similarities between things and putting them in categories so that we can understand them, like the difference between "plant" and "animal." Although they're all living things, we create categories to differentiate them, because the world is easier to understand if we compartmentalise everything. But a result of this is that we see patterns everywhere, even if they weren't necessarily intended. A lot of academic analysis is based on this, like literary theory. I'm not saying literary theory is garbage (it's a large part of my education) but it is largely based upon the science of seeing patterns, and it can often enter the realm of the ridiculous.

There is a theory, for example, that Donald Duck cartoons endorse soulless consumerism. It sounds ridiculous to say that the adventures of a pantsless duck with a speech impediment doubles as some kind of Randian love letter to self interested capitalism, but in Dorfman and Mattelart's book *How to Read Donald Duck*, the sociologist authors weave a complex theory about the hidden agenda behind Disney's most famous half-naked misanthrope.[25] Consider the difference between Scrooge McDuck and his nephew Donald – the former a self-made billionaire constantly battling against those villains who would steal his money rather than earn their own, and the former a mooching goofball who can never do anything right and who is ultimately useless to society. The analysis goes on to point out that

---

[25] Dorfman, A. and Mattelart, A. (1975). *How to Read Donald Duck: Imperialist ideology in the Disney comic*. International General, New York.

there are no direct parental relationships in Donald Duck cartoons, Scrooge is an uncle to Donald, who is himself an uncle to Huey, Dewey and Louie. This means there are no immediate family ties, so everyone is an island responsible for his or her own success, a direct allusion to the anti-communal nature of a capitalist society.

This is an oddly compelling analysis, because it totally makes sense. All of the pieces fit. But is Donald Duck actually a propaganda tool for capitalist interests? We can't really say, based on this analysis alone. It's just an interpretation of patterns, and though fascinating, it doesn't prove a thing.

Pattern-finding in Illuminati/Masonic/New World Order theories is essentially the same thing taken to an extreme. And although it may be fun to find allusions to left-wing politics in vampire fiction, I would never attempt to formulate real-world ideology or policy based on this. It's much more an art than a science. Creating an Illuminati narrative from a Lady Gaga video is really the same sort of thing, but the difference is that people interpret this as a real and immediate threat that must be combatted. In reality, *there are a thousand different interpretations that I could make about this same video*, based upon whichever pattern I choose to look for.

The obsessive phenomenon of seeing patterns where there aren't really any patterns to speak of has a name in psychology. They call it "pareidolia." And before anyone protests that it's unfair and naïve to dismiss anything as mental illness, let me assure that mental illness is not what I'm talking about. Pareidolia is an inbuilt mechanism of the human mind. It's a part of all of us. As an example, consider this image:

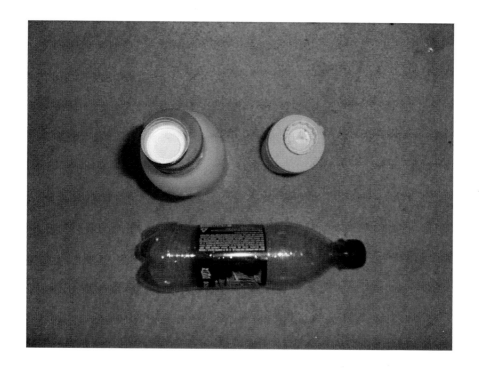

Most people will see this for what it really is – three bottles. But then, there's more to it than that. What if I told you that it's not a pile of garbage, it's a *face?*

Look again. You can't un-see it now. For some of you, it may have actually been the first thing you saw, you may have had a sense of unease like you're being watched, even before you saw the plumbing. It depends on how attuned you are to seeing faces. And we all are, to some degree. It's how we recognise our friends and relatives from strangers on the street. Our brain actually has a specific area dedicated to decoding visual signs on somebody's head (the distance between two eyes, the shape of the cheekbones and lips, the size of the nose) and not only recognises who is speaking to you, but knows whether they are happy, or sad, or want to leave a boot print on your face.

Some people have difficulty doing this. Many conditions along the autism/Asperger spectrum are partially characterised by a difficulty in reading expressions. People who suffer from an extreme condition called *prosopagnosia* are unable to recognise faces at all – they can't tell the difference between their wife, their boss, or in some cases, their own reflection. The healthy brain can differentiate between human faces immediately, it's part of our ability to form tight social bonds.

The glitch in this programming means that our brains are looking for faces everywhere. And if you consciously know that you're looking for a face, it makes your brain's job a lot easier.

Go ahead and check out your environment right now. Pick out any three objects in front of you. It could be two picture frames and a television set, or two cups and a plate. Even a doorknob, a clock and a packet of crisps. Any three objects. Now, tell yourself that they form a face. Sometimes it may take a little more imagination, but as long as the objects are arranged in some kind of triangle, you should be able to tell yourself that you can see two eyes and a mouth. The face's expression depends largely upon the shape of the objects. Incorporate more objects and you might even be able to see noses, eyebrows and ears. Creepy, right?

Another well-known example of this is the so-called "Face on Mars" in the Martian region of Cydonia. In 1976, blurry photographs of

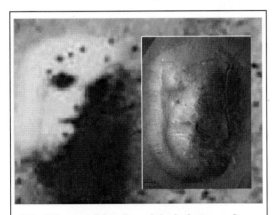

The "Face on Mars" - original photograph vs enhanced photograph (right).

the surface of Mars sparked little-green-men speculation the likes of which hadn't been seen since the infamous "Martian canals" fiasco, when people spotted what appears to be a human face on the surface of the Red Planet. The image is so chilling that it's stayed with us to this day, being used by alien aficionados as evidence that another civilization has built crap all over the solar system, even though another photograph was later taken of the same structure with much better camera technology, and found that it looks a lot more like something a doctor once removed from my neck. The human mind saw three indentations in a mountain, roughly where eye sockets and a mouth are on a human face, and it drew its own conclusions.

What does any of this have to do with Illuminati symbology? Well, seeing faces in objects is just one example of the brain's pre-programmed ability to see patterns in the world. It can be consciously altered. Imagine that what you're looking for is not faces, but symbols of the Illuminati. That means triangles, pyramids and eyes. Symbol-seekers often also mention owls (the logo of the Bohemian Club) as well as the "devil horns" gesture, a fist with the pointer and pinkie fingers extended, which is mainly popularised by fans of heavy metal music. Even butterflies, apparently a symbol of CIA mind control, are significant. The triangle is doubly significant for its resemblance to the logo of Freemasonry, which is simply a depiction of a square and compass set against each other, which has the added benefit of looking a little like the Jewish Star of David, if you have a little imagination.

The simplicity of all these different symbols means that, just like you can make a face from any three objects, you can see an Illuminati narrative in any logo, design, film or music video. Symbol-seekers don't even stop at the obvious. It's a popular theory that the American dollar bill, for example, is modelled on the face of an owl. The two circular stamps either side of Washington's bust are the eyes, and the man's face becomes the beak. It's a lopsided, surrealistic image that you can only see if you squint your eyes and have the imagination of Dorothy Gale, but they swear it's there.

The bottom line is, there's no limit to how obscure or unlikely an Illuminati symbol might be, someone will see an owl, or a pyramid, or a butterfly if they look hard enough. Indeed, it's assumed to be in the Illuminati's interest to keep these symbols from the public by hiding them really well. But that just raises the original question – why hide these codes everywhere to begin with? Conspiracy theorists seem to believe that the symbols are some kind of method the Illuminati uses to "tag" itself as an Illuminati organisation, kind of like how dogs piss on mailboxes to tell other dogs they were there. But even if we are to assume that the Illuminati is so huge, so sprawling, so billion-strong that they cannot themselves identify the entire scope of their operation, isn't this simplistic code-based communication system kind of a really poor way to communicate with one another?

Consider, for example, if an organisation that was not affiliated with the Illuminati decided to adopt a logo that featured triangles, eyes, owls or butterflies. Wouldn't this falsely advertise itself as an Illuminati organisation, thus polluting the message that the Illuminati is trying to send to its co-conspirators? How would the Illuminati deal with this complication? Would they somehow prevent the unaffiliated organisation from using this logo? Wouldn't they then risk revealing themselves? Has any organisation ever complained that it was blocked from using a logo solely because it used Illuminati symbology?

Some might say that this risk never arises, because people simply cannot establish organisations without being associated with the Illuminati. But doesn't this invalidate the entire point of leaving symbols all over the place? What point is there to secretly labelling your organisation as an Illuminati affiliate if all organisations are such by definition?

There are likely many other explanations for why the Illuminati, Masons and NWO shills leave their mark everywhere. I've heard it suggested that they're trying to "desensitise" us or something, that by seeing triangles and eyes everywhere, we are subconsciously being conditioned toward Illuminati control (as though the human brain came already equipped with knowledge of the Illuminati and a symbol-code for making us accept it). But again, this is just reasoning in the wrong direction. If you cannot think of any solid motive beyond idle speculation for why the Illuminati would leave its mark everywhere, then what reason is there to believe that these triangles, owls and eyes actually have a deliberate symbolic purpose? Presumably, you started to believe in Illuminati symbology *because* you expected some reason for it to exist, so to turn around and declare it exists without knowing the reason for it is just thinking in circles.


## The Conspiracy that Dare Not Speak its Name

One of the great things about living in a democracy is that, generally speaking, you can't be prosecuted for believing something. Believe me, I've spent enough time on the internet to fully appreciate the phenomenon. It doesn't matter how stupid your dumb ideas are, you're allowed to have them and even promote them, just as long as you're not actually harming anyone. There are repercussions to being a massively ignorant but generally benign douchebag, but they're not usually legal repercussions. More often they are knuckles-to-face repercussions. Or a sad and lonely descent into obscurity, alcoholism, and premature death, depending on how much more you value never having to challenge your own point of view over having friends or being loved by anyone.

That's the boon of living in a free society. Conspiracy theories, offensive and idiotic as they may often be, are generally legal to believe. Except one. After centuries of particularly horrible side-effects arising from one specific manifestation of ignorance, one kind of belief has been cracked down upon with unusual ferocity, and in some places in the world, actually has been made illegal. The belief is thus so taboo, and so dangerous to be even tangentially associated with, that many have been expelled from the general conspiracy community for espousing it, and those who do espouse it publically have often spent some time in prison for it. That is the belief formally known as anti-Semitism, or informally, "Jewsdunnit."

There seems some bizarre and hitherto unknown glitch in human nature that leads to racism in general, but anti-Semitism in particular. Even communities that are actively and unapologetically dedicated to racism as a philosophy will regularly draw the line at anti-Semitism, because advocating for the return of black slavery isn't illegal, but questioning the official story behind the Holocaust is.

I'm not coming down on either side of the debate about whether the special treatment of anti-Semitism as opposed to other manifestations of racism and prejudice is well handled, but it does seem to be true that the fear of prosecution or heavy-handed consequences to anti-Semitic beliefs tends to drive these beliefs underground. It can be sometimes difficult, for example, to disentangle anti-Zionism, an opposition to the state of Israel, from genuine anti-Semitism, hating Jews because they are Jews. On the one hand, anti-Zionists have a political point to make that should not be censored through accusations of racism. On the other hand, the anti-Zionist community have to worry about being polluted by people who are actually against Israel because it has a bunch of Jews in it, and anti-Zionism is the closest thing to anti-Semitism that they can safely sign up for.

The seriousness and borderline illegality of anti-Semitism also makes it a good tool for those who want to silence others, whether they're actually anti-Semitic or not. David Icke, the conspiracy researcher about whom I'll be going into detail later in this chapter, has faced serious static all through his life as various anti-Semitism watchdog organisations shut him down as an anti-Semite. Icke may be a lot of crazy things, but anti-Semitic is probably not one of them – the theory goes that when Icke discusses his theory that lizard people secretly rule the world, he's actually using a code to refer to Jews. Of course, Icke contends that he actually, literally means lizard people. Actual alien reptiles from the physical constellation Draco. Still, the Anti-Defamation League has gone to great lengths to tease out the metaphors that they insist exist in Icke's work, to the enormous frustration of Icke and his followers who cannot possibly stress enough that they are opposed to *actual, literal alien beings*. Presumably, it is Icke's charisma and apparent sanity that confuses people – it's a deeply entrenched but mistaken belief that you have to be crazy to believe in alien conspiracies, so non-crazy people who go on about it must simply be encoding meat-and-potatoes style old fashioned racism. This simplistic view makes the psychology of conspiracy theory difficult to study.

But there is a further complication. While conspiracy theory does not necessitate anti-Semitism, there is an undeniable correlation. The relationship between anti-Semitism and conspiracy culture is difficult to tease apart, because although most of the leading figures in conspiracy literature today are not, themselves, anti-Semites, it's nevertheless a historical fact that anti-Semitism practically gave birth to their entire culture. As far as you can trace back modern conspiracy culture to its philosophical origins, all roads lead to the same starting point – 1919, Europe, emerging from the rubble of World War I, the greatest cataclysm to ever befall humanity. The dazed and impoverished population was looking for answers. And then somebody went and published a small pamphlet called *The Protocols of the Elders of Zion*. It was the first modern Illuminati-style conspiracy theory, and its eventual conclusion would come to be known as *the Holocaust*. You may have heard of it.

Unlike most racial groups who have been systematically persecuted on racial grounds, hard times for the Jews throughout their history in Europe have been interspersed between periods of them doing extremely well for themselves, or at least, that is the perception. The Jewish people were and are stereotypically seen as Shylocks and banking magnates, particularly the Rothschild dynasty, and historically they have been regarded with suspicion for the extent to which they control the world's money supply. Ironically, this was a position that the Jews were forced into to begin with.

In the middle ages, during the time of Pope Alexander III, Christians were struggling with an inconvenient Biblical law that essentially forbids charging interest on loans. While this sounds like a nice principle for anyone who has had their house repossessed, it basically means that the banking system can't work. But Christian rulers in Europe found a loophole, as they often do when God sets inconvenient rules – the law against usury only applied to Christians, not Jews. So the Jews were given the exclusive responsibility of running Christian banks, and forced to charge ridiculous interest rates to rake in money for the king. Hell, you execute one culture's deity and they never stop beating you up about it.

So, for a time, Jews were put in charge of the banking institutions and they prospered in that line of work because it was the only job that Christians were allowing them to do. The tradition passed from father to son throughout time, and before long people began to notice that all the banks were run by Jews and concluded that it must have something to do with Jews being money-hungry, when it was actually the Christians who put them there because *they* were money-hungry and needed a way to get around the Biblical law about greed.

The late 19th century and early 20th century came at the end of an exhausting series of worldwide upheavals which culminated with the worst, the Great War. This was a miserable time for the human race, and just like conspiracy theorists today, the vulnerable and disillusioned citizens of the world were looking for a simple way to explain everything – if possible, one group to blame, their own Illuminati, who could be fingered as the villains behind all of this madness.

Journalist David Aaronovitch, in his book *Voodoo Histories*, points out the suspicions that several different groups must have held about one group in particular. The Communists in the new Russia already felt that the capitalists (many of them Jewish bankers) were responsible for the ills of times past. Those unsympathetic to the Bolshevik cause also noticed that Jewish men played a not insignificant role in the rebuilding after the Revolution. Capitalists in the west, suffering from economic woes, turned their suspicions also toward the Jews. Over the past century or so, many of the great revolutions, the American and French and Russian, had all benefited the Jewish race in terms of their greater emancipation. Basically, when you lived in the early years of the 20th century, it didn't matter what your background, political persuasion or personal grievance, you started to suspect that an awful lot of the people you blamed had names with some combination of gold, silver, berg, and stein in them.

It didn't help that the Jews were already seen as a suspiciously insular and secret-society-like group, with strange traditions and a resistance to marriage or socialisation outside of their own people. In many people's minds, this presented similarities with real secret societies that people already feared for their secrecy, like the Freemasons and the real Bavarian Illuminati.

The *Protocols of the Elders of Zion* document had already been circulating in Europe for some time, possibly since the beginning of the century, but after the war ended, people began to take notice of the then obscure pamphlet. The Protocols were an 80 page booklet that constituted the minutes of some meeting between the leaders of the grand Jewish conspiratorial society that people had begun to suspect existed. A modern equivalent would be to smuggle a tape recorder into a meeting of the Illuminati or the Draco reptoids. The document outlined, in specific detail and Machiavellian style, the Jewish plot to overthrow the world through slow infiltration and gradual desensitisation of the masses. It detailed how the Jews planned to take over the media so that they owned all sources of information from every political point of view – left, right, republican, monarchist, socialist and anarchical. Just like the tyrannical Ingsoc organisation from Orwell's *1984*, the Jewish elders would control the minds of the populace by controlling both the media that supported their rule *and* the media that opposed it. On top of all this, they would flood the world with the most depraved pornography so as to keep the population dumb and malleable.

This is exactly what the believers of Illuminati-style conspiracies believe today. Compare the "pornography" tactic of the Elders with the Hollywood-brainwashed "sheeple" of today. Indisputably, the Protocols are the philosophical origin for today's Illuminati/NWO/Zionist/Reptoid family of conspiracy beliefs – they pay the same homage to Machiavelli and, retroactively, Orwell. The difference is that most of today's leading conspiracy personalities, not themselves anti-Semites, pay no respect to the Protocols as the genesis of their philosophy. There are notable exceptions, such as David Icke, who believe the Protocols are real, but misattributed to Jews as a misdirection from the real authors – those crafty Illuminatis.

LE PERIL JUIF

LES PROTOCOLES DES
SAGES DE SION

But the Protocols are not real. There's a reason that it so closely resembles the work of Machiavelli – it took a few years to work it out, but the book is a plagiarisation of an earlier philosophical work, a fictional Machiavelli-style treatise called *Dialogues in Hell Between Machiavelli and Montesquieu*, by French satirist Maurice Joly. The *Dialogues* were not meant to be taken seriously, but were in fact a satirical attack on the Napoleonic government (just as many, in turn, argue that Machiavelli's own famous treatise, *The Prince*, was a satirical attack on the Medici tyranny of his own time.) Joly was imprisoned by Napoleon III for having written the book, but despite efforts to eliminate it, copies leaked out of France and found their way into Switzerland, and then into Russia.

Authorship of the Protocols document is disputed, but it was almost certainly written by elements within the Russian government in the opening years of the $20^{th}$ century as a propaganda device to demonise the Jews. A short time after Joly's Dialogues found their way into Russia, the Protocols mysteriously appeared, which by astounding coincidence varied between a superficial editing job and in some cases a word-for-word ripoff of the former text. Due to the obvious amateur hack-job of Joly's biting satire, there isn't a single reputable scholar who thinks the Protocols are even an original work, let alone the genuine minutes of some clandestine secret society bent on world domination.

Regrettably, by the time the true nature of the Protocols started to gain a foothold in academia, they had already taken the world by storm. By horrible, horrible racist storm. The document had become popularised in America by, of all people, Henry Ford, father of the motor car. Ford was, by all accounts, a pretty decent human being with a good heart who nevertheless is responsible for half of the horrible things that have happened in the world over the past century (but you know what they say about what paves the road to Hell). He was a man of great ambition who took the rich man's luxury, the car, and made it accessible to the masses (and Al Gore has a few words to say to him about that one). He was also a damn good boss who fought all his life for better work conditions for his employees, and opposed war in all its forms. He was a really nice dude.

Unfortunately, he was also a conspiracy theorist and a crackpot. It's actually easy in retrospect to compare him with the leading conspiracists of today, who are also, for the most part, fun guys to hang out with. He had some strange alternative health beliefs (to the chagrin of his family, a large portion of his diet involved common

94

garden weeds, which he called "roadside greens," and served them as meals at very awkward dinner parties). He also, like most leading figures in conspiracy belief today, opposed war and believed that all war was the work of one shadowy, universally evil cabal. He knew who they were when he got his hands on a copy of the Protocols. In the heat of the Great War, Ford used his financial and popular muscle to make the Protocols as accessible as possible to the American public, while shrieking about the insidious Elders of Zion to anyone who would listen. If he were alive today, Ford would no doubt have a lot to say about how 9/11 was an inside job. As a result of the nature of conspiracy theory in his time, Henry Ford, pioneer of human rights and all-round nice guy, did almost as much to spread anti-Semitism in the early 20th century as another nice guy with a peculiar moustache did across the pond in Europe.

Speaking of which…

By this time, coming into the Great Depression and a time when the human race was about to be pretty much as miserable as it had ever been since the Dark Ages, a disillusioned college dropout named Adolf was one of many who was looking for someone to blame about Germany's woes. Although the Protocols had been thoroughly debunked as a forgery by the time Hitler came to power, the damage had already been done in the minds of the Nazi party and their supporters, and Hitler spoke at length about the work in *Mein Kampf*, about its influence on him and his ideals. The rest, as they say, is history. This is my response to those who suggest that conspiracy theory is the domain of loners and wackjobs who have no influence upon the world at large – Hitler was a conspiracy theorist. And without pointing fingers at any one, simple explanation for large-scale human tragedies (far too much of that happens already), it is worth at least mentioning that some of the names of people heavily involved in conspiracy culture include Timothy McVeigh, Jared Loughner and Anders Breivik. While most conspiracy theorists are pretty much content to shriek about aliens and Jews from the safety of their homes, most of them secretly hope that another guy will be the one to actually pick up a gun and do something about it. And, tragically, a few of them do pick up that gun. It's happened before, and it will happen again. The question is whether that weirdo you run into at a party who tries to educate you about mysterious planets, alien plots and government cover-ups is going to be the next one to take matters into his own hands.

## Conspiracy Over the Airwaves

Consistently ignored by mainstream media, conspiracy theories have, since the 20th century, found their home among the alternative media. Although conspiracies like that developed by the *Protocols* have been able to simmer through alternative print journalism and word of mouth throughout time, it's only since the advent of accessible electronic media that we can see the rise of what can be considered a "conspiracy culture" – where such theories can reach a wide audience and allow the formation of a community where people with strange ideas can find each other around the world and develop a forum to discuss those ideas. Before the internet, it was radio.

Possibly the single most important figure in bringing conspiracies and various other woo beliefs out into the mainstream is Art Bell, who founded *Coast to Coast AM*, which was at one time one of the most popular radio shows in the United States. Since the age of 13, Bell was obsessed with radio. During his tour of Vietnam, Bell hosted a pirate radio program that made him the real life *Good Morning Vietnam*. I mean, except for the actual real life *Good Morning Vietnam*.

After the war, Bell hosted *West Coast AM*, a political talk show out of Las Vegas. But it wasn't until he decided to make a small, unconventional change to his format that his ratings began to skyrocket – he moved from dry politics to fringe politics, UFOs and conspiracy theories. It's a change that immediately paid off after the Oklahoma City bombing of 1995. Conspiracy theories peak after any terrorist event, but this time, they found a forum.

In 1997, *Coast to Coast AM with Art Bell* was pulling 15 million listeners per night, syndicated on over 500 stations. But Bell is not, himself, a very political man, nor is he carried away with conspiracy theories and paranormal claims. For the most part, he never made much comment as to the validity of anything that came up on his show – it is, in his words, "absolute entertainment." Merely a forum for people to discuss theories that, in some cases, would see them ridiculed for their beliefs. To that end, *Coast to Coast* never denied anybody an audience, no matter how attention-seeking or just plain nuts they may have been.

Art Bell's success is attributed to having single-handedly rescued the overnight radio timeslot from its reputation as a black hole. People who listen to radio from 10pm to daybreak are a peculiar audience, composed of truckers, late-shift workers, and people listening alone in the dark, and for many years, radio had difficulty figuring out how to reach those folks. Bell found exactly what they were craving.

To this day, you can trace just about every new conspiracy theory of the 21$^{st}$ century back to the time it was awarded on *Coast to Coast AM*. In fact, it was even implicated (with or without merit) to the Heaven's Gate cult suicide in 1997 – the fringe-of-the-fringe conspiracy theory, a tentpole of Heaven's Gate, that the comet Hale-Bopp was being followed by a UFO, was given credence on *Coast to Coast* shortly before 39 people swallowed a cup full of cyanide in order to rendezvous with said UFO. It's disputed whether or not the radio show ever had anything to do with the tragedy, but it does serve to illustrate that nothing, not even the principles of a man who claimed to be Space Jesus, was too weird for Art Bell. In fact, even Andrew Basiago, the time traveler who met Barack Obama on Mars, found his 15 minutes of fame on *Coast to Coast AM*.

In 2003, after Bell retired, the show was taken over by his successor, George Noory. Unlike Bell, Noory was always taken in by stories of the supernatural. He takes a more active role in asserting the New World Order as a reality. Rather than simply a mere entertainment, for the most part a way for people to laugh at the lunatic fringe, Noory's version of *Coast to Coast* takes more of an informative role in preparing its insomniac listeners for the coming (any day now, we promise) global takeover by the Illuminati. As Noory states: "This push for more of a world government that so many people laughed at five or six years ago, including me—we aren't laughing anymore…Because you begin to see the pieces of a puzzle, and when you put them together you begin to see a picture you really don't like. This incredible need to control and manipulate—I think our program cuts to the heart of that."[26]

With this kind of mentality, Noory's words sound peculiarly like they could have come from another mouth. While *Coast to Coast* might serve as kind of a soft introduction to fringe beliefs, more hardcore participants in conspiracy culture recognise a different cult hero on the airwaves. While Art Bell was coming into the mainstream, so too was a hard-nosed shock-jock named Alex Jones.

Jones is a difficult nut to crack. His biography is elusive – he grew up in Austen, Texas, the son of a dentist, neither of his parents particularly political. In one of the few insights into his early life, Jones

---

[26] Lavin, Timothy. (2010). The Listener. *Atlantic Magazine*. Jan/Feb.

told The Rolling Stone that his introduction to conspiracy culture came from neighbours who were members of the John Birch Society. But more importantly, Jones learned first-hand to distrust authority through his dealings with corrupt police as a teenager. As he recounts, cops would deal drugs to his friends while off-duty, and then test the football team for drugs when their uniforms were on. But while most people conclude that such things are evidence that the system is broken, Jones got his hands on a John Birch Society publication called *None Dare Call it Conspiracy*, a primer on the New World Order as understood (invented) by the JBS, which taught him everything he needed to know about the secret rulers of the world and their plans.[27]

Alex Jones is the ideal and foremost example of what I like to think of as the *secular* conspiracy theorist. That is, his narrative is entirely non-supernatural. In that respect, he is possibly the last of the very old school of conspiracy theorists, the school of John Robison and the John Birch Society, of those who pushed the *Protocols* document as fact and mused on political motives for the JFK assassination. His is the pure strain of secular conspiracy culture that existed before the culture joined and became intermingled with Lovecraft-inspired pseudoarchaeology, 1960s ufology, and New Age spiritualism. Alex Jones exists one generation removed from when he should have been born. He's like Germaine Greer exasperatedly trying to push second-wave ideology onto a third-wave world. As such, he's largely *respected* by conspiracy culture, even if it considers him behind the times in a culture ruled by David Icke, who we'll

Molech, the pagan idol that Alex Jones refers to as the "owl god," after no doubt tireless research.

[27] Zaitchik, Alexander. (2011). Meet Alex Jones. *Rolling Stone Online*. March 2. http://tinyurl.com/6c3jc7p

get to next.

Jones knows that he's dealing with an audience who, since the 1970s, have been deeply obsessed with UFOs, and since the 80s, Satanic panic. While he claims often that he does not himself believe in aliens or demons, he believes that the Illuminati believe. His vast success on radio and as an idol of conspiracy culture comes from his ability to appeal to both mainstream secular and supernatural/extraterrestrial conspiracists, by arguing that it *doesn't matter* whether the Illuminati are aliens/demons, controlled by aliens/demons or simply believe in aliens/demons, because the outcome is the same.

I have to combine "aliens/demons" like this in discussing Jones' views, because his views are so elusive and difficult to pin down. I have a suspicion that they're designed that way. Jones is, after all, a showman, a man who needs to keep his finger on the pulse of his audience. As much of an effect as he may have on conspiracy culture, conspiracy culture also has an effect on him. In the 90s and early 2000s, Jones believed that the Illuminati and New World Order were a Satanic cult, and that politicians, bankers and business moguls practiced ritual human sacrifice in secret. This was the era in which Jones was obsessed with the Bohemian Club, a private gentlemen's resort that Jones likes to make seem much more mysterious than it actually is. On one notorious occasion, he snuck into the Bohemian Club with Jon Ronson, and the two of them have a very different interpretation of what they saw – for Jones, they bore secret witness to an evil, Satanic ritual, whose participants staged mock sacrifices under a 40 foot Pagan idol of an owl god named Molech. (Interestingly, this Molech owl business has been a large part of premillenialist conspiracy theory for some time now, and I'm not sure how it emerged, considering the apocryphal Biblical character of "Molech" has never been represented as an owl, but as a bull.) Ronson, on the other hand, saw a bunch of rich people trying pathetically to revisit their college days by pissing up and playing silly-buggers around a silly owl statue with a bunch of Elvis impersonators. Despite what Jones would like you to think, the Bohemian Club is not only not frightening, it's not even very secret. As far as secret societies go, we know an embarrassing amount of what goes on inside. Jones and Ronson "infiltrated" the club, as a matter of fact, by simply walking through the front entrance.

In more recent times, however, Jones has drifted away from claiming that the New World Order are Satanists, and has been more

interested in keeping up with the technology fetishism of his audience by incorporating aliens into the narrative. The New World Order, now, are part of a cult of alien-worshippers who believe in the Sitchin story of genetic manipulation, and the Illuminati's end goal is to play God with our genetics. The film *Prometheus*, he explains, is a surreptitious admission about what they actually believe, and Erich von Däniken's life work explains not how aliens built ancient civilisations, but rather, how these ancient civilisations were part of the same evil alien-worship cult that rules the world from the shadows today.

In an interview with George Noory on *Coast to Coast AM* in 2008 or thereabouts,[28] Jones spoke about a legend that arose from the secular conspiracy community in reaction to the growing influence of ufology on their culture – a family of beliefs centred on what they call "Project Blue Beam." In short, the concept of aliens and UFOs is an invention of the New World Order, and throughout the 20th century, they have been working toward introducing us slowly to the idea of aliens through ufology and science fiction, gearing us up to fear an alien invasion. Eventually, Project Blue Beam will culminate in a staged alien invasion pulled off by advanced hologram technology which would project UFOs into the sky, and also fake the second coming of Christ somehow, and this would somehow lead immediately to the complete global takeover of the New World Order. The idea was first put forward by conspiracy theorist Serge Monast in 1994, and I'm sure it's a total coincidence that Monast's theory is identical to an aborted *Star Trek* script by Gene Roddenberry that was released earlier in the same year. It's probably the same reason David Wilcock's narrative follows the plot of *Total Recall*.

But then, Alex Jones has never managed to produce one central thesis about what he thinks is really going on in the world. What Jones

---

[28] http://tinyurl.com/aucloh

promotes is a pretty good example of what researchers have studied about the mentality of conspiracy theorists who form what is known as a "monological belief system." It's very similar to what George Orwell called "doublethink" – the tendency to hold several *contradictory* beliefs, simultaneously, and accept all of them as true. It sounds impossible, but it's a natural consequence of inverted logic. For the conspiracy theorist, truth is defined as whatever the evidence put forward by an authoritative body rules out, because all authoritative bodies (scientific, political, etc.) are lying, and furthermore, they are lying 100% of the time. But sometimes, even often, believing the opposite of what you are told leaves you open to multiple possibilities. Rather than take this opportunity to discriminate, the conspiracy theorist believes *all of them*.

In a paper titled *Dead and alive: Beliefs in contradictory conspiracy theories*, researchers surveyed 137 students to gauge their beliefs in popular conspiracies, while sneakily throwing in some contradictory ones to see if people would bite. Notably, the participants were asked to rate, on a scale from 1 to 7, their level of agreement with the following statements about the death of Princess Diana: That she was murdered by rogue elements within the British Secret Service; That she was the victim of an official MI6 sting; That she faked her own death; That Diana was collateral damage in the assassination of Dodi Al-Fayed, committed by his business rivals; That she was ordered to be killed by the Royal Family, who could not allow her to marry a Muslim.

Some of these statements are more contradictory than others. But some just don't fit together no matter how hard you try to cram them. Nevertheless, the results showed that a tendency to believe in any one of these theories is positively associated with a belief in *all* of them. The fact that Diana can't have simultaneously been murdered by MI6, murdered by Dodi's business partners, and not murdered, didn't matter. The researchers realised that the coherence of theories with the belief that there is a grand conspiracy is *more important than their coherence with each other.*[29]

Alex Jones is skilled in managing to weave his doublethink in such a way as you can't easily see the contradictions between his views. Perhaps it's because he's so loud and enthusiastic; he's like a Pentecostal minister who gets worked up into such fervor about the

---

[29] Wood, Michael J., Douglas, Karen M., and Sutton, Robbie M. (2012). Dead and alive: Beliefs in contradictory conspiracy theories. *Social Psychological and Personality Science*: 3(6).

truth that you don't notice when the truth doesn't make any sense. And so Jones simultaneously claims that the New World Order are an elite Satanic cult who believe they derive their power from demons, and that they are an atheistic UFO cult who believe they are honouring their alien masters with genetic engineering. He has also claimed simultaneously that Barack Obama is a Manchurian candidate in the pocket of big business, and that he is a socialist whose plan is to destroy capitalism. In trying to describe who the New World Order are, he has variously claimed that they are the Freemasons, the Illuminati, the Bohemian Grove, the United Nations, a collaboration between some of those groups, or else it's a Chinese plot, or else it's the American government, or else it's a rogue element within the American government who intend to usurp it, or else it's the English government who intend to take back America, or else it's a collaboration between the American and English governments who intend to take over the world. For Jones, these are all true, at the same time. To think critically about any one of them is to run dangerously close to what *they* want you to believe. Better to believe twelve mutually contradictory scenarios than to admit *they* are true in denying any one of them.

Conspiracy radio fans were more divided in the 90s, as several hosts competed with each other for the same audience. Before the internet age merged all conspiracy theories into the same homogenous soup, there was more than one cohesive narrative about how the world really was, depending on who you tuned into in the evenings. Another of the most important figures in conspiracy radio was Milton William Cooper, who operated at the same time, and there was no love lost between him and Jones.

Though both jocks came from the hard-right fringe, they disagreed about elements of the grand conspiracy. While Jones focused on Satanism as the tentpole of his narrative, Cooper belonged initially to traditional Roswell style ufology, although he later changed his narrative (as Jones does) when these ideas went out of vogue, eventually abandoning the alien hypothesis and claiming that UFOs were a government hoax.

We have Cooper to thank for coining (or at least popularizing) the term "sheeple," a word that he used approximately infinity times per sentence. An old fashioned radio pirate, right-wing patriot and gun enthusiast, Cooper was also aggressively isolationist about his conspiracy narrative. He appeared as a guest on Alex Jones' show once in the 90s, but claimed not to know who Jones was at the time, and would later regularly berate Jones as a liar and a fearmonger. It's likely, though, that Cooper saw Jones' rising star as a threat to his dominance over conspiracy radio, and actively propagated a rivalry in an attempt to wrestle his audience back.

Cooper's significance to conspiracy culture is significant, even if his audience was never as large as that of Jones or David Icke. He's the model for the stereotype of the hard-right conspiracy nut broadcasting from inside a van, an image which is popular in films and television series' such as *The X Files*. He gets a lot of respect from the conspiracy community for the fact that he mostly operated on pirated or self-funded radio, rather than the big-budget commercial operations of Jones and Icke.

But although Cooper also hated Icke and the New Age movement in general, he can possibly be credited for actually instigating the merger of New Age and conspiracy culture in the 1990s. When his only book, *Behold a Pale Horse*, was published, it became a bestseller, but bookstores didn't really know where to put it. One of the first prominent books about Illuminati-style grand conspiracy, *Behold* wound up occupying real estate in bookstores' New Age sections, which exposed spiritually-minded hippies to ideas about the secret government and UFO cover-ups. David Icke owes much of his own conspiracy narrative to Cooper, though Cooper would never have approved of the spin that Icke puts on it.

Perhaps most significant is the way that "Bill" Cooper ultimately died. It's significant to note that most of the ringleaders of conspiracy culture never put their money where their mouth is when it comes to doing something about this secret fascist government – they leave it to their followers to take up arms, but rarely will a Jones or an Icke wind up on the news for having been involved in a gunfight. In this sense, Cooper merits a kind of horrible kudos.

In the late 90s, Cooper began to believe that he was on the top of a "hit list" put out by then president Bill Clinton, and began to refuse to pay taxes to what he believed was a socialist, Illuminati government. Having become deeply entrenched in the American militia movement, he believed strongly that the time would soon come when the gun owners of the nation were going to have to rise up in revolution against the government.

He got his chance to stick it to the government in November of 2001—a month after 9/11, no less—when sheriff's deputies arrived at his home to serve a warrant for his non-payment of taxes. Cooper, assuming that the police were there to execute him as per Clinton's orders, fired upon them. One deputy was shot in the head, and the law returned fire, killing Cooper and launching a thousand more conspiracy theories. It was an ironic end to a man whose advice to the militia movement was always "whoever shoots first loses." For what it's worth, he had always warned the prospective revolutionaries who listened to his show that the public would never support their cause if they fired the first shot. He should have heeded his own advice.

Jones and Cooper are an example of conspiracy theory in its raw form. Although they are living in an inverted sociological world, they're still living in a world where the planets orbit the sun and water is wet. They believe in corruption at an impossible scale, but in the end that it's a human problem that can be eradicated politically. Their worst case scenario is fascism on the scale of the Holocaust, but the world is going to keep spinning regardless. But what happens when your distrust of authority scales up even from there? What happens when the laws of physics become the unjust laws you're fighting against, and gods are part of the conspiracy? It won't take ten minute's study into postmodern conspiracy culture to find reference to its portly, blonde, British king.


## Yesterday's Nut

Human beings have a fetish for the concept of extraterrestrials. Jason Colavito suggests that this emerged naturally from the decline of religion and mythology, and the ascension of technology to replace it since the technological revolutions of the past two centuries.[30] It's easy to see how this might be the case – abductions by and interactions with mysterious creatures are common in western mythology. The stories are exactly the same, it's just that what we used to call "fairies" we now call "aliens," and what we used to call "will-o'-the-wisps" we now call "UFOs." The encroachment of science and exploration onto the mysteries of reality has reached a point where we've basically searched under every rock for the fairies, and, having found none, we're forced to search off-world for them. Having found no magic in the world, we're forced to look to advanced technology in our desire for there to still be stuff out there that we can't fathom.

UFO culture has been conspicuously absent from this book so far. I opted not to include a chapter on it because, unlike many other

---

[30] Colavito, Jason. (2005). *The Cult of Alien Gods: H.P. Lovecraft and Extraterrestrial Pop Culture*. Prometheus Books: New York.

aspects of conspiracy culture, critical analysis of the UFO phenomenon has been done to death more often than vampire/human romance novels. Also, I would argue, ufology's influence on conspiracy culture has been slightly tangential, and as a fad during the middle-to-late 20th century, it has more or less died out. It's easy to see why – UFO culture, with the "greys" popularised by Whitley Strieber and others, was *huge* in popular culture. It's difficult to maintain that the government is still desperately trying to hide the existence of creatures who now appear on the backs of cereal boxes.

There are two distinct threads of extraterrestrial mythology in the world today, I believe. Distinct, but not fully separate. The UFO culture that emerged with the Roswell incident, involving abductions, black helicopters, anal probes, cattle mutilations, and which jumped the shark at around *The X-Files'* sixth season, was one. The narrative of ancient aliens who visited long ago and built the pyramids is the other. Both emerged from the same primordial soup of early 20th century pulp science fiction. The ancient aliens narrative, however, is slightly older, and with the steady decline of alien abduction reports and UFO sightings over the past couple of decades, it seems it has also endured longer. Mainstream, secular conspiracy culture had its flirtations with the ufology fad, probably most notable in the work of Milton Cooper, but the alien "greys" didn't quite have the staying power that we needed in a conspiracy mythology. They were inquisitive little scientists who shoved rods up people's arses and otherwise bled like we do. The ancient aliens were different – their power knew no bounds. They were *gods*. Who is more likely to sit at the pinnacle of the sinister, all-powerful Illuminati? Sitchin's awesome, planet-shaping Annunaki? Or the gnome creatures who recently starred in a Simon Pegg vehicle voiced by Seth Rogen?

At some point during the 20th century, three distinct threads of alternative culture began to come together to merge into one culture: the adherents to pseudoarchaeology espoused by von Däniken and others; the conspiracy culture that descended from the *Protocols* document and Cold War hysteria; and what became known as the New Age movement. Nowhere else is the combination of these three movements better personified than in the beliefs of David Icke, the pope of the postmodern conspiracy culture. You might know him as the lizard guy.

Before we get too into the Icke phenomenon, it's necessary to talk a little about the New Age movement. What we call "new age" is a fusion of very poorly-defined spiritual principles that draw on both eastern and western religious traditions, but perhaps primarily it owes its origins to a late 19th century group called the Theosophical Society, formed by one Helena Blavatsky, which posited a number of hippy-dippy metaphysical philosophies (interestingly, Theosophy also heavily inspired the early pseudoarchaeologists such as the Thule society, through their obsession with Atlantis, so it's perhaps unsurprising that alternative archaeology would reunite with the New Age movement a century later). In particular, it was the writings of a later Theosophist named Alice Bailey in the 20th century that laid much of the foundation for the modern New Age, and put a lot of familiar terms in our lexicon like the Age of Aquarius and the Earth spirit Gaia. Much of what you see in recent New Age revival films such as *Thrive*, *Zeitgeist*, *What the Bleep Do We Know* and *The Secret* also derive much from Bailey and the Theosophical teachings.

The teachings of David Icke, which are commonly downloaded to the public by way of expensive 11-plus-hour-long lectures, are notoriously difficult to understand. This is primarily because they are gibberish – technobabble (or spiritubabble) without objective meaning, and journalists who try to cover the Icke phenomenon find nothing but tortuous nonsense when they cover his seminars, unprepared for the fact that none of his concepts have any genuine definition. But although the media likes to paint Icke as a lovable eccentric who makes all of this stuff up from whole cloth, very little that he says is original. His New Age and spiritual ideas are almost pure Alice Bailey, even if he doesn't always credit Theosophy. His pseudoarchaeological conceits are pulled direct from Zecharia Sitchin, and his conspiratorial ideas are the product of the *Protocols* document, the John Birch Society, and mainstream conspiracy culture.

It's no coincidence that we arrive at David Icke at the centre of this book, as he is at the centre of most studies of conspiracy culture, because Icke believes in every single alternative science, conspiracy, and woo theory that has ever been posited (though I believe he draws the line at the flat Earth, as he often mocks people who don't believe his theories as "flat Earthers.") He is an extremely impressionable man, and one can trace the history of his ideas pretty clearly along with the ideologies various woomeisters he's picked up into his inner circle along his career.

David Vaughan Icke has the rare privilege of having risen to celebrity twice in his lifetime, for two unconnected reasons. The son of a domineering father, Icke grew up in destitute poverty and found his calling in the game of soccer, being recruited by a talent scout as goalkeeper by the Coventry City Football Club in the 60s. He might have precursed Beckham as a household name in soccer had he not tragically been struck down with rheumatoid arthritis at a very early age, forcing him to retire from the game. But in 1973, good luck granted him a job as a sports reporter, first in radio and then television, becoming a popular addition to the BBC's breakfast lineup. He published his first book in 1983, *It's a Tough Game Son!*, a decidedly un-weird book about how to break into football.

For almost a decade, Icke worked for BBC Sports, until 1989 when his freak flag first began to fly. It was then when, still crippled with arthritis and no relief in sight, he resorted to consulting a psychic healer. He burned his bridges with the BBC in 1990 when he started refusing to pay certain taxes, an early sign of his anti-government leanings that led the BBC to terminate his contract to distance themselves from him. By this time, he'd developed a soft spot for environmentalism and joined the British Green Party, and his second book (slightly weirder than the first) was published – *It Doesn't Have to Be Like This*, an environmental treatise.

Icke continued to rise through the ranks of the Green Party, eventually becoming its spokesman for a short time. But this is where Icke began to enter the period he refers to as his "awakening," and he soon resigned from the party because they just weren't weird enough to keep up with him. He'd begun to hear voices in his head telling him that he was destined for greatness, and he decided to pursue this calling full-time. His third book, *Truth Vibrations*, would turn out much weirder than the previous two.

For a time, he began to only strictly wear blue-green clothing, which he referred to as his "turquoise period," because that colour is somehow a conduit for positive energy.[31] This is surely where he became first acquainted with Theosophy – the colour of turquoise is important to Alice Bailey's central astrological theory of the "seven rays." He began sleeping with his psychic healer, who bore him a son, and for a time, Icke, his wife and his psychic entered into a polyamorous relationship that the media referred to as the "turquoise triangle."

---

[31] A friend of mine from the Isle of Wight, where Icke lives, told me that Icke obsessively purchased all of the turquoise jewellery from his town of Ryde during this period of his life.

The end of David Icke's first celebrity and the beginning of his second came with his 1991 interview on the Terry Wogan talk show. In front of a live studio audience, donned in a turquoise jumpsuit, he declared himself to be the son of God. The audience naturally broke out into laughter, which Icke regarded to be completely childish. Back in ancient Rome when some kid named Jesus started saying the same thing, Icke quipped, people probably laughed then as well. Then he went on to prophesise a bunch of earthquakes and volcanic eruptions that never happened. Of course, Icke thinks that pointing out that he turned out not to be the son of God and that his prophecies were wrong is also childish behaviour, as we should instead be respecting the changes he was going through at the time. This philosophy doesn't stop Icke from sarcastically laughing at anyone who says anything he disagrees with, to this day.

After the Wogan interview, Icke sulked for a few years about having been unfairly laughed at for the minor transgression of announcing himself to be the Second Coming on national television. But although his credibility as a journalist had been, let's say, thrown under a bus, he found a new celebrity among conspiracy theorists as the voices in his head continued to reveal truths of the universe to him, and he wrote books about them. It's worth noting that his earliest work, such as *Truth Vibrations*, is heavily influenced by Christianity (he discussed conversations he had with Jesus and the Archangel Michael, and asserted that Satan, uh, threw the moon at the Earth in an effort to destroy it, but Michael caught it like a baseball and that's why we have a moon now). Icke is now vehemently against Christianity, and would presumably laugh at anyone else who claimed to be Jesus.

Astute students of the David Icke mythology can see a fairly direct line from his views back to those of Zecharia Sitchin. He speaks at length in his lectures about Sitchin, the Sumerian texts, and the inaccessibility of modern knowledge to ancient people. From Sitchin's theory of the Annunaki race of Nibiru, Icke formulates his unique contribution to the New World Order conspiracy. Unlike the secular view that paints the Illuminati as simply a group of powerful men, Icke believes that the architects of his grand conspiracy are literally the descendants of Sitchin's Annunaki. Every world leader, according to Icke, is part of one single ancient bloodline that dates back to old Sumer when one dastardly Annunaki decided to get it on with a human woman and create the Illuminati, the overlord race. Icke believes that the Annunaki are shape-shifting reptiles, as evidenced by the fact that many ancient religions featured reptiles heavily in their mythologies.

It's important to note that Icke uses the term "research" a lot, but the research he does is not the same kind of thing that most of us mean when we talk about research. Icke freely admits that his primary source for most of his information is a voice in his head. It shouldn't really need to be said, but you should be wary of anyone who cites a voice in their head as evidence to prove any kind of hypothesis unless that hypothesis is "Guys help, I think I might have brain problems." Here we find again the difficulty in discerning the mentally ill from the charlatans. Of course, for all I know, he really is receiving telepathic messages from an interdimensional intelligence who has decided to let Icke and only Icke in on this incredible, world-changing revelation. The problem is, if you really are receiving mental transmissions from an alien telepath, there's no way that we can distinguish you from someone who is mentally ill and the victim of mental delusions. Unless someone is willing to claim that *all* schizophrenics are genuinely in telepathic contact with aliens or ghosts, you have to admit that this distinction is a problem.

At this point, we might legitimately wonder why David Icke has a mainstream following, while your average mental patient who claims he's speaking to Abraham Lincoln can't sell so much as five tickets to his world tour. The answer possibly lies with Icke's genuine charisma, lucidity, and self-awareness. He doesn't sound like your average lunatic, staring blankly into the middle-distance and ignoring every criticism that comes his way. Icke has learned an important lesson from the ridicule he faced after the Wogan interview, and he prefaces his descriptions of shapeshifting reptile overlords with assurances that he knows they sound crazy. Icke, if he *is* crazy, is nevertheless in touch with reality to a degree that most crazy people are not. Genuinely crazy people don't seem to be able to differentiate between sane statements and crazy statements. When somebody segues smoothly between saying they don't like the Republicans' fiscal policy and saying that the Republicans are time travelling spider people, and they don't understand your weirded-out expression, that's crazy. But when David Icke *tells you* that what he's about to say is crazy, it lends a kind of legitimacy to it. As Icke often says about his newfound success: "Today's mighty oak is just yesterday's nut that held its ground."

Icke has a way of attracting support by making you feel bad for making fun of him. His comeback from random kook to charismatic public speaker was so phenomenal that it almost makes you forget that he's talking about reptilian alien invasions. Watching the infamous Wogan interview, you see a pathetic-looking waif of a man, a soft-spoken hippie plagued but enlightened by his newfound talent for prophecy, eager to tell the world about his divine revelations. When the audience laughs, the hurt on his face is palpable. You can see the man's heart break the moment after Wogan tells him, "They're laughing *at* you, they're not laughing *with* you." It's the image of humiliation.

But Icke did not respond the way that many less successful individuals have. Instead, he took it on the chin. He handled it *brilliantly*. And when Terry Wogan brought him on the show for a second time sixteen years later, David Icke *cleaned the floor* with him. No longer the timid, hurt little victim, Icke strode into the studio with confidence and told everyone how it was. David Icke was *loud*, now. And after a rousing speech about refusing to conform, dealing with ridicule and bullying, and damn well surviving, he finally earned his applause. This time, the audience *was* laughing with him. To be honest, I felt like applauding him too.[32]

If you take a slightly closer look at what's happened, though, you realise that he's taken some lessons in how to speak like a politician. If he hasn't read up on it explicitly, then he's certainly done some personal research. Because David Icke plays his audiences brilliantly. In the second interview, when Wogan asks him about his claim that he's the son of God and that he predicted a bunch of earthquakes that never happened, Icke's reply is:

"What I am is frustrated at watching Orwell's *Nineteen Eighty-Four* unfold in front of our eyes by the day, while people focus on who shot Phil Mitchell."

It's not an answer to Wogan's question, in fact it's an absolute deflection, but this being the years shortly after 9/11, and the interview taking place in Britain, he hits the nail on the head in terms of the biggest hot-button issue of the time. Nobody realises that he didn't address the question. They applaud. Indeed, Icke has made a killing glomming on to popular conspiracy theories that have hit mainstream in the wake of the War on Terror, as has Alex Jones.

Focusing on the less mystical and science-fiction aspects of his grand theory, at least in the public sphere, is another tactic Icke employs to sell the conspiracy to a more skeptical population. Secular conspiracy culture, stripped of its New Age and extraterrestrial elements, is easier for people to accept than a full space opera. This is another lesson that Icke clearly learned from his humiliating appearance on the Wogan show, declaring openly the more freakydeaky aspects of his narrative. It's very similar to the way in which scientologists (also expert self-promoters) sell themselves. On the surface, scientology is some kind of New Age self-help philosophy that isn't that easily distinguishable from tested science, at least to the layman. It's not until you really get into it that you find out that philosophy is based upon the belief that the tyrannical dictator of a galactic confederacy used Earth as a kind of Nazi gas chamber for convict aliens and we are depressed or mentally ill because our bodies are haunted by their ghosts. Scientologists fight tooth and nail to avoid this narrative from becoming public knowledge, at least before you've

---

[32] I wasn't able to find a full version of the original Wogan interview online, but there is a segment available from his return to Wogan sixteen years later, which includes a partial clip of the original interview: http://tinyurl.com/yjd4ff8

paid your membership fees. In the same way, Icke doesn't put his New Age and extraterrestrial beliefs at the forefront of his interaction with the media. In public, he sticks to the secular narratives of the New World Order, banking conspiracies and government corruption.

Not all of Icke's contemporaries are pleased with his marriage of New Age beliefs and Reptilian puppet masters with secular conspiracy theory. Alex Jones in particular feels that the inclusion of extraterrestrial concepts is counterproductive to the broader movement. In an interview for a documentary on Icke, *David Icke, the Jews and the Lizards*, Jones tells what he thinks about Icke's unique worldview as opposed to his own, non-supernatural "meat and potatoes" conspiracy narrative:

> So what does David Icke do? He talks about the Federal Reserve, the Bank of England, these global elitists, these power structures, all real, all true, all demonstrated by bills and executive orders and prime ministers and premiers and presidents. All real, meat and potatoes, something you can bite into. Something that is easily demonstratable (sic). And then you've got David Icke at the end of all this, he says "by the way, they're blood-drinking lizards." Al Gore needs blood to drink, so does Prince Phillip, I mean, it's asinine. And it's being picked up by people, and so it discredits all of the reality that people are talking about. And that's a problem, that's the problem with David Icke – he's got a good line to a point, and then he discredits it all. It's like a turd in the punchbowl. That's his job, you've got this nice big thing, you know, this nice fruit punch, nice ice cubes floating around in it, you know, and then he takes a big dump right in the middle of it, and no-one's going to drink out of that punchbowl.[33]

Although Jones has since backpedalled slightly on this view, opting to think of Icke as simply a fringe theorist of the same school, assumedly because, as conspiracy culture's opinion shifts away from Satanic panic and toward New Age theories, Jones needs to change his focus to stay relevant.

---

[33] This interview with Jones can be found here: http://tinyurl.com/3as76dv. Later in the same video, we see David Icke being interviewed on Alex Jones' show, and here we see an immediate comparison between secular and New Age conspiracy narratives: Icke asserts that a conspiracy of this magnitude must be the work of greater forces than human, and Jones counters that the conspirators merely *think* they're in contact with greater forces than human.

So what does David Icke actually believe? His reptilian theory, his "Xenu narrative," if you will, began with a pilgrimage to South Africa early in his career, where he met with a Zulu shaman named Credo Mutwa, who educated him on ancient African religions based around reptilian entities. From there, Icke became obsessed with pseudoarchaeology and looked further into mythologies from around the world that mentioned reptilian or serpentine entities. As many old-world religions have some basis in animism, this isn't too difficult – the scholar of ancient mythologies can easily see reptile-gods everywhere, from the lizard people of Africa to the serpent of the Garden of Eden. Of course, it requires a selective study to conclude that reptiles are so significant – one has to ignore cultures who worshipped goats or lions or sloths. Mixed with an avid reading of Zecharia Sitchin, David Icke concluded that ancient aliens, Sitchin's Annunaki, arrived early in human evolution and set up their grand plot to enslave modern humanity via the Illuminati conspiracy.

This "reptilian bloodline," idea, which he also calls the Babylonian Brotherhood (as another way of obscuring his alien elements for those who might be made uncomfortable by it) is now the tentpole concept in Icke's narrative. In short, one of these alien beings got frisky with our ancient ancestors and created a hybrid bloodline, and it's these half-alien beings who have controlled the world from the year dot. Most or all of the current western world leaders and other influential people are descendants of this hybrid bloodline, from Queen Elizabeth to Boxcar Willie.[34]

They're all alien half-reptiles, working for the alien agenda, and although their true forms are those of alien lizards, they shape-shift to appear human. Because that's a thing that they can do.

His evidence for this is initially compelling. Here's a fascinating, kind of frightening bit of trivia – all the American presidents, with the sole exception of the eighth, Martin van Buren, are descended from British royalty. Specifically, King John, the 13th century ruler of England and nemesis of Robin Hood. In Icke's theory, the ancient tradition of kings, emperors and pharaohs marrying their

---

[34] A constant source of ridicule and confusion, of course, has been the inclusion of Boxcar Willie and Kris Kristofferson on Icke's list. He's not accusing Elvis, Johnny Cash and Bob Dylan of being reptiles – apparently the reptilian project to dominate the country/folk scene of the 60s and 70s just didn't work out as well as their political aspirations.

own family members has been a deliberate attempt to preserve the alien bloodline and not dilute it too much by procreating with too many humans. Apparently, this is why you can trace all the presidents back to King John, and King John back to Charlemagne, and Charlemagne probably to a common ancestor of King Tut, Alexander the Great and Elvis. All the powerful people in the world today are from the same family! There must be a deliberate reason for that. To David Icke, this *cannot* be coincidence. It proves that there is something fishy about that particular line of DNA, and this greatly assists the reptilian hypothesis. This also puts Martin van Buren, otherwise a fairly forgettable president, in the lofty position of having been the nation's only human leader. It seems that, sometime in the 1830s, one of the alien bureaucrats messed up the election rig.

Intrigued? Okay, so let's apply a bit of critical thinking that David Icke didn't bother to do. It's true that all of the presidents save van Buren are descended from British royal stock. What Icke fails to tell you is that *you are, too*. Or, you're very likely to be. So is everybody else. The presidents are related to King John because it would be unusual if they weren't. It's actually likely, given the evidence, that *van Buren* was the alien.

Think about this: One generation back, you're descended from two people, your parents. Another generation back, you're descended from four people, your four grandparents. They each have two parents, so you have eight great grandparents. You have sixteen great great grandparents. If you step into a time machine and travel back a hundred years or so, there might be thirty-two people walking around who are in your direct parental ancestry, and this doubles roughly every 20-30 years you go back. If you get back in your time machine and travel back to the 13$^{th}$ century when Bad King John was luring Robin Hood into a rigged archery competition, then your direct family line constitutes roughly the order of everybody on the planet.

Imagine yourself there, at the competition, everyone watching the archers take aim in their silly hats and those weird skirts with the square trims and green tights. Everyone you can see in the audience, including the royal family, are probably your great-whatever grandparents. There's a certain amount of random, unknowing incest that's going to go on through the ages (like, two of your grandparents in a single generation might turn out to be the same person) but by and large, you're going to have millions of people in your family tree back then. Martin van Buren stands out solely because he came from a very Dutch pedigree with little or no British blood in his family line. Most or all of the other presidents (including Obama through his mother) have been of British or Irish descent. That's all it takes. Basically, if there's even a single white person in your family tree over the past few hundred years, then you're related to nearly everyone in Europe who lived at the time of King John, and possibly King John himself. Everyone alive today is a distant cousin, we all share the same family line only a thousand or so years old.

This sounds *astonishing*, doesn't it? Because it's easy to miss this mathematical reality. When Marty McFly goes back to the Wild West, he runs into a guy who looks exactly like him, his paternal ancestor. If they made another instalment and sent McFly back to the Middle Ages (to fight the evil Lord Tannen of Biff, perhaps) then you'd bet they'd have a lowly peasant played by Michael J. Fox to represent Marty's dozen-great grandfather. The Da Vinci Code managed to get away with a ridiculous plotline involving Jesus's descendent – assuming somehow that, if he *did* have kids, there'd only be one descendent alive today. We think of ourselves as having a blood*line*, which probably has something rooted in patriarchal gender politics and carrying only the name of our father. So when David Icke traces a direct line between Barack Obama and King John, he thinks he's found some kind of smoking gun. In reality, there's nothing fishy about that.

David Icke has written roughly seven trillion books on the subject of his Grand Unified Conspiracy Theory, but his magnum opus, probably, is *The Biggest Secret*, the 1999 book in which he first reveals the reptilian hypothesis. It's not just notable for that, but it stands as a near-perfect cross-section of every field of pseudoscience. It's practically an encyclopaedia of terrible logic. One can watch in awe as he expertly falls for every logical fallacy that we've ever discovered, even the really obscure ones. It's tempting to believe that David Icke is one of the world's greatest satirists. Had his life taken another turn, he would have been a fantastic novelist.

*The Biggest Secret* is possibly the most elaborate example of obsessive pattern-recognition (or misrecognition) that you will ever find. If there's a superficial similarity between a hieroglyph etched onto the wall of some lesser known Mesoamerican tomb and an explicit sketch doodled onto the wall of a gas station bathroom stall in Minnesota, Icke has found it, and found great meaning in it. From beginning to end, the book is filled with obsessive symbol correlation, attempts to conflate historical figures as co-conspirators through elaborate genealogies, and lots of word and phrase etymologies that seem to be based entirely on Icke's guesswork. (At one point, he cites the Cross of Lorraine, the double-barred crucifix, as the origin of the phrase "double-crossed." Though he states this without reference as though it's self-explanatory, I cannot find any evidence to back this up. Consensus suggests that the etymology of "cross" in this context is in contrast with "square," i.e. fair or honest. A "double-cross" in this instance meaning to double-back and betray. But maybe language etymologists are part of the reptilian conspiracy to dispute Icke's best guess. Certainly every other professional in every field is.)

In the opening chapter of *The Biggest Secret*, Icke begins with the pseudoarchaeological genesis of his beliefs. Beginning as I do with Erich von Däniken, he starts by describing all the ancient structures he believes could not have been built without extraterrestrial help, like pyramids and the Nazca lines. After this, he turns to Sitchin, Velikovsky, and the Atlantis mythology as authoritative sources who completely trump mainstream science's conclusions on all of the above.[35]

From here, he immediately introduces his reptilian theory, with a disclaimer – "Don't Mention the Reptiles" is the title of his second chapter, and he repeats his assurance that what he's about to say sounds crazy to the average joe. "I wish I didn't have to introduce the following information because it complicates the story and opens me up to mass ridicule," he writes, "But stuff it. If this is where the evidence takes me, that is where I shall go every time." He admits that what he's about to reveal (the reptilian alien conspiracy) makes him seem mad, but if you don't unconditionally believe what he's about to tell you, then your mind is closed, you are brainwashed by the establishment, and you're a victim of Illuminati control. (Disbelief thus proves that it is true, and alternatively, belief proves that it is true.)

David Icke has been plagued throughout his career by the worst accusation that can be leveled against the modern conspiracy theorist – that of anti-Semitism. It is the view of many of his opponents—most notably, the Anti-Defamation League—that Icke is speaking in "coded" anti-Semitism. Quite simply, that when he says "reptiles," he means "Jews." I think that this is, in part, because Icke is seen as too sane and too mainstream to truly believe in a shapeshifting alien narrative.

---

[35] He admits that Plato is the sole originator of the Atlantis story, but alludes to the idea that Plato was a secret society initiate, maybe an early Illuminati, and possibly a reptile. As to why he broke the Atlantis story while simultaneously trying to cover it up, maybe he fell victim to the same curse as George H.W. Bush, trying not to mention the global conspiracy but constantly and accidentally doing so.

I would argue that the idea that Icke is speaking in code when he mentions "reptiles" is ignorant of the genealogy of Icke's narrative. Nothing that he says is original. He didn't invent the reptile hypothesis, he cribbed it wholly from Sitchin, who was himself Jewish and in no way proposing an anti-Semitic viewpoint. In fact, the Anti-Defamation League often act like conspiracy theorists themselves, searching for the codes of the secret anti-Semites as fervently as Icke searches for the codes of the Illuminati. Sometimes, lizards are just lizards.

That said, it's important to note that Icke's narrative of conspiracy theory does owe its origins to an anti-Semitic tradition. He maintains that the *Protocols of the Elders of Zion* is an authentic document, but insists that it was written by the Illuminati and not by Jews. Ascribing the *Protocols* to Jews, he insists, is a false-flag tactic to erroneously implicate them (another example of the Illuminati admitting their existence and then trying to cover up their admission.) This is a theory he takes from Milton Cooper, who argued the same thing. Modern conspiracy theorists may not be anti-Semitic, but they cannot run from the fact that their entire culture was deliberately created by authoritarian governments in the $19^{th}$ and $20^{th}$ centuries as a way to vilify the Jews. It's like if David Icke got a copy of *The Lord of the Rings* and simply changed all instances of the word "orc" to "reptoid," and then claimed that Tolkien had meant reptoids all along.

Nevertheless, the idea that a single, small group of highly organised people is knowingly responsible for all the bad things that happen in the world is as absurd a proposition when it was the Jews as it was when it was space reptiles. Icke is just taking Dan Brown's hammer further than most who are restrained by secularity are willing to take it – Icke recognises that ascribing the kind of omniscience required to pull off a conspiracy of this magnitude is beyond the reach of squabbling, short-sighted human beings. But rather than concluding that the conspiracy must not exist (because there's no mechanism through which it can exist), he hammers a new complexity onto it and invokes omnipotent aliens to carry out the conspiracy. In doing so, he undercuts any rebuttal that suggests what he's saying is impossible. It's a circular argument: The conspiracy is impossible for humans to carry out; the conspiracy wouldn't be impossible for omnipotent aliens; therefore, the aliens exist; therefore, the conspiracy exists.

David Icke is probably the most successful career conspiracy theorist working today. I don't mean the most successful person who believes in conspiracy theories, but the most successful person for whom conspiracy theories are their sole occupation. The reasons for his popularity are different, I think, to the reasons for Alex Jones' success. Jones appeals to the white, militant, anti-Communist, American patriots who used conspiracy theory as the club with which to beat the encroaching Soviet menace back during the Cold War. Jones' enemies, the authoritarian menace of the early 20$^{th}$ century, are a thing of the past. He needs to construct a kind of straw man version of these threats to keep his audience tuned in and afraid. But it's a specific audience.

Icke, on the other hand, has proposed with his reptilian hypothesis a blank slate that people are free to substitute for their own villain of choice. For some people, it's fascists; for others, it's communists; for others, it's Jews; for others, it's corporations. His writings offer a smorgasbord of information that appeals to any fringe ideology, and although not all of his fans accept everything he has to say, they all have their favourite talking points to take away. His lectures are attended by hippies and New Agers, by Christian patriots, by UFO aficionados, and by white supremacists, to name a few. His work has been cited by anti-vaccination activist Meryl Dorey, and was passed around the Occupy movement. And then there are those who are just curious – few people who don't fully agree with Alex Jones' ideology would buy tickets to hear him be an obnoxious asshole live, but people flock to hear Britain's most public eccentric speak about the lizard people to thousands in a stadium. He's friendly, receptive to discussion, and bulletproof to criticism.

In a way, his opponents make him look better for their inability to shake him down – it's not just his stunning recovery on the Terry Wogan reunion that makes him a hero. On one occasion, recounted by Jon Ronson in his book *Them*, a group of activists crashed one of Icke's book signings with the intention of hitting him in the face with a cream pie. Had they done enough research into Icke's career, they would presumably have known how futile it was to try to humiliate him in this way—he who recovered his reputation after proclaiming himself the son of God—but nevertheless, the activists missed, and the cream pie hit the children's book section instead. Sometimes, all you need to sound reasonable is for your opponents to be more childish than you are.

## The Slow Kill

Up to now, we've said very little about the actual motive of this shadowy elite, which seems like an important question considering they already apparently have total control and infinite money. In the anti-

Semitic and Cold War origins of the theory, the goal of the New World Order was to take over the world. But in the current era of Alex Jones and David Icke, they have already taken over the world. Where is there to go from here?

It's simple – current consensus among conspiracy theorists is that they intend to *kill us all*.

As overpopulation began to become a hot button issue in world politics during the 20th century, governments began to speculate on how they could slow down the rapidly escalating population of humans before we literally starve ourselves to death. Conspiracy theorists misinterpreted this plan as "kill everybody," and proceeded to hysterically stock up on guns to fight against the NWO's coming genocide attempt against the US population.

Fears that the government was about to storm in any day and just straight kill the shit out of everybody were prominent during the 1900s, among what became known as the *militia movement*. In the wake of the bungled Ruby Ridge and Waco sieges, panicky right-wingers decided to band together and form private armies, because a certain mentality among the American right is that every problem is the result of too few guns. At its peak, Timothy McVeigh decided to put his conspiracy theory where his mouth was, and blew up a federal building in Oklahoma City. Conspiracy theorists maintain that this was actually committed by the government in order to destroy the militia movement, because a bunch of jittery gun nuts are the only thing standing between them and their dastardly Malthusian genocide plan. If McVeigh wasn't enough to make people polish up their tin foil hats, Milton Cooper was then killed in a siege at his home. If Cooper had wanted to prove to the world that the Illuminati were there to kill him, he probably shouldn't have fired first.

With America's last hope—gun nuts—out of the way, the Illuminati, as commanded by either Satan or aliens, are now free to enact their plan to exterminate the human race. And boy, are they ever! According to proponents of the depopulation agenda theory, like Alex Jones, the tools of the extermination effort include genetically modified crops, fluoride in the water supply, vaccinations and prescription drugs, the availability of birth control and abortions, outbreaks of diseases (which are always manufactured in a lab) and the packaging on your food. Alex Jones in particular warns about dyes used in plastics, textiles, and even money, which poison you when you touch it. In one notorious rant, he complains that the plastic lining on the inside of juice boxes is making people gay.[36] The New World Order has been engaged in a secret, massive-scale extermination program for decades now. They're killing you with every substance you put inside your body.

The only problem is that the planet's population has continued to rise steadily, the entire time.

This is a point that I've never heard a proponent of the "depopulation agenda" even try to address. If the secret government are currently engaged in a holocaust program against the human species, then they are *mindblowingly* incompetent at it. One would think that we'd be able to notice such an absurd increase in mysterious deaths over the past couple of decades. The insidiousness of the NWO's plan seems to be to hide their activities by killing everybody at exactly the rate that everyone has always been dying naturally. Those *bastards!*

One thing that conspiracists often cite to prove the global depopulation program is happening is something called "Agenda 21." Argue with them, and they'll frequently tell you to educate yourself by Googling "Agenda 21," the boldly admitted truth that the NWO intends to murder all of us. Agenda 21 is the *Protocols* of the depopulation agenda, pursuant to the NWO's tendency to make secret plans, then publish a document outlining them in explicit detail, then try to cover it up. I did Google "Agenda 21" to educate myself, and the results are mainly conspiracy sites, which are the only people who have any interest in whatever Agenda 21 is. But conservative politicians are also in a tizzy about it – Newt Gingrich thinks that it's a plan by the United Nations to take over the United States. During his race for the 2012 Republican Presidential nomination, he explained: "It's a United Nations proposal to create a series of centralized planning provisions where your local city government can't do something because of some agreement they signed with some private group who are all committed to taking control of your private property and turning it into a publicly controlled property."[37] He could have saved breath by simply saying it's a "communist plot."

Agenda 21, despite the ominous sounding name, was a non-binding series of guidelines published by the UN in the early 1990s for sustainability. The "21" refers to the 21$^{st}$ century, and it's intended to

---

[36] http://tinyurl.com/3nx7rtp

[37] Acosta, Jim. (2011). What's with Newt Gingrich and Agenda 21? *CNN Politics*. November 18$^{th}$. http://tinyurl.com/7u9vprv

be a bunch of advice for gearing toward sustainable growth in the 2000s. It's not a treaty, nor is it enforceable by the UN. The American militia movement seized on it when George H.W. Bush signed on in 1992 (one year after his infamous "New World Order" speech) and the John Birch Society decided that it was the first sign that the world government was about to come to fruition. 20 years later (with no sign of the world government or the global cull in sight) right-wing conspiracists suddenly remembered that Agenda 21 existed when Glenn Beck discovered it in 2012 and told his followers that it was a new plan by the UN to strip Americans of all their rights and establish a tyrannical UN government. In reality, it's as much that as a recipe for key lime pie is a nefarious mandate to forcibly bring your household under the authoritarian control of the lime cartel. Of course, it doesn't help that the UN *did* name it like a Bond villain's plot.

The global human cull might be moving absurdly slowly, but conspiracists believe that things are about to ramp up a notch. Any year now. Well, any decade now. Among right-wing militia movement groups and libertarian radicals, steps have been taken since the 90s to prepare for (as it's said in hushed whispers) martial law. During the eight years of the Bush Jr presidency, conspiracists expressed certainty that Bush would, at some point, declare a national emergency, enact martial law, and announce himself Dictator For Life, throwing away term limits and re-establishing the USA as a dictatorship with himself at the helm. That didn't happen, but the conspiracists are certain that Obama will do it tomorrow. In 2016, the next president *definitely* will.

For some reason, it's FEMA (the Federal Emergency Management Agency) who the conspiracists are most scared of. The federal body in charge of mopping up after hurricanes and meteor strikes are the ones who will be issuing the marching orders to the millions of Americans who will be interred in the hundreds of "FEMA camps" that have already been set up, to be gassed like Holocaust victims. Conspiracists trot out photographs of these concentration camps with the fervour of people throwing up photos of Nibiru. And likewise, the photos they show are usually just random buildings that someone has decided must be a concentration camp in disguise.

One of the most bizarre phenomena linked in with the depopulation conspiracy was the discovery, in 2008 or thereabouts, by conspiratorially-minded rubberneckers, of a site in Georgia along the Interstate 20, of thousands of stacks of coffins. Conspiracy theorists cite this as irrefutable evidence that the government is about to gas millions of people to death. Alex Jones and Jesse Ventura, on Ventura's ridiculous and dumb-as-hammers *Conspiracy Theory* program, stalked through the underbrush in hushed whispers to discuss this top secret government site. What possible reason, they asked, could the government have to stockpile thousands of coffins, if not for a planned holocaust event in the very near future?

The mystery becomes a little less mysterious when you learn that the site is not owned by the government, but rather, a company who manufacture coffins. And the reason they're stockpiling them is probably the same reason that any company would stockpile the product that it produces. Nobody breaks into a Ford factory to reveal to a stunned populace that Ford appears to be manufacturing *thousands of cars*.

But if you believe this is a cover story and the coffins are indeed evidence of a coming holocaust, you have to admit it's awfully strange that the government intends to slaughter us and then give each of us a respectful individual burial. That's going to take a lot of time.

When it comes to conspiracies about secret government programs, especially enacted on a global scale, much of it relies on a phenomenon of human perception that we don't tend to notice mundane things until they have been explicitly pointed out to us. Like the number of buildings that have tall fences around them. When you're told that these are FEMA camps, you suddenly notice that there are a *lot* of buildings with security fences out there. It's called "blue car syndrome," presumably because you can trigger it simply by asking someone if they've ever noticed there are a lot of blue cars out there. They hadn't, but they do *now*. What's more, they think it's a conspiracy, because they don't remember there having been so many blue cars on the road before. Where did they all come from?

One of the most notable examples of this phenomenon is also the most hilarious and frustratingly widespread. It's the belief that *clouds* are a New World Order conspiracy. More specifically, they are really chemicals that are being sprayed into the air to slowly poison all of humanity. It's a conspiracy theory borne from equal parts of blue car syndrome, scientific ignorance, and the fervent *need* to believe in a government plot to reduce all the complicated reasons we get sick to one very simple, preventable cause.

We live in a world of incredible scientific accomplishment. Less than a hundred years ago, my grandmother lived in a house that wasn't even hooked up to a power grid. Now we're walking around with iPhones the size of our palm that connect wirelessly to a worldwide virtual reality called the internet. And that's pretty remarkable considering that, when we first woke up on this blue-green rock, all we had to work with was dirt, trees, and the corpses of whatever we were fast enough to catch.

But despite all of this, there are thousands of people running around today, in the 21$^{st}$ century, ordinary people with their iPhones and computers and fast food restaurants, people in first-world cities with middle-class jobs, who become completely and utterly terrified whenever they crane their necks upward, due to an inability to understand how clouds work. It's just like someone seeing a lit match and calling it witchcraft.

For those who aren't sure of the technical specifics, clouds are quite literally condensed water vapour. It's the exact same phenomenon that occurs when you pour a cold drink on a hot day and the outside of the glass becomes wet. The air around you, everywhere, contains a certain amount of evaporated water (humidity), and that turns back into liquid water when it touches something cold. Likewise, when warm, humid air from the ground floats up to a certain height in the atmosphere, it mixes with cold air and turns into this semi-liquid steam-blob that we call cloud.

Through the same process, you can create clouds yourself if you take warm, moist air and blow it out into cool, dry air, like, through an aircraft engine. Under the right conditions, aircraft create thin, straight clouds along their path of travel. They're called "contrails" or condensation trails.

Most people get this, but some people don't. It's possible to understand, I suppose, why they don't – clouds are natural formations, and planes are human-built machines, and when we all have ingrained in our minds that "human" and "nature" constitute some kind of binary opposition, adversaries which are in no way compatible, then clouds shooting out of planes is something akin to trees sprouting out of lawnmowers and baby birds being forged inside a nuclear fission reactor. Whatever is billowing out of those aircraft engines, they figure, it's definitely not fluffy cotton-candy clouds. It must be something insidious, toxic, *evil*. We say contrails, but they mockingly call them "chemtrails," and whatever they are, we can be reasonably sure they're *baaaaad news*.

The chemtrails theory is possibly the first conspiracy theory to be spread entirely via the internet. But speculation about contrails hasn't been limited to the internet age. Unsurprisingly, people have been curious about the billowing white trails left behind aircraft since aircraft existed. Before mankind learned to fly, we had no idea about the physics of the upper atmosphere, so for the first half of the 20th century, contrails were a strange novelty, especially since planes just didn't appear that often. Take a search through the mainstream news from last century, and you can occasionally find articles puzzling over those white lines in the sky, like this one from the Waterloo Courier, April 16, 1950:

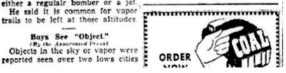

Page Sixteen                    SUNDAY, APRIL 16, 1950.

# Sky 'Objects' Probably Plane Vapor

Des Moines —(P)— The control tower at the Des Moines municipal airport said yesterday that "objects" reported sighted in the sky at Clinton, Davenport and Ottumwa yesterday morning "undoubtedly were vapor trails left by a high flying plane."

"What probably was the same plane came over Des Moines shortly before noon and the vapor trail still was visible here from a long distance off about half an hour later," a spokesman in the control tower said.

He added that the plane was flying at between 20,000 and 30,000 feet and that it may have been either a regular bomber or a jet.

He said it is common for vapor trails to be left at those altitudes.

**Boys See "Object."**
(By the Associated Press)
Objects in the sky or vapor were reported seen over two Iowa cities

yesterday.

At Davenport, two boys, aged 10 and 12, called police when they saw an object they thought was a flying saucer in the sky.

A few minutes later newspaper switchboards were flooded with calls from residents reporting they had seen a mysterious object.

At Ottumwa, a number of persons reported seeing a streak of vapor that extended from horizon to horizon across the sky.

One woman was hysterical with fright as she called the office of the Ottumwa Courier to report the vapor.

Persons who reported seeing an object at Davenport said it flashed, then became black and flashed again before disappearing.

A group watching the vapor at Ottumwa said no airplane was visible although one boy said he could hear a sound like that of an airplane. The vapor streak remained in the sky for quite some time, similar to the vapor train left by a "sky-writer."

ORDER NOW

Scan courtesy of Contrail Science[38]

But confusion about what contrails were was scattered and generally content to be set straight by the scientists who explained the physics of cloud formation. It was the internet that allowed people with strange theories to come together and collaborate. In much the same way as paranoid schizophrenics collaborate online to form the "gang-stalking" community to reinforce their shared delusion, so too does the "chemtrail" community collaborate their own suspicions that clouds are

---

[38] http://tinyurl.com/bu6qve7

not a natural phenomenon, and they reinforce each other's unwillingness to listen to the scientists' explanation, which is part of the cover up.

The first known reference to the conspiracy theory is an online article[39] by a journalist named William Thomas, who can probably be considered the father and originator of the chemtrails theory, as he later went on Art Bell's *Coast to Coast* to tell him all about this amazing scoop. The conspiratorially-minded Bell fans all looked up after Thomas told them that contrails were a new thing, and lo and behold, suddenly the sky was full of blue cars, figuratively speaking.

As usual, who is doing it, why they're doing it, and even exactly what they are doing are all unknown. But one thing is for sure – somebody is spraying something for some reason, and I'm sure as hell not believing those corporate funded scientists who say they're just clouds. Nice try, but clouds are *round!*

In the early days of the chemtrails theory, it seems that the assumption was that the government was secretly spraying the atmosphere in an attempt to mitigate climate change. Of course, this was back in the days when governments denied that climate change existed. Here's some hilarious insight into how conspiracy theories work – when climate change was still being debated among scientists, conspiracy theorists believed that it was real, that the government was covering it up, and that contrails were a secret "geoengineering" project designed to fight it while denying it at the same time. But now that the official line has changed, and scientists and governments say that climate change is real now, conspiracy theorists have changed their minds too. Now, climate change is a hoax, and "chemtrails" must be for some other purpose. This is the point where chemtrail theorists glommed onto the "global depopulation agenda" narrative.

For whatever reason, it's most commonly claimed that aircraft vapour trails are made up of barium, aluminium and other metallic aerosols. Of course, nobody has ever actually flown up there with a bunch of beakers and Bunsen burners to take samples and test what contrails are actually made of (after all, if they did, they would just find water). These arbitrary chemicals have been chosen by the echo chamber nature of the conspiracy theory of the internet age. Intrepid conspiracists who tried to find out exactly what was in these mysterious white lines actually attempted to do some real science – but it was

---

[39] http://tinyurl.com/bolq2av

terrible science, because instead of testing contrails directly, they tested rainwater, figuring that whatever chemicals exist inside contrails would come down with the rain. Most of the "chemtrail tests" that appear online are tests taken of muddy puddles or groundwater sediment, in which the testers miraculously found elements apart from hydrogen and oxygen. Elements such as aluminium. And, for the same reasoning that demands that natural clouds can't come billowing out the engines of a man-made aircraft, so too do people assume that the stuff that makes up your *Coca-Cola* cans can't possibly be lying around in nature. But it is – in fact, it's plentiful.

People who try to argue that "chemtrails" are real use a handful of common arguments. I use the term "argument" loosely, because it's not much of an argument when they never respond to or even read your rebuttal. The most common is that real contrails, vapour exhaust from plane engines, wouldn't stick around in the atmosphere. There is no explanation for this belief except that they're repeating what somebody else told them. People who use this argument always fail to explain how it is that clouds stick around in the atmosphere, considering they believe that water vapour simply cannot do that. Nevertheless, there is another very serious problem with the "I've seen vapour trails and they don't persist, therefore persistent trails can't be contrails" argument.

Imagine if I told you that cars are pushed by ghosts. You might reply that's absurd – cars move under their own power, through a mechanism called an "internal combustion engine." I can reply, no man, I've seen cars, in parking lots and driveways, and *they don't move*. I can show you plenty of photographs of cars not moving to back up this fact. Then I can reiterate that, since cars do not move, it's obvious that cars which are seen moving *must* be being pushed along by ghosts. It's the same argument – a particular phenomenon cannot behave one way under one set of conditions, and another way under another set of conditions. Normal contrails evaporate quickly, and normal cars don't move.

Another common argument is that people simply don't remember contrails in their youth. Therefore, there weren't any contrails before modern times. There are a number of explanations for this – the most obvious is the blue car phenomenon I mentioned earlier, but there's also the fact that there are simply more planes now. Saying you don't remember there being so many contrails is like saying that you don't remember there being so many paved streets. That doesn't mean that paved streets are a conspiracy.

Mainly, people just like to try to figure out what singular phenomenon they can blame for the existence of diseases. Like I'll discuss in the third section, nobody likes to think that disease is something that is out of our control, that we might just come down with cancer one day and it might be nobody's fault. Better to imagine it's the government who are poisoning the air supply, and the water supply, and the food supply. So, in the event that you die sometime over the next 100 years, then you're probably a victim of the slowest genocide in history. By the 30th century, the New World Order might even manage to kill people faster than they're being born.

## Osama Blockbuster

The terrorist attack of September 11th, 2001, was one of the most implausible series' of events in human history. Make no mistake, Osama bin Laden had some pretty over-ambitious plans. I can only imagine how many of his fellow jihadists thought that he was off his tree – the plan, after all, was to hijack several large aircraft and kamikaze-bomb them into a whole catalogue of American landmarks. That's basically the plot of every Roland Emmerich film ever made, but it's not the blueprint of a traditional terrorist attack.

In fact, 9/11 was a stupid plan from the beginning. Sure, if it was pulled off, it would change the world as we knew it, but there were so many variables to consider, so many things that could go wrong along the multiple steps that have to fall in place. Terrorists prefer simplicity – (1) make a bomb, (2) drive it up to a target, (3) detonate said bomb. It doesn't do much damage, but the goal is to make the people abandon their trust in their security, and lots of successful, small-scale explosions are more effective than one big, lumbering, idiotic landmark apocalypse that fails miserably. When bin Laden was describing his plan to his lieutenants, we can only imagine the incredulity in their expressions when he got up to around step 47. If 9/11 had failed, it would have made them look like idiots.

But 9/11 didn't fail. It didn't entirely succeed (the fourth plane they captured, probably headed to either the White House or the Capitol Building, crashed 30 minutes away from its target) but three out of four hits is still better than anyone in their right mind could have expected, and it got the point across quite nicely. Some aspects didn't go as well as Al Qaida probably would have expected (though 125 died, the plane that hit the Pentagon may as well have been a Buick for all the damage it did), but others probably went much better (the New

York towers collapsing was probably a pleasant surprise for them, like finding a carton of beer that turns out to be padded with winning lottery tickets).

The point is, bin Laden was an idiot who got lucky. He's the bowler who tripped over his own shoelaces and managed to knock down eight pins. He didn't even get a strike. He's just one fool in history who managed to achieve better-than-average success despite the odds, sandwiched in between a whole bunch of idiots through history who failed where failure was expected. The laws of chance dictate that some of those idiots are going to fail upward.

But conspiracy theorists don't believe in chance or idiots. Because of the whole implausible Hollywood blockbuster feel of the entire event, it has become perhaps the most widespread conspiracy theory of all time. People who already subscribed to all the Illuminati business jumped on board immediately, as they were always going to, but even people who didn't otherwise believe in UFOs and Masonic weather machines started looking at the affair with a certain degree of scepticism. 3000 people died that day, and not a shot had been fired, not a bomb detonated – the only thing close to a weapon that anyone used was, reportedly, some box cutters.

(Interestingly, "box cutters" is one of those terms that people spit out with a chuckle when trying to highlight the ridiculousness of the hijacking story. "They didn't even have knives, they had *box cutters!*" Let me tell you, as someone who actually cuts boxes as part of his job, I'd be every bit as nervous of someone holding one of those up to my jugular than one of those unwieldy looking Rambo knives. It's a six-inch-long holstered razor blade, come on.)

The 9/11 story, the official story, kind of is ridiculous. This was no car bomb. This was something a Bond villain would do. And it's the unlikelihood of the story that drives the conspiracists into a feeding frenzy. We are expected to believe not only that 19 hijackers with limited flight experience hijacked four planes with box cutters and managed to crash three of them directly into American landmarks, but that both towers of the World Trade Centre, steel-reinforced skyscrapers, would collapse due to fire (which can't ordinarily bring down buildings at all) and that all of this happened without the omniscient CIA knowing anything about it. Yes, it is a crazy-ass storyline. You'd be silly to think it could happen if not for the fact that it did, and many people think you'd still be silly.

First of all, if you think the 9/11 plot is implausible, you haven't heard anything yet. Like any blockbuster script, the final version of the 9/11 attacks went through a lot of rewrites, and was adapted from a much earlier, much stupider version. What ultimately came to fruition as the 9/11 attacks started with an epic, cataclysmic, jihadist stoner fantasy known as the "Bojinka Plot."

In the early 1990s, Khalid Shaikh Muhammad and Ramzi Yousef (masterminds of 9/11 and the 1993 World Trade Centre bombing respectively) got together in Manila to hang out, play a little pool perhaps, and talk about good times past. While there, they began to draft the ultimate big-budget, infidel-crippling terrorist extravaganza, a plan that they simply called "Bojinka," a nonsense word that in Serbian means, literally, "kaboom." Here's how it was going to play out:

First, a suicide bomber would kill the Pope. This would happen when the pontiff visited the Philippines on January 12, 1995 – a bomber, disguised as a priest, would approach John Paul II and trigger a fatal popesplosion. While everybody was mourning the assassination of the Catholic leader, five terrorists would then embark upon a worldwide flying holiday, jumping from flight to flight and planting time bombs on every plane that would be set to detonate after the bombers had already disembarked. After blowing up 12 flights and thus killing an estimated 4000 people, the intrepid jihadists would serve up the *pièce de résistance*, hijack a whole fleet of airliners and crash them into the CIA headquarters, the World Trade Centre, the Pentagon, the Sears Tower, the Capitol Building, the White House, and the Transamerica Pyramid.

Bojinka!

The plot was foiled, officially, when some wanker messed with the explosives and set himself on fire, alerting the police to the existence of a terrorist den in Manila. But one can suppose that the plot would have foiled itself at some point along its ludicrously detailed chain of events. What Khalid Shaikh Muhammad and his buddies eventually settled upon to take the last third of the Bojinka Plot, pare it down a little and run with that. It was still a ridiculous plan, but in comparison to what they had tried first, maybe not so much.

The problem with using the implausibility of 9/11's official story as a means to debunk it, quite simply, is that no matter how ridiculous it is, *it is still the most plausible theory*. Whenever conspiracists try to formulate an alternative theory to how 9/11 took place, whenever they try to fill in the gaps and patch up the perceived problems, what they inevitably wind up with is a *more complicated* and *less plausible* theory. Although the actual events were indeed unlikely and everyone is trying to think up an alternative, all the alternatives that people are thinking up are *retarded*.

For example, the alternative that is most widely accepted among conspiracy theorists, the one that is supposed to answer all of the mysteries and patch up the unlikelihoods, goes something like this:

On the morning of September 11$^{th}$, 2001, four domestic passenger jets take off as usual from their respective points of origin. The pilots of these planes, however, are either part of the conspiracy and act on their own accord, or else they are ordered for reasons unknown to them, to divert their course and land at a secret location, probably a military base.

From here, two different aircraft are launched. These are empty, remote controlled aircraft which are painted up in the American Airlines and United Airlines colours, in order to fool eyewitnesses. The two remote controlled planes are flown toward Manhattan. In the meantime, the passengers on the ground, under military arrest, are forced to call their loved ones on their cell phones and pretend they have been hijacked by terrorists (alternative theories: Those who made the calls were part of the conspiracy, OR, the calls were never made, and those people and their entire families were *all* in on the conspiracy.)

The two empty, remote controlled planes are flown into the two towers of the World Trade Centre. These buildings, however, have already been wired up days in advance with thermite devices and explosives. After the towers have been allowed to billow smoke for a while, and after enough firefighters have been allowed to enter the building to maximise the tragedy, the conspirators set off the explosives which collapse both towers in a controlled demolition in order to make it appear as though they collapsed due to fire damage. Also demolished is a nearby office building, WTC7, which was not hit by a plane but needed to be destroyed for reasons known only to the conspirators (theory has it that it contained documentation damning to Bush's corporate interests).

While this is all happening, the military shoots a missile at the Pentagon. All security footage is confiscated so that it can be claimed that what hit the Pentagon was, in fact, a hijacked aircraft. Every eyewitness who can attest to the fact that it was actually a missile is either eliminated or is a part of the conspiracy and lies about the planes.

Everyone who, at this point, needs to be murdered (the passengers on all those planes and the eyewitnesses who refuse to cooperate) is bundled onto one of the planes they confiscated United flight 93 (at this point they are all either alive or dead) and the plane is piloted toward Pennsylvania and shot down under Dick Cheney's command over a field in Somerset County. All the other planes need to either be dismantled and destroyed in secret, or flown out over the ocean and scuttled.

At some point, Larry Silverstein, the lease holder for the World Trade Centre, who is in on the entire conspiracy, accidentally forgets that it's supposed to be a secret and goes on television to make some vague remarks, one interpretation of which is that he gave the order for the buildings to be demolished. The government then launches an investigation into the attacks but secretly ships all of the debris from the buildings out to China to be destroyed, and the investigators are either not permitted to actually inspect real WTC wreckage, or are in on the conspiracy and lie about everything.

Later, when too many people catch wind of the *truth* about 9/11, the magazine *Popular Mechanics* does its own full investigation into the attacks, consulting leading professionals in every field of science and engineering to fully reconstruct the events of that day, and their consensus is that, although remarkable, the official explanation is the only plausible one and all of the questions of conspiracy theorists can be explained within that framework of phenomena. *Popular Mechanics* is, of course, backed by the CIA, and every single one of the professionals they consulted is in on the conspiracy.

This, according to a baffling number of people, is how 9/11 *really* went down. Of course, a lot of them probably don't realise, *per se*, that this is what they believe. They haven't seen it written all out like this. Subscribers to the "inside job" hypotheses tend to see trees, but not a forest. Each individual point in the theory is used as a band-aid to patch up perceived problems in the official story.

"You know, fire usually can't burn hot enough to breach a building's foundations."

"Funny, I thought cell phones couldn't work from inside planes."

"World Trade Centre 7 wasn't hit by a plane, how did that collapse?"

"Sure seems fishy that some terrorists were able to do all this with box cutters."

"I hate George Bush. I bet he did it."

These seem like reasonable points to make, but when you put them all together and see the grand narrative, you should find that all of these little fixes add up to a story that is vastly more ridiculous and has many, many more holes in it than the official story that they're trying to probe into. And the narrative I've just provided is only the most popularly held one. A smaller minority of "9/11 truth" advocates have offered alternatives that go even further down the rabbit hole. The so-called "no planes theory" puts forward the idea that no planes hit any buildings at all. Instead, explosives were rigged inside to blow out the sides of the buildings, and the government used hologram technology to broadcast fake planes into the sky, creating the illusion that planes hit the buildings. Those who think that hologram technology is too crazy, but the mainstream theory isn't crazy enough, assert that all of the footage of 9/11 was doctored to add CGI planes, and everyone who actually claims to have been in New York and have seen the planes are simply in on it, or victims of mind manipulation. Beyond even that, there are the David Icke "aliens did it" crowd.

Personally, I prefer the alternative "single plane theory" offered by the comedy site *The Onion*:

> At 8:46 a.m., a lone commercial airliner flew diagonally through the North Tower of the World Trade Center, maintained a circular holding pattern for approximately 17 minutes, then struck the South Tower before heading to the Pentagon. After its collision with the center of American military operations, the so-called "magic plane"—which variously and ingeniously identified itself to air-traffic controllers as "American Airlines Flight 11," "United Airlines Flight 175," "American Airlines Flight 77" and "United Airlines Flight 93"—took to the skies once again, landing at a top-secret "black-ops" Air Force base in West Virginia, where it was reloaded with a group of clones from another shadowy government program that [Oliver] Stone described as "shocking." [40]

---

[40] http://www.theonion.com/articles/new-oliver-stone-911-film-introduces-single-plane,2017/

As always, conspiracy theories started up immediately after the event happened. People who would have believed from the outset that such an event was orchestrated by the government, the shadow government or the Illuminati immediately started looking for evidence that this was so. But the theory didn't really hit the mainstream until 2005, when an aspiring filmmaker named Dylan Avery started selling an independent film that he'd made. Statistically, you've probably seen "Loose Change." This is the film that turned a fringe conspiracy theory into a mainstream belief, that rocketed conspiracists into prime time television talk shows, that gave it credibility up there with Watergate and the Clinton sex scandals, that ultimately forced publications such as *Popular Mechanics* to launch mainstream investigations into the matter. At least at the time, 9/11 conspiracy wasn't something only tin-hat wearing UFO nuts believed. It was believed by *lots of people*. Of course, thousands of firefighters and victims' families wanted to punch those people in the face.

So where did Loose Change come from? Well, as I said, Dylan Avery was an aspiring filmmaker, and those who have followed his career know that Loose Change began as a work of fiction. To his credit, this isn't something that he hides. The original intention was to create a fake documentary, a kind of "what if" scenario, like the Blair Witch, using doctored and cherry-picked footage to build a fictional case. But Avery had no real way to finance and promote his project – it was only when Phillip Jayhan, an Illuminati believer, offered funding to produce and distribute the film, and Kory Rowe, another believer in the secret shadow government cabal, came on as producer, that Dylan Avery mysteriously came to believe that what he was saying was real. Or at least, that's the way he presents the story.

I don't want to spend much time impugning Avery's motives. Demanding that everyone else is "in on it" is more the job of the conspiracy believers, and I'll leave that tactic to them (though, while I'm casting out ad hominims, I'd like to mention that Jason Bermas, Avery's other producer and frequent interview partner, is quite possibly the single biggest asshole on the planet, and to research this issue, and have to wade through interviews with him shrieking red-faced about how everyone is a liar, it really makes you wonder how often he just gets punched right in the face in the middle of a conversation.)

Generally, the entire 9/11 "truth" movement, from its most mainstream adherents up to its nutty UFO fringe, rests upon four points of contention. They all have explanations that line up with the official story, but giving these explanations to a 9/11 conspiracist will ordinarily result in them ignoring you or telling you without further clarification that the answer you gave is "a lie." It's clear to see why – you can argue about the finer points of the different kinds of explosives that might have been used or whether or not the planes were equipped with missiles, but to debunk these core, load-bearing arguments at the base of 9/11 truthism will make the entire conspiracy theory collapse upon itself like a couple of skyscrapers hit by passenger jets. Believers just cannot allow that to happen, and so they hold firm to the basic atomic elements of 9/11 conspiracism:

1) No source of heat inside the World Trade Centre was sufficient to melt steel. This is why fire generally does not demolish steel reinforced buildings. You can compare (as they frequently do) the WTC with other famous building fires and see that the buildings never actually collapse, because the melting point of steel is greater than any fire can reach. Only demolition-grade tools like thermite can melt through steel.

Conspiracists did adjust this argument after it was pointed out that, while steel will not melt in a fire, it will lose 50% of its strength, which was more than sufficient to collapse the towers. The truthers then found quotes from people who went to Ground Zero after the disaster and said they found molten steel in the area. They also scoured through photographs of the collapsing buildings and pointed out stuff dripping out the windows that they contend is molten steel. The intent here is to build the case that steel *did in fact melt*, so the "weakened steel" argument in the official story is bunk.

What they refuse to entertain even remotely, of course, is the possibility, however slight, that they may be in any way mistaken about their amateur analysis of the red dots they see on a vastly blown-up low-resolution image of a collapsing tower taken from a news report from over a decade ago. They argue that it is a cop-out and a dodge to argue that red dots pouring out of the World Trade Centre might actually be something other than steel, like aluminium (also very plentiful within the buildings), or various flammable liquids, or, you know, anything. They also will not allow you to point out that the quotes they mine from visitors to Ground Zero only ever report seeing "molten metal" at the site, except for one quote by one Peter Tully, president of a construction company, who does utter the words "molten steel." But it's a mystery exactly how anyone, even the president of a construction company, might be able to distinguish between different kinds of molten metal from just a brief glimpse.

The contention that fire absolutely cannot demolish a building is probably the central lynchpin for the whole conspiracy theory. More often than not, they will direct you to photographs of the Windsor Tower in Madrid, which was on fire for 26 hours straight, but, although gutted, did not collapse.

Understandably, conspiracy theorists are unable to find too many examples of buildings that continued standing after passenger airliners were flown into them, so structurally sound towers in which someone dropped a cigarette will have to suffice for comparison with the 9/11 disaster. But another very important aspect to the WTC collapse that is difficult or impossible for conspiracy theorists to wrap their heads around is that the twin towers were remarkably, and unusually, shitty skyscrapers.

We live in a bit of a "plastic scissors" state in the west. Workplace health and safety officials spend so much time up our arses that they've pinned pictures of their kids winning track and field medals up in there. If we try to build a gazebo too close to the fence line or within marathon distance from an underground pipe, council officials smash through our windows like SWAT. Maybe I'm exaggerating a little here, but what seems an unspoken assumption to us these days is that buildings are built to be able to withstand fire, and in many cases, even greater disasters like being bombed or hit by planes. Building codes demand that buildings can survive greater mishaps than they are sanely expected to ever actually face. That's true, for the most part. But what most people don't realise, and what Osama bin Laden probably didn't realise (although maybe he did – rumours suggest he may have had a degree in civil engineering despite the conspiracists' worryingly racist "towel wearing caveman" caricature) is that the World Trade Centre did not conform to building codes. It conformed to building codes about as well as Charlie Sheen conforms to codes of social etiquette.

In the United States, federal buildings are exempt, for some reason, from adhering to building codes. These codes are the reason that fire won't usually topple a building – a sturdy core of steel columns supports the structure in such a way that the building just can't collapse. Imagine a tree enveloped with fire – it'll burn off the leaves, but the trunk will still be there. Skyscrapers have to be particularly rigorous when it comes to ensuring they have a solid core, because it's particularly disastrous when they fall over, and they're particularly susceptible to things like turbulent weather and, I dunno, getting hit by planes. But due to its not adhering to anything remotely resembling a building code, the twin towers were not "skyscrapers" so much as 110 Home Depots stacked on top of each other.

The primary concern for the designers of the World Trade Centre was floor space, and nothing interferes with floor space so much as a bunch of inconvenient central columns. So the architects instead built the towers with an "exoskeleton" of steel supports, fine for a short, flat building but not so good for a towering skyscraper. The resulting towers were basically structurally dodgy steel tubes shooting up into the sky. A further result of its not having to adhere to codes was that tenants within the WTC got to choose whether or not to spend extra money on stuff like fire precautions. Predictably, few bothered.

If any skyscraper in the world was going to fall down after getting hit by planes, it was the twin towers of the WTC. If the terrorists had struck the Empire State building instead, this story might have gone a little differently. But there would have been conspiracies attached to that as well – whatever suspicious details can be extracted from the actual events of 9/11, it remains so that a government conspiracy was already a foregone conclusion among truthers before the planes even hit. The rest, as they say, are details.

You'd imagine, though, that a government smart enough to pull off a conspiracy like 9/11 would have been smart enough from the outset not to create a scenario that every engineer and physicist in the world could immediately see was totally impossible, like a couple of skyscrapers collapsing due to fire. Of course, almost every engineer and physicist in the world actually agrees that the buildings *did* collapse due to fire, but conspiracists latch on to the one or two exceptions and hold fast to their own poor understanding of physics to argue that 999 out of a thousand scientists are either wrong or lying about basic science.

So they hold their hands over their ears and scream "lalala" until the room is silent enough for them to repeat their mantra that steel does not melt in fire, and because all the vertical beams in the WTC melted as evidenced by the oceans of molten steel they found there, clearly the building was brought down by thermite.

Don't tell them that thermite can only melt downward and thus cannot melt vertical beams. We don't want them to start bleeding into their brains.

2) World Trade Centre 7 was never hit by an aircraft, and yet it collapsed in what really, really, really looks like a controlled

demolition. Also, the owner of the building admitted that it was a controlled demolition.

The collapse of "building 7" on 9/11 gives conspiracy theorists a massive boner. Because even if you convince people that the twin towers were somehow brought down by such an insignificant event as having two Boeing 767s flown into them, you can't explain why building 7 came down. And this is the kicker – the collapse of WTC 7 is indeed more complicated and less thoroughly studied than the relatively simple explanations behind the collapse of the towers. Conspiracists thus employ a strategy similar to what atheists refer to as the "god of the gaps" argument, invoking the existence of God wherever we find something that science legitimately can't yet explain confidently. Building 7 is the "conspiracy of the gaps," and after the whole melted-steel bulldust has been debunked again and again for a decade, truthers will now stand there yelling "building 7!" at you because they know it poses some more difficult questions.

There are, however, some things that we know the conspiracy theorists are wrong about. They are wrong about building 7 having sustained no damage. They may not have flown a plane into it, but it had parts of the twin towers falling on it the entire time they were burning, and by the time it came down, it looked as though it *may as well* have been hit by a plane. They are also wrong about the building coming down symmetrically as though by controlled demolition – a close analysis of the footage of the collapse shows that the damaged side fell first and pulled the rest of the building down with it. But I'm not going to argue those points here, first of all because you can find much more concise websites that explain it with images, and also because these arguments *don't matter* to truthers. Building 7 is the last desperate stronghold that they have, and they'll be damned if they're going to let you convince them that it doesn't look like they brought that building down with bombs.

Instead, I'm going to focus on the sillier points that have to be made here to support the building 7 conspiracy. For instance, much has been made of the fact that the owner of the World Trade Centre, Larry Silverstein, later said this in an interview about the collapse of building 7:

> I remember getting a call from the Fire Department commander, telling me they were not sure they were gonna be able to contain the fire, and I said, you know, **"We've had such terrible loss of life, maybe the smartest thing to do is**

**just pull it.**" And they made that decision to pull and then we watched the building collapse.

Conspiracy theorists regard this quote to be one of their smoking guns – the word "pull" is an industry term used by demolitions crews. The dictionary also provides about 30 alternative definitions of the word "pull," but the important thing is that one of them is building demolition lingo and thus this constitutes an admission by Silverstein that building 7 was a controlled demolition.

Altogether too many words have been spent debunking what Silverstein said and what conspiracy theorists thought he said. To summarise a few inconvenient truths: Silverstein is quoting himself talking to firemen, not a building demolitions crew; Silverstein himself is not a demolitions expert, so it's bizarre that he would use insider demolitions lingo that neither he nor the firemen he's talking to are equipped to understand (kind of like an engineer describing chemistry to a landscape artist by using medical shorthand); the *actual definition* of the word "pull" within the demolitions industry refers to a method of pulling a building down using cables, which even conspiracists agree was not how WTC7 was brought down; Although "pull" can be used as an industry term, another definition of the word happens to be "pulling firemen out of a building because it is about to collapse," which for some reason conspiracists do not agree is more likely to be what he was saying here.

You can go on the internet and see pages and pages and pages of rebuttal detailing what Silverstein was probably actually trying to say here as opposed to the assumption made by truthers that he was really saying "Haha, fools, I blew up the World Trade Centre" in thinly veiled code. But any attempt to put his quote in context pales before the glaringly massive and incomprehensibly ridiculous assumption that truthers are clinging to – the idea that Larry Silverstein accidentally forgot to not go on national television and casually declare that 9/11 was an inside job. Freaking *whoops!* This is the same insane logic that is used by people who look for Illuminati codes in corporate logos, or who argue that George Bush was admitting his plans when he uttered the words "new world order," or who think they see news anchors' eyes momentarily become reptilian in a blurry, low-resolution news broadcast. It's the idea that, if there is indeed a conspiracy, the best way to figure it out is through the many casual encoded admissions that the conspirators are flooding the media with, because supposedly it never occurred to them that the best way to hide a conspiracy is to not put a guy in front of the cameras and make him admit to it.

I've heard a lot of people explain this away with simple hubris. The conspirators deliberately go on TV and admit that 9/11 was an inside job because they know that most people will not work out their code, and so they are flaunting their superiority to the minority of people who *know* they really did it. People seriously believe this, and I'm sure it makes conspiracy theorists feel very validated, to know that their personal nemesis Larry Silverstein considers them worthy enough opponents to go on television and speak directly to them in code that only they are intelligent to understand. Kind of like in the *Superman* movie when Lex Luthor broadcasts his evil plot over the whole of Metropolis, but does it in a frequency that only Clark Kent's super-ears can pick up. Real life, however, is not a comic book, and the "hubris" explanation is just an example of conspiracy theorists trying to understand world events in terms of how they roll out in action movies and Spider-Man issues. Nothing more.

If anything, the collapse of World Trade Centre 7 does more to *harm* the conspiracy theory than to back it up. Because, if it was a conspiracy, there's no reason why they should have bombed that building. People are trying to understand the collapse of WTC7 from within the framework of assuming it must have been deliberate. But the fact is, if it really was an inside job, then the government could have brought down those towers alone and nobody would be left scratching their heads about why building 7 was still there. If the government did bring down the twin towers, then bombing WTC7 as well was a random, meaningless expense that achieved nothing but to have conspiracy theorists ask a bunch of questions that they wouldn't have been able to ask if the conspirators had simply not bothered to do so. Why would they do this? Is this hubris again? Did the conspirators think that the demolition of the twin towers looked too much like the work of Arab terrorists and so they decided to throw conspiracy theorists a bone and make this a real challenge for themselves by randomly blowing up a different building? Once again, this whole scheme sounds like it was masterminded by The Riddler.

When things happen in reality, they are messy. The official conspiracy theory, the conspiracy of terrorists, doesn't require any mention of building 7. The terrorists didn't plan on knocking down building 7. They didn't even plan on knocking down the twin towers, beyond *possibly* expecting that was their best case scenario. It doesn't require us to imagine Osama bin Laden as some omnipotent master villain, orchestrating every detail of the scenario, rigging every building to collapse, micro-managing the exact chain of events deliberately to the letter. They just flew some planes into the buildings, and what happened, happened. It is thus a simpler explanation. The alternative, the "Bush did it" explanation, *does* require such a master villain, and *does* require micro-managing of every fire, every impact, and every collapse, down to the smallest possible detail, even the ones that occurred for no reason. Let me remind you that the simpler explanation, despite racist assumptions about towelheads in caves, was carried out by a professional terrorist and master guerrilla leader with several university degrees under his belt. The more complex and difficult to pull off scenario was masterminded by a man who once coined the term "misunderestimated."

   3) It is impossible to use cell phones from the altitude of a plane in flight. They say that the victims of the hijackings called their families before they died. The truth must be that the calls were made from the ground, or were not made at all.

This is a strange point for conspiracy theorists to get caught up on, because it makes life more difficult for themselves. Their absolute refusal to let go of the "can't use phones on a plane" argument forces them to revise their own theory from "staged hijackings" to something like "remote control planes, faked phone calls, and a hundred or so civilians secretly part of the plot." I think we can all agree that this is a more complicated scenario, and it seems like the government could have saved themselves a lot of expense by simply dressing up like Arab terrorists and staging a hijacking, instead of the whole remote control planes business.

    This point is also more easily dismissed than most of them – some of the calls that were made were made from air phones (specifically designed to be able to be used in flight, because that's what they're for) and others were made from cell phones while the planes were at extremely low altitude. Which they were because, you know, they were about to fly them into some buildings.

    Conspiracy theorists generally sweep all of this kind of thing under the carpet as "a likely story" and "don't you just have an answer for everything." As though having an answer to everything and telling likely stories isn't the only possible avenue to rational explanation that we have available to us. How do we better reach our conclusions? Do we rely, as David Icke does, on voices in our heads to reveal the true story?

140

The "phones don't work on planes" theory is most popularly championed by one of the foremost figures in 9/11 conspiracism, Prof. David Ray Griffin, Ph.D. The truth movement loves to invoke Prof. David Ray Griffin, Ph.D., wherever possible, because while facing a barrage of charges that 9/11 truthers are generally amateurs whose entire position is built upon an unprofessional opinion of a tenuous grasp of science, it helps their case to mention that Prof. David Ray Griffin, Ph.D. is on their side. Prof. David Ray Griffin, Ph.D. thinks that the planes were remote-controlled, so what do you debunkers with your undergraduate educations and so-so grade point averages think about *that?*

Prof. David Ray Griffin, Ph.D. is a professor of philosophy of religion. Apparently he is very good when it comes to analysis of the work of Alfred North Whitehead and process philosophy. Considering my own background, I am certainly not going to mock a man for having a degree in philosophy. But constantly invoking Griffin's status as a professor and his status within the field of philosophy in order to put weight behind his interpretation of the laws of physics is a case of what is known as the "appeal to authority" fallacy. Griffin's opinion, in reality, carries no more weight than the opinion of Charlie Sheen about how 9/11 really went down.

Now, many conspiracists are aware of logical fallacies. But, just like Occam's razor, they have their own upside-down and backward version of it. Conspiracists will often tell you that you are falling for the appeal to authority fallacy when you listen to *Popular Mechanics* and other articles written by physicists and engineers. That you should instead get your facts from Dylan Avery, Charlie Sheen and David Ray Griffin. Paradoxically, they are more reliable because they are not authorities and thus it's not fallacious to appeal to them.

An appeal to authority is not fallacious when the appeal is to a direct authority in the exact field of the question that you are asking, if said authority is able to back the answer up with verifiable facts. An appeal to authority is only fallacious if you are using the mere fact of authority, albeit in an entirely different profession, to beef up the apparent reliability of an opinion that is not and cannot be backed up with facts or evidence because it is *freaking wrong.*

Really, the apparent problem with the phone calls is the point at which 9/11 conspiracism moves from an entertaining thought experiment into outright cartoon fantasy. This small and easily explained hang-up is where a story about a faked hijacking turns into a story about weird future remote-control technology, complicity on a downright *X Files* scale, and an incredibly complicated plane-shuffling plot that makes you wonder why the CIA didn't just plant a nuclear device and leave a few turbans and a signed portrait of Osama bin Laden in the rubble.

4) The hole on the side of the Pentagon isn't the shape of a passenger aircraft. The Pentagon must have been hit by a missile.

Even when I was very young, I thought that it was implausible that, when Wile E. Coyote ran through a solid wall, he left a hole in the wall that completely matched his exact silhouette, down to the shape of his hair and whiskers. I mean, obviously that wasn't the only thing I thought was implausible about Roadrunner cartoons and that they were otherwise totally legit, but that was something I was clearly able to discern, even at the age of 5, was meant as comedy because it was so silly.

Imagine my surprise in my cynical mid-20s when I discovered that one of the primary arguments of the 9/11 conspiracy crowd is that the Boeing 767 that hit the side of the Pentagon didn't leave a hole in the wall that was the size and exact shape of a Boeing 767.

Remarkably, this is one of those positions that can be clearly distinguished as cognitive dissonance, conspiracy theorists holding two simultaneous and contradictory views and believing them both. Not an awful lot of damage was done to the Pentagon on that day, though I am not trying to minimise the tragedy of those who died by saying that. To that end, the Pentagon behaved just as conspiracy theorists believe the twin towers should have behaved upon being hit by planes – not much happened.

But the conspiracists are not convinced, and so the superficial damage to the Pentagon is itself used as proof of a conspiracy. The bizarre position of the 9/11 truth movement can thus be described something like this: Because the twin towers, fragile and vulnerable as they were, collapsed upon being hit by aircraft, this proves a government conspiracy. Because the Pentagon, built to withstand a nuclear war, did not collapse upon being hit by aircraft, this also proves a government conspiracy.

To the rest of us, those to whom up is up, red is red, and water is wet, this scenario played out pretty much just as you would expect that it should. While Dylan Avery and his followers contend that the superficial damage sustained by the Pentagon is not consistent with the size and shape of a passenger aircraft, the rest of us, those who recognised as children that Wile E. Coyote was a fantasy and a comedy, can understand pretty easily what happened to the Pentagon on 9/11. The hole in the building, consistent with the shape of a "missile" or some other cigar shaped object, looks the way it does because the cigar-shaped body of a 767 was the only part strong enough to damage the wall. Flimsy extraneous features such as the wings and wheels didn't make it through. If you really need a demonstration of this phenomenon, grab a fist full of chopsticks and punch the wall as hard as you can. You will probably find that your fist makes a hole in the wall, but the chopsticks simply snap. (The broken bones in your hand, for this analogy, represent all the dead people in the Pentagon that you're pretending never existed.)

I could write an entire book debunking the technical aspects of the 9/11 conspiracy theories, but others have already done that (the NIST, for example, spent 298 pages doing so). There comes a point where conspiracists and conspiracy debunkers wind up debating highly technical jargon-riddled micro-aspects of the trajectory of steel beams during individual frames of the WTC collapse footage, where the details become lost for the layman, who wants a simple and plain language reason to take one side or the other. For those people, and for most every day situations, I prefer one argument that few people in the heat of the debate invoke, but which I personally think is the elephant in the room when it comes to 9/11 conspiracy. It's the argument that the pseudonymous author and editor David Wong pointed out[41] not long after the attacks themselves, which has been somewhat neglected through the course of the discussion. Once again, it's an appeal to Occam's razor.

Think about how many people it would take to pull off a conspiracy on the scale that 9/11 truthism implies. It cannot be, as many people tacitly suggest, the work of Bush, Cheney and Rumsfeld

---

[41] Via *Cracked*: Was 9/11 an Inside Job? http://tinyurl.com/36ma5v

alone. At the very least, the team of people who wired the World Trade Centre with explosives must be in on the plot. To set three high-rise buildings up for a controlled demolition (two of them being two of the tallest buildings in the world) must have taken a crew of hundreds, working for months by cover of night so that nobody who worked in any of those buildings knew what was happening (unless you want to add thousands to that number by suggesting the people who worked in those towers were complicit). You need to incriminate everyone who was directing aircraft on that day, who would have seen the passenger airlines disappear from their radar and be replaced by the military's top-secret remote control planes. For some versions of the theory, you need to incriminate the firemen who reportedly heard bombs going off (many of whom gave their lives) and also the victims of the tragedy who made fake phone calls to their grieving families, and all of the military personnel who directed the events.

Most notably, you have to implicate all of the scientists and engineers in the world who support the official story even though they know better. Whether you insist that these people were all in on it, or that they were bribed or paid off by the conspirators, you are looking at either thousands of conspirators, or tens of millions of dollars paid in bribes. As Wong points out, for the 9/11 conspiracy to be viable, the 9/11 conspiracy must have been the single biggest employer in the history of the world.

Add to that the notion of risk. The philosopher Noam Chomsky, an outspoken critic of the Bush administration's treatment of 9/11 (and thus an adopted darling of the truth movement despite his disagreement with it) rightly points out that if the government did in fact orchestrate the 9/11 attacks and they were ever discovered, every conspirator from Bush himself down to the captain of the firehouse, would only have a firing squad to look forward to, and it would in fact very probably be the end of the existence of the Republican party. This is one hell of a risk for the Bush administration to take, being that they relied upon not a single one of these thousands of conspirators, from government agents to bureaucrats down to air traffic controllers and the demolitions crew who orchestrated the event, from Silverstein to the military personnel, to the firemen who lost their lives that day and the families of the victims who were paid to remain silent, to the thousands if not millions of scientists who know better and were told to keep their mouths shut, for not a single, solitary one of these people to ever develop a conscience and go to the media about their role in the 9/11 conspiracy. That none of them would ever do this for the remainder of their natural lives.

The events of September 11$^{th}$, 2001, cannot be explained simply. What happened that day was one of two very implausible stories. One requires thousands, if not tens of thousands, of psychopaths working through every level of society from president to housewife, all of whom have no desire to open up about their knowledge about the true events of that day. As for the other... I don't know how many conspirators exist in that version of events, but I do know that most of them were operating in a country that both turned a blind eye to terrorism and had an open antagonism toward the United States, and the breadth of the conspiracy upon American soil need only extend to 19 individuals and some box cutters. All uncertainties about the mechanism of the events aside, I know which one I'm putting my money on.


## Sour Grapes

In 1960, the height of the Cold War, a dastardly plan was hatched by the worldwide communist conspiracy, a long-term plan that would take almost 50 years to come to fruition – but when it did, it would mean the total destruction of the United States of America, and its absorption into the growing union of communist empires that spanned the globe. It was an unconventional plan, ambitious in its cunning. Little did the communists know that the events they had set in motion would ultimately outlive them, bringing the spectre of a long dead Soviet empire back to haunt the nation that had defeated it.

The scene is Kenya, a small nation on the coast of Africa, bordering on Ethiopia and Somalia ("where all those poor skeleton kids are,") and Uganda, home to a guy named Kony who kidnaps the poor skeleton kids and uses them to form a skeleton army. Also, apparently, Tanzania, where that spinning tornado monster from the Bugs Bunny cartoons lives. Africa is a very strange country. But this is where the American Communist Party set the stage for the ultimate overthrow of the United States government. To that end, they sent their ambassador, their twisted parody of the Virgin Mary, a staunch communist woman with the unlikely name of Stanley. While there, she would get knocked up by a Muslim terrorist, creating a spawn who was the ultimate unholy hybrid of everything America opposes – a communist atheist Muslim, who was also gay, but it's uncertain whether his gayness was planned or just a fortunate accident.

Barack "Saddam" Hussein Obama II, whose first name rhymes with "Iraq" and whose last name rhymes with "Osama," was a child born to great potential. He was to be raised within a communist household while absorbing the fundamentalist Islamic ideology of his home in Kenya. As an aside, Kenya is a Christian nation. Perhaps the communists had intended to raise Obama in neighbouring Sudan but got confused because all these black countries look the same. Nevertheless, the seeds of America's ultimate destruction were sown in this young Kenyan national whose greatest feat was yet to be realised.

After an ideological brainwashing tour of Islamic terrorist Indonesia, Obama immigrated to the United States at the age of ten by way of its newest, least American gateway state, Hawaii, now the most devout Marxist Muslim terrorist who ever gayed. The next stage of the plan was underway. Obama was groomed to eventually rise in the ranks to be President of the United States. First, the communists fabricated for him a fictional American past life, complete with a forged short-form Hawaiian birth certificate, to create the illusion that he was an American citizen. For the remainder of his youth, he was locked in a room with the Reverend Jeremiah White, violent black liberation activist Frank Marshall Davis and domestic terrorist Bill Ayers, who took turns beating ideologies into him until he became a powder keg of anti-American rage.

Obama lived a lurid political life as a Chicago senator full of drug-fuelled gay sex limo parties with some guy named Larry Sinclair whose career as a con-artist is unrelated to his totally true accusations. Eventually, this ineligible Kenyan citizen, a secret Muslim, a secret communist, a secret homosexual, was installed as President of the United States largely through the actions of the New Black Panther Party who threatened citizens with physical violence if they failed to vote for him. Now that the greatest conspiracy ever hatched by the international communist cabal had finally come to fruition, Obama immediately took advantage of his power... to become one of the most moderate presidents in American history.[42] *BUT,* we can safely assume that this was just a ruse to lull everyone into a false sense of security. All the real Muslimification and conversion to a new Soviet bloc and whatever else will happen during his second term.

If this sounds like it might be a far-fetched plotline even for a Bond movie or a Superman villain, the depressing fact is that this story

---

[42] http://tinyurl.com/7u3sazc

or something very similar to it is either believed or espoused by a number of high-profile politicians who should know better. It should be clarified that it's very important to distinguish between people who believe it's true and people who only imply it might be true in order to gain acceptance with the depressingly large percentage of the American public who believes it's true, which doesn't really make them any better. Members of one category or the other included several of the presidential hopefuls for the 2012 election cycle, such as Donald Trump, Sarah Palin, Newt Gingrich and Michelle Bachmann. All made comments in the lead-up to the Republican primaries implying, at the very least, that Obama's citizenship question is one that is worth investigating. If that sounds fair, imagine Obama himself suggesting that we re-open the investigation as to whether the moon landings were faked. That narrative is no less plausible than the constellation of Obama conspiracies.

Now, there is probably an important ideological component to the belief that Barack Obama can't possibly be eligible to be President. Something that distinguishes him from, say, his 2012 opponent Mitt Romney, whose father was also not born in the United States but who is never questioned about his eligibility. Perhaps the real issue here has more to do with some feature of Barack Obama that distinguishes him as an "other" in people's minds and they just can't accept him as fully "American" in the way that Donald Trump is "American." Some physical feature perhaps that makes it seem plausible that he's a foreigner while at the same time it would be considered absurd to demand George Bush produce his birth certificate before taking office. Some feature that indeed no previous president has shared (I'm not sure what that could be.)

Nevertheless, election time is the one time that conspiracy theories really leap out of the land of kooks and crazies and suddenly seem completely legit to a disturbingly high percentage of the population. For those who think that crazy is the sovereign territory of the right wing, I'd urge you to remember eight years of high profile spokespeople of the left insisting that George W. Bush stole two elections and usurped the presidency in a Lex Luthor-esque coup.

The "Bush rigged the elections" conspiracy theory is granted legitimacy on the grounds that its adherents aren't usually the kinds of people who espouse conspiracy theories. Michael Moore doesn't think that Bush was behind 9/11 (as far as I'm aware) but he does think Bush's presidency was illegitimate. Though the conspiracy by the Republicans to rig an election like a game show implies about the same

Illuminati-esque reach of power that they would need to bring down the Twin Towers.

Conspiracy theories go into overdrive after an election. It makes sense – it never seems to add up that most people voted for the other guy. When you believe something and believe it strongly, it's difficult to understand that most people disagree with you, especially when your whole circle of friends share your beliefs. People tend to disregard the fact that they gravitate toward people of a similar ideology. When you voted for Joe Blow and all your friends did too, then who voted for Joe Schmo? If Joe Schmo won the election, it's tempting for even the most seasoned skeptics to believe that he cheated somehow. Thus every election is accompanied by a controversy about how the winner "stole" the election, and in America, this is often followed by accusations that the current president will be the last – he stole this election, and it will inevitably follow that he'll pass some legislation outlawing the democratic selection process, and before we know it, the president is calling himself emperor and we're all in FEMA camps.

Conspiracy culture comes full circle with the "Birther" movement, in two ways – it goes back to the New World Order theory's origin as a fear of communist usurpation, and conspiracy culture's origin as basically a racist thing. At least the Birthers are giving the Jews a bit of a break this time, because now the racial enemy is black people.

The history of anti-African conspiracy theory in America is short and really depressing. Like anti-Semitic conspiracies, those who indulge in them harbour a deep terror that the feared race is going to infiltrate, usurp, and ultimately overthrow and destroy the white race. Anti-black racism most often features the accusation that black races are more violent, and so they will ultimately seize control the only way they know how – violent riots.

One of the most famous versions of this conspiracy theory was that espoused by Charles Manson. He believed that the blacks were going to rise up and kill all the whites in a race war that he called "Helter Skelter" (because he believed The Beatles were sending him coded messages about this war through the lyrics of the song by the same name.) Manson and his cult had prepared to hide in underground bunkers until the war was over, at which time they believed the blacks would realise they weren't smart enough to run a country and Manson and his followers would be able to return to the surface. Also, for some reason, they were going to have to kill Sharon Tate.

Manson was and is a stark raving lunatic. But the "Helter Skelter" theory seems to be implicitly believed by a depressing number of people – the only real difference is that they don't believe it comes from secret codes in Beatles records. During the 2012 election campaign, there were significant warnings from the far right that the race riots were coming. Conspiracy theorists who don't want

"Do you feel blame? Are you mad? Do you feel like woofskabab a ruff flamich ga-flamich booch booch booch bojuju, beo-ramich degeech degeech degeech degeech degoogoo, beaghgablachablemichblagagabagle?"

Charles Manson, responding to the question of whether he feels any remorse.

to be seen as racist (and might be deluded enough not to realise that they are racist) don't go out and say that Obama is ineligible due to the colour of his skin. Their explanation requires some hefty mental gymnastics to escape the racism accusation, and even accuse their ideological opponents of racism. The idea goes that the left are so racist that they don't think blacks can achieve anything on their own, so instead, they install unqualified black people into the system. Therefore, the system has been infiltrated by unqualified black victims of liberalism who are relegated to laziness because of their communist education, and their secret mission is to spread this communism. The ultimate goal of this mission, of course, is to install an unqualified "affirmative action" president, which is more or less what the Birthers think has happened. So once again, white people are terrified that people with a different skin colour are going to kill them in their sleep. The "birth certificate" fiasco is the new Protocols, and the whole wheel comes spinning right round to the beginning again.

I wanted to end the section on conspiracy theories on this particular note, not just because of the similarities between Birtherism and anti-Semitism, but also because election cycle conspiracies in general, I think, highlight an important point – conspiracy theory isn't the exclusive domain of the radical, paranoid right-wing. Popular conspiracy theories such as the New World Order do traditionally have their roots in right-wing fears of communism, and before that, Jews and Catholics. But this is the result of the age in which we're living. The idea that world events we don't like are caused by an organised conspiracy by our ideological enemies is a way for us to make sense of the fact that there are a lot of people out there who don't agree with us. It's easier to believe that *everyone* agrees with us, but there are a group of people who want to oppose us anyway for reasons of evil, or else they are deluded by an irrational dogma.

Deep conspiracy theorists—the really entrenched ones, like David Icke and Alex Jones—don't really slot into any political ideology. The lords of conspiracy do not have the level of understanding of politics necessary to form a political ideology. Similarly, you can't really ascribe a political ideology to Sauron or the hobbits. They are living in a fantasy world of evil *qua* evil. Their politics are purely utopian – get rid of the evil, and the world will simply right itself.

Most other people fall into conspiracy theories on a case-by-case basis. The idea that global warming is an orchestrated hoax would fall into this category. A lot of people who wouldn't for a moment entertain the idea that a conspiracy of engineers could keep quiet about what really brought down the twin towers nevertheless seem to think it's possible that a conspiracy of climatologists could keep quiet about how the climate really works. Such people are skeptical of some outrageous claims but not others, or else they may be trying to be skeptics but they're mistaken about which side of the argument is more reasonable. People who apply skepticism on an ideological basis might reasonably be called *cynics.*

The problem with the term "skeptic" is that the people on both sides of any debate tend to think that they have the monopoly on skepticism. Dr Steven Novella, a neurologist and prominent figure in the skeptic community, recounted a time when he was sent an email criticising him for not applying skepticism to the government's story about the killing of Osama bin Laden.[43] The misconception for some is that to assume the government is lying about everything until proven otherwise is true skepticism. If you're just taking the government's word for everything, aren't you failing to apply critical reasoning to government claims in the same way that you apply them to a conspiracy theorist's claims?

Cynicism is kind of the cheap, slutty cousin to skepticism. The cynic doesn't just weigh the evidence between one claim and another,

---

[43] From SkepticBlog, December 19, 2011: http://tinyurl.com/bkrqlg4

but they apply the entirety of the burden of truth on whichever side of the argument they've already decided isn't to be trusted. We'll see an excellent example of cynicism in the next section when I'll talk about the anti-vaccination movement, who declare themselves "skeptics" because they question the scientific consensus, and berate the skeptic community for insufficient questioning of authority.

The misconception is that skepticism isn't about declaring a claim to be invalid simply because it's a claim. Particularly not just because it's a claim by someone you happen not to like or not to trust. It is of course naïve to assume that nobody lies, even people in authority or in the scientific establishment. But it is cynical to assume that they are lying all the time. That's why we have to try to put our ideological bias behind us and investigate individual claims on their own merit. Any one political ideology doesn't have a monopoly on bullshit.

Sometimes this cynicism can just make an entire ideology look really bad. Certainly, the Birther movement is one of the most embarrassing things that the conservative side of politics has had to be associated with in a very long time. It's embarrassing for the Democrats, too – in April of 2011, Obama released his birth certificate to the public to prove that he was born in the United States. It's always embarrassing when a president is forced to respond to a conspiracy theory, and humiliating for the nation when that conspiracy theory is based on the colour of the president's skin. Of course, there's some possibility that, since Obama was planning a secret mission to kill bin Laden at the time, he was just distracting the media like dangling a rubber spider in front of a cat while the vet shoves a needle in its arse.

The job of the skeptic is not to prove that conspiracies don't exist. We know that they do. Governments, politicians and organisations conspire and misdirect all the time. Sometimes it may be justified, other times they're just greedy dickbags. Skeptics do not, for example, argue that Watergate did not happen. That was a conspiracy theory that happened to be true. By applying proper skeptical analysis to it, the facts came out. And, unfortunately for Tricky Dick, the truth about government conspiracies tends to be less than impressive. Conspiracy theorists believe that the president is capable of arranging a conspiracy of thousands, to fake the fall of the twin towers, to convert the entire air travel system into an aerosol spraying program, to poison the air and the water, to pull off a staged space program where interplanetary travel is faked from a studio lot in Los Angeles, to arrange the death of anyone who gets in his way.

But he can't break into a hotel room without alerting security.

That's the truth about conspiracies. They are usually sad, humiliating affairs that fall apart when they require more than half a dozen participants. That Watergate was pretty much the pinnacle of conspiracy scandals says a lot about how badly the conspiracy theorists overestimate their villain's capability. It brought down a president, and it wasn't even exciting enough to get Jesse Ventura out of bed an hour early.

# SECTION THREE:
# CARGO CULT SCIENCE

*"By definition (I begin),*
*Alternative medicine (I continue)*
*Has either not been proved to work,*
*Or been proved not to work.*
*Do you know what they call alternative medicine that's been proved to*
*work?*
*Medicine."*

*Tim Minchin*

It's a couple of hours into the seminar when Wilcock begins to build up the scientific thesis he's formulated. The world's most "published" author on "quantum physics" is about to lay down some hard science. I can hardly wait. Wilcock can very well be an expert on his own metaphysical beliefs, and I have no problem with letting him alone with his non-overlapping magisteria. But he's about to start overlapping, and I think it's a fairly safe bet that he isn't going to know what the fuck he's talking about.

"Scientists set up a quartz room," he begins, "What do you think happened when they shone light into that room?" As he explains, the light did whatever you'd expect it to do when you switch the lights on. The room lit up.

"But then, they put a strand of DNA in the middle of that room," he continues, "And do you know what happened then?"

No, but I bet you're going to tell us.

"All of the light in the room got sucked into that DNA."

As Wilcock explains, it was like the whole room went dark, and the only thing that you could see was that strand of DNA, because it had sucked up all the light. The first thing that occurs to me is that it sounds like the DNA is emitting light, not absorbing it, which is the reason we can see stars but not black holes. Actually, that's not true – the first thing that occurs to me is that is the stupidest thing I've ever heard. But, scout's honour, this totally legit scientific experiment happened in 1984 by two scientists in Russia named Gariaev and

Poponin[44]. You can Google it, it's true. At least, there's a bizarre and incomprehensible experiment with that citation – the truth of it is hard to discern when it's so difficult to understand what the article is actually saying.

Even more astonishing, however, is what apparently happened when they took the DNA sample away. The light, Wilcock explains, stayed exactly where it was. The photons just kept swirling around in midair, where the DNA had been, creating a hologram of a DNA strand! And it stayed there for *30 days!* The audience gasps. I think I feel my brain bleed a little into my skull cavity.

From here, Wilcock just starts blinding his audience with science. At least, they think he's blinding them with science. To someone who is really ignorant about science, there's no difference between science and gibberish. If you try to explain, for example, string theory to me, then to me it sounds like you're speaking gibberish. But it also works the other way around. If I speak gibberish to someone who knows less about science than I do, then to them it might sound like science.

There's actually a term for this – technobabble. I could explain, for example, that an experiment was conducted in which scientists revealed subatomic fluctuations in the hadron field after reversing the polarity of a beam of antimatter upon a nanostring of Carbon 7, and this is how they proved ghosts exist. If you say that to a room full of ordinary people and they think that you're a real expert on the matter, then some of them are going to believe you by default. They might not realise that, while those are all real words, and some of them are even real *science* words, that sentence doesn't make any sense. It is literally nonsense, as meaningful as saying "scientists bleeped the bloop and blippety bloo the zip zap zonk, and because the zippety doo lippy blomp, this proves ghosts exist."

Bullshitting is an actual art. It's an art that's used benignly in a lot of cases. You know it if you've ever watched an episode of Star Trek or grew up reading science fiction. But there are those who will use their skill in this art for evil, to so dazzle you with bullshit that you

---

[44] Gariaev, PP; Grigor'ev, K.V.; Vasil'ev, A.A.; Poponin, V.P.; Shcheglov, V.A. (1999). Investigation of the fluctuation dynamics of DNA solutions by laser correlation spectroscopy. *Bulletin of the Lebedev Physics Institute.* No. 11-12 pp. 23-30

can't pick out the lies, inaccuracies and bad science that you're being fed.

David Wilcock's science lecture moves on to the work of one Dr Fritz-Albert Popp, who seems to have discovered that DNA is made of photons, or something, and that the answer to disease is to eat food that is "high in photons." For a moment, I think that Wilcock is mispronouncing "protein." But no, he really means for us to eat photons, as though you could take a bite out of a torch beam. He tells us about an experiment in which they removed the pancreas from a rat to give it diabetes, and then they "shot a laser through a healthy rat pancreas" and into the rat, and it regrew its pancreas. I guess the pancreas must have been transparent, otherwise I'm not sure how that worked.

Another scientist, V. Budakovski, did research on curing a cancerous tumour on a raspberry plant. "He took a healthy raspberry," Wilcock explains, "and he made a hologram of that raspberry. A perfectly detailed hologram, down to the structure of the DNA. Then, he zapped it into the tumour." Cancer, he says, is just the result of cells getting confused. The raspberry hologram reminded those cells where each of them belonged and what they were supposed to be doing.

Now, I know a lot of people might find this a reasonable claim if they are blinded by the gibberish. So let me assure you, you cannot "make a hologram of a raspberry," at least not one so detailed that you can make out its DNA structure. Even if you did, you couldn't "zap it into" a raspberry plant – disregarding the ambiguous nature of the term "zap," you can't put a hologram into something as though it's a flu shot. Even if you did that somehow, you certainly couldn't cure cancer, especially not by somehow reminding the individual cells that they shouldn't be cancer anymore.

As Wilcock continues, I notice a similarity between most of the scientific studies that he's quoting – they're all Russian names, all dated in the later 20th century, research that spilled out from the cracks in the crumbling iron curtain. Wilcock has based his science entirely on vague late-Soviet research. All his references come out of the second world, with not a single first world study among them. It's probably not surprising – the first world, for Wilcock, is the dominion controlled totally by the Illuminati.

There has for some time been a significant problem with pseudoscience in Russian academia. When the Soviet Union—uncompromisingly harsh on religion and spiritualism—collapsed, society kind of snapped back like a rubber band, overcompensating for the weird ideas they hadn't been allowed to have.[45] On one hand, the academic freedom was a boon for science, but the opposite side of that coin was that low scientific literacy filled the universities full of ghostbusters and ufologists. Academics from the Soviet era didn't, by and large, have the scientific tools to be able to sort good science from the wacky stuff. In the early 21st century, the Russian Academy of Sciences had to put together a committee to combat the terrible state of affairs in Russian academia, where astrology was as good as chemistry in the scientific arena.

The pseudoscience community, naturally, saw it as a witch hunt. The name that pops up the most throughout Wilcock's list of citations is one Dr Peter Gariaev – I did a search for his name, and he's frequently referred to as the father of something called "wave genetics." I can't seem to find any mainstream science that refers to this field, but it's discussed a lot on conspiracy theorist websites, used a lot to bolster alternative medicine claims, and turns up on David Icke's discussion forums. Other than that, I found an article by Gariaev himself in which he complains that the Russian Academy's pseudoscience watchdog is trying to shut him down by withholding his funding. Commentators remark that of course they are – they're run by Monsanto, the Bilderbergs and the Illuminati.[46]

By now, I'm feeling as though I'm at a lecture by one of Oprah Winfrey's less credible pals, but a few hours into the seminar, after Wilcock has disposed of the "hard science" portion of the day, things

---

[45] Kurtz, P. (2002). Science and Pseudoscience in Russia: The First Skeptics' Congress Convenes in Russia. *Skeptical Inquirer.* 26(4).
"Belief in pseudoscience and antiscience has been rising in Russia, as it has in other countries of the world. This is especially true in the mass media and popular press, but pseudoscience has also entered into Russian science, largely because skeptical points of view have not been heard. This has been of special concern to many Russian scientists, who believe that the scientific community needs to provide critical examinations of paranormal claims-which mainstream scientists heretofore have largely deplored but ignored. ...
"During the long period of the Soviet Union, the official dogma of the Communist Party ruled the country, and alternative viewpoints were suppressed, though the rulers defended what they called "scientific Marxism." With the collapse of the Soviet Union, all sorts of paranormal and religious claims proliferated, but there were few defenders of critical thinking."

[46] Via Laleva.org - http://tinyurl.com/cre4jjv

suddenly turn a little weird. And by "weird," I mean like sitting in on a Heaven's Gate meeting before they busted out the Kool-Aid. The reason for all this talk about photons and their life-giving energy is that the universe is made of photons. Specifically, photons of different densities – first density photons are what make up inanimate matter, second density photons create non-human life. Humanity is composed of third-density photons. At the end of 2012, when the Mayan calendar ends, we are going to move up to the fourth density. The way he speaks, he sounds like Marshall Applewhite describing how we were to be sucked up into space into the comet Hale-Bopp.

These "densities" that he's talking about aren't couched in scientific terms, Russian or otherwise. The terminology comes to us through channeling sessions that Wilcock and others have undertaken where they made contact with the Egyptian sun god, Ra.[47] Wilcock is pretty good buddies with Ra, they shoot the shit all the time, and there are soundtracks on the internet where you can hear Ra speaking through Wilcock, albeit with Wilcock's accent, his prose style, and a manner of speaking that sounds suspiciously like he's reading off a script. But I guess that's just the way alien gods speak.[48]

Ra/Wilcock has a lot to tell us about the coming ascension of mankind. He's been telling us about it for a long time. In the 1990s, Wilcock ran a website called *Ascension 2000*, in which he claimed that mankind would ascend in the year 2000, and a good thing too, because the world would be useless to us after the Y2K apocalypse. When 2000 came and went, seeing neither ascension nor technological failure, the Ascension 2000 website fell into an uncomfortable silence, then vanished. In its place arose *Divine Cosmos*, the Official David Wilcock Website, preparing mankind for the coming ascension in December 2012. In a rather Orwellian wordplay, it seems the date of ascension has always been 2012. It occurs to me that he must recognise the feeling that's creeping up on him – the date is creeping up on him again, the moment of truth for all of his prophecies. If the next six months pass without incident, if the Illuminati doesn't fall and the

---

[47] As far as I can tell, "densities" in this context came out of conversations that clairvoyants had with Ra back in the 80s, as published in some obscure monographs called "The Law of One." I wonder whether Ra pronounced his own name with the same American accent approximation that he uses through Wilcock.

[48] http://tinyurl.com/c4dguwj

ascension again fails to materialise, what then for David Wilcock? I rather suspect he'll pick a new date, like the constantly moving goalposts of the Jehovah's Witness apocalypse, he'll merely assert that he forgot to carry the 1 and lecture upon the impending ascension of 2023.

For hours, Wilcock has been mercilessly berating mainstream science for its idiocy. He makes fun of the big bang theory – the idea that "there was nothing, and then it exploded." He ridicules Darwinism in its entirety. "It's a 120 year old theory," he says "For God sakes, let's get rid of it." He's having fun showing off, buckles over laughing at his own jokes and wearing his snake-oil-salesman grin. He admires Einstein, but feels that he got the theory of relativity wrong. Einstein suggested that, as an object approaches the speed of light, its mass approaches infinity. "What if we flip that upside-down?" he asks. What if, as we approach the speed of light, mass approaches zero? Doesn't that make more sense? Of course it does. The faster we move, the closer we approach our real reality – massless beings of pure light and consciousness, one with the universal source field. Adherence to Einstein's formula is an Illuminati cover-up – it's time to move forward.

David Wilcock actually has a very straw-man opinion of today's scientific consensus – the ideas he ridicules aren't actually the ideas that science puts forward, except perhaps in junior textbooks that greatly simplify concepts for young minds to grasp.

"I flunked chemistry in school," he says, and he's embarrassed about it because (true to his ego) he claims never to have done badly in anything else, ever. But he did fail chemistry, because he didn't understand it. "It didn't make sense," he says. This idea that atoms are made up of little particles, like tiny planets in a solar system. Of course, to characterise this as the true belief of scientists is misguided, and it does sound silly, as Wilcock intends it. But he only flunked chemistry because it's wrong – what he's since come to believe makes much more sense to him, and therefore must be correct. Atoms, he argues, are merely geometry.

"Oxygen is the most predominant element. And the most stable. Because it's a cube."

He laughs at the silly idea that there is no perpetual energy – atoms are always energetic, they are always moving, they never run out of energy (what then, might I ask, is radiation?) and they are held together by gravity. Actually, gravity is the weakest of forces, and what holds atoms together is the strong nuclear force. On an atomic scale, the force of gravity is practically negligible. But Wilcock doesn't seem to know about, or simply disregards, the existence of the strong force. Atoms, he says, are bound by gravity, and actually powered by gravity.

"And what is gravity?" he asks, "It's the power that flows from space into the Earth to make it exist. As it flows in, it blows everything down with it."

## Coconut Radios

Let's face it, science is a bit of a petulant child at the best of times. It doesn't matter how hard we might wish, hope or believe against them, the laws of science refuse to give any wiggle room to our demands. I'm reminded of a circulating email joke that floated around at the beginning of the Obama presidency – that, as part of his platform for change, Obama promised to repeal the laws of thermodynamics. Without those, we would be able to build a free energy machine to solve all our problems. Science, as it turns out, is not so easily voted down. We can't simply legislate away those laws that we don't like, block them in the senate like a constitutional amendment. Newton didn't establish the laws of thermodynamics because he hated whales and held a controlling interest in Exxon Mobil. Science is what it is, whether we like it or not.

Or is it?

As it turns out, we're told, there is an alternative. You don't have to be held down by the tyranny of science. You don't have to march in lockstep with what the laws of science tell you to do. Alternatives exist. I'm not just talking about alternative theories within science, like string theory and loop quantum gravity, both accepted (though competing) scientific theories about how the world operates. I'm talking about alternatives *to* science. There is a prevailing view among many that science is just one way of doing things, one way among many. Science says that a machine can't give out more energy than it takes in? Or that disease is caused by tiny organisms called germs and viruses? Or that ozone turns into bleach when it comes into contact with your lungs? In the timeless words of The Dude, "Yeah, well, you know, that's just, like, your opinion, man."

The physicist Richard Feynman coined the term "cargo cult science" to describe things that use the language of science and appear on the surface, perhaps, to be science, but are actual nonsense. The term "cargo cult" refers to a phenomenon which occurred among remote tribal societies around the time of the Second World War. Because all of the industrialised populations of the world were busy trying to kill one another at this time, this was the first time that some of these remote tribes were exposed to things like planes and large ships, as they watched vehicles come and go, transporting various goods, weapons, and people from one place to another.

Now, these people had the same ability as the rest of us to see patterns in events and work out cause and effect, but they also had the ability to make false theories and incorrect correlations. They saw white people building airports and things, and they saw planes coming and going and dropping off cargo. When the war ended and the white people packed up and went home, the cargo stopped coming. So the tribespeople, using a basic but insufficient understanding of the science of what was going on, assumed that the white people were making the cargo appear by building airports. So they built their own airports and planes out of wood and vines and made coconut radios and trained monkey butlers, probably. None of these effigies actually worked, but they resembled devices that the white people were using, and the tribes hoped that this was enough to make the crates fall from the sky again.

As Feynman put it in his own words:

> During the war they saw airplanes land with lots of good materials, and they want the same thing to happen now. So they've arranged to imitate things like runways, to put fires along the sides of the runways, to make a wooden hut for a man to sit in, with two wooden pieces on his head like headphones and bars of bamboo sticking out like antennas--he's the controller--and they wait for the airplanes to land. They're doing everything right. The form is perfect. It looks exactly the way it looked before. But it doesn't work. No airplanes land. So I call these things cargo cult science, because they follow all the apparent precepts and forms of scientific investigation, but they're missing something essential, because the planes don't land.[49]

This might just look like dumb people doing dumb things, but it's actually the result of humans using ingenuity and "best guess" to figure out technology they didn't understand. They were only wrong

---

[49] From Richard Feynman's Caltech commencement address given in 1974. http://tinyurl.com/ybgfa3p

because they understood a little, but not enough, of the science of what was going on. If you explain to a cargo cult the real relationship between airports, planes and cargo, they will hopefully nod their heads and understand.

When people are engaged in cargo cult science, like most of the people in this section, they usually understand just enough about how science works to be able to establish some basic framework through which to explain things. They've just made some fundamental mistake in how to apply the science. The processes that most of the people in this book are going through to formulate their theories are a kind of cargo cult science – whether they're pseudoarchaeologists using a perverted form of archaeology to come to some crazy conclusions, or conspiracy theorists poring over photos of the moon landing to find discrepancies with their limited understanding of physics, most of the time they think they're putting their theories through due scientific process, but what they're really doing is a poorly understood mimicry of science. Taking their theories as scientific is kind of like talking to a parrot and thinking you're having a meaningful conversation. And, unfortunately, they're still building those planes out of bark even after the scientists explain they're wrong. They like the coconut radios better than the real ones.

## The Personality Cult of Nikola Tesla

Every so often, history spits out a real human being who more closely resembles a character out of a comic book than anyone from the mundane real world, and by virtue of this, that person becomes a hero to geeks. The Serbian-American inventor and engineer Nikola Tesla probably fits that definition better than anyone who came before or after him. He has the perfect story to enamour himself to geek culture – he was a genuine mad scientist who worked with electricity in its early days, building a lot of steampunk lightning coils and particle beam rays that wouldn't look out of place in Frankenstein's laboratory. He was under-appreciated for his genius in his own time, plagued by bad luck and the jealousy of his wealthier, intellectually inferior contemporaries. And as far as we know, he died a virgin.

Tesla's story has taken on a folklorish life of its own in recent history, and has become particularly popular among the alternative science crowd. The most important aspect of Tesla's story is his role in the "current wars," which were basically the nerd version of the cola wars in the late 1800s. At the beginning of the campaign to create

infrastructure to deliver electricity to homes, the debate over the best kind of electricity was fought between Thomas Edison's company, which was sort of the Coca Cola for this particular analogy, and George Westinghouse, our Pepsi-esque underdog.

Okay, my analogy is falling apart because Westinghouse actually won the current wars whereas Pepsi remains the Nickelback of colas – it still exists but nobody knows anyone who pays money for it. Westinghouse advocated alternating current, or AC, which is the system that we use today to bring electricity from the power station to our home. It usurped the frontrunner of the time, Edison's direct current, DC, which lost the war in part because it can't be transported long distances and you'd basically have to build a power plant on every street corner.

Tesla's role in the whole affair is that he was instrumental in the development of AC, and in modern pop culture, public understanding of the current wars has been simplified so that rather than two huge companies battling for dominance in the market, we just think of it as an evil rich dude versus a smarter underdog. So the meme of Edison vs Tesla was born.

There are a number of reasons why Tesla may have won the affection of geek culture while Edison is derided, but the most telling, I think, is what cartoonist Matthew Inman says about the issue in his piece *Why Nikola Tesla was the Greatest Geek Who Ever Lived*:

> Edison is a good example of a non-geek who operated in a geek space. He believed the value of his inventions could be gauged by how much money they made. He was neither a mathematician nor a scientist – he believed he could just hire people to do that for him. Edison was not a geek; he was a CEO.[50]

Human beings have a tendency to see every human conflict in terms of the "good guy" and the "bad guy," and we get aggravated if we can't

---

[50] http://theoatmeal.com/comics/tesla

figure out which is which. Try entering into any discussion about Israel and Palestine to see exactly what I mean. Which side is blameless and which is responsible for the entire situation? People get confused and irritated when you ask them about the atomic bombing of Hiroshima and Nagasaki – as though implying that this was a bad thing to have happened means that we have to vindicate everything that the Japanese Empire ever did. We need to make a simple narrative that makes sense.

We do this for corporations, too. Popular culture frequently sorts competing organisations into two camps – Apple good, Microsoft bad. Or Google good, Facebook bad. Sometimes society commits so strongly to the bad guy/good guy dichotomy that we grant absolute power to one giant corporation in an effort to send a message to the other one, and that's why every computer on the market looks like a giant iPhone now.

The conflict between Tesla and Edison was likewise not as simple as most people paint it, but it can in essence be distilled down to the characterisation of Nikola Tesla as a geek hero, whereas Thomas Edison, not a geek but a businessman, is seen to have insidiously co-opted the illusion of being a geek so that he could make a profit. Though I don't think either Tesla or Edison would have busied themselves playing Dungeons and Dragons or wearing a beard confined only to their necks, and I think it's disingenuous for geeks to equate handsome Tesla's unwillingness to have sex with their own inability to have sex, that's more or less the core of the issue. Tesla was an eccentric genius, kept down in his own time, and the necessary good guy to balance Edison's pretentious douchbaggery.

But some people go beyond seeing Tesla as an unusually smart guy who lived a hundred years ago, and have taken to seeing him as the smartest human being who ever lived, who invented a bunch of things that could have solved all of today's problems if not for the fact that a conspiracy is keeping his work a secret. Depressingly, proponents of most of the weird ideas in this book like to posthumously claim support from Tesla – if he was alive, he would surely have agreed that the pyramids were built by aliens, and he would have invented something to fight the chemtrails, that's just how smart he was. Fans of Tesla like to attribute just about every invention of the 20th century almost exclusively to him, but there's perhaps a little hypocrisy to the fact that they like to downplay Edison's own inventions (like the lightbulb) by pointing out that he didn't invent them from whole cloth, but merely improved upon other people's ideas. In a way, the same comment could be made of Tesla, or indeed, most of the great inventors – that's kind of the way invention works. As electrical engineer Jeff Johnson writes of Tesla:

> Tesla fans credit him with a long list of inventions and discoveries. These include radio, a bladeless steam turbine, fluorescent lighting, robotics, diathermy, the laser, vertical takeoff aircraft, pulsars, and much more. Ironically, these people seem least enthusiastic toward the one area in which historians of science and technology give Tesla unqualified credit: AC power technology. He is generally credited with two ubiquitous inventions: the induction motor and "polyphase" power transmission. All Tesla fans love his induction motor, but many fear the current that makes it go. Yet this is really the only area in which Tesla succeeded in developing a concept into a practical reality. (In his honor, the scientific unit of magnetic induction, or magnetic flux density, is named the "tesla.") In other areas Tesla's achievements are not so impressive. A good example is radio. In the mid-1890s Tesla developed all the components needed to construct a practical radio system, but then seems to have lost interest — he never took his ideas beyond some very short-range demonstrations. This left the field to Guglielmo Marconi — whom Tesla despised — who would prove the feasibility of long-range wireless communication just a few years later. This leads to a Tesla Paradox: Although he anticipated Marconi and others in many ways, excellent histories of early radio need make only incidental mention of Tesla. (Two books that together make an excellent history of early radio technology are *Syntony and Spark* and *The Continuous Wave*, both by Hugh G. J. Aitken.) This paradox recurs throughout Tesla's life.
>
> His bladeless turbine may have been conceptually sound, but difficult and expensive to manufacture, and it may have had technical characteristics that limited its appeal. Tesla fans are inclined to resent this.
>
> Other claims are even more dubious: Tesla fans broaden the definition of *invention* until it loses all meaning. Tesla found that gas-filled glass tubes glowed in the presence of his high-voltage apparatus, but modern neon and fluorescent lighting don't work this way and were developed by others. The claim that Tesla is the father of robotics stems from a story of a demonstration he performed in 1898 in which he steered a model boat in a water tank by remote control. He speculated

that electricity had curative powers and built Tesla coils for this purpose — therefore it is claimed that he invented diathermy. He rambled about death rays — hence, he "invented" the laser. Little more than a sketch from the 1920s of a very peculiar biplane on casters makes Tesla the "inventor" of vertical take-off and landing (VTOL) aircraft. All this may be remarkably prescient, but by similar reasoning Leonardo da Vinci invented the helicopter and Hero of Alexandria (first century) invented the steam locomotive.

About 1900 Tesla was playing with a radio receiver when he picked up a series of regular pulses. He instantly concluded he had made contact with Martians — an announcement that got him considerable ridicule. Tesla's modern admirers, perhaps a bit embarrassed for their hero, are equally sure he had tuned in on a pulsar — 60 years before radio astronomers did. Considering what radio technology was in 1900 this may not be the true explanation.

Tesla's "death ray" is something of a mystery. Some (not all) admirers insist it was actually built and used to shoot down a plane. Descriptions vary: sometimes it is a particle beam of some sort. My favorite is that it was "a kind of radio-wave-scalar weapon or what might be called an ultra-sound gun" (*The Fantastic Inventions of Nikola Tesla*, by D. H. Childress, 1993).

The most intriguing of Tesla's inventions are the ones that got away. Visitors to the Tesla Museum in Colorado Springs are told a story reminiscent of UFO conspiracy tales: In a raid on his house immediately after his death, government agents seized all of Tesla's apparatus — some 85 trunks full — either because timid bureaucrats felt the world wasn't ready for the wonders of Tesla technology or for more sinister reasons. Exactly what all this top-secret Tesla technology may be isn't known, but some of it, so goes the story, may make time travel possible.[51]

Our friend David Hatcher Childress, who thinks that the pyramids were power plants and that ancient civilizations had access to rocket ships, is

---

[51] Johnson, Jeff. (1994). 'Extraordinary Science' and the Strange Legacy of Nikola Tesla. *Skeptical Inquirer.* 18(4).

a card-carrying member of Tesla's personality cult. He believes that the mysterious "Tunguska event," an immense explosion in Siberia in 1908 that mainstream science agrees was a large meteor impact, was in fact Tesla testing one of his incredible weapons. In one of Childress' more outrageous scenarios is that Tesla and one of his colleagues, Guglielmo Marconi, faked their deaths and travelled to South America to invent UFOs. In one baffling conjecture, he says:

> Time travel experiments, teleportation, pyramids on Mars, Armageddon, and an eventual Golden Age on earth, may all have something to do with Tesla, Marconi and their suppressed inventions. While UFO experts and former intelligence agents tell us that flying saucers are extraterrestrial and are being currently retro-engineered by military scientists, Tesla, Marconi and their friends may be waiting for us at their space base at the pyramids and Face on Mars.[52]

Apparently, Childress decided that even aliens were too likely an explanation for pyramids and other mundane phenomena, and decided to go even further afield and suggest that *Tesla* is behind all the mysteries of the universe. Though I suspect that he's just making up some nonsense here to meet an article deadline.

Another figure who is often lumped together with Tesla, for some reason, in alternative science circles is Wilhelm Reich. Reich was an influential psychoanalyst of the Freudian tradition, and though he enjoyed a successful career asking people about their mothers, he later seemingly went batshit insane and claimed to have discovered some kind of life force energy that he called "orgone."

It probably says something about the field of psychoanalysis that crazy people are indistinguishable from geniuses until they apply their theories to the real world and we realise that they were just regular old nuts. Reich, being a Freudian, thought that everything came back to sex, but went further than most psychoanalysts by claiming to have located some kind of sex energy in the universe that was responsible for orgasms. Or something. Apparently this entire theory came about when he was looking at something under a microscope and saw some blue glow around the edges of whatever he was looking at, and rather than wonder whether his microscope was out of focus, he figured the most likely explanation was radiant blue sex energy.

---

[52] From "Tesla and Marconi" by David Hatcher Childress: http://tinyurl.com/c4qmlrt

As his mental state began to diminish (and with it his academic credibility), Reich began to use his orgone energy theory to build makeshift backyard contraptions out of pipes and hoses that he claimed could shoot orgone into the stratosphere and destroy clouds. It's not clear how Reich came to the conclusion that it was possible or even desirable to destroy clouds by shooting orgasms at them from a brass tube in his backyard, but today, crazy people make use of Reich's "cloudbusters" to clear up all the chemtrails that the Illuminati are bombarding us with, and shrewd people are making a lot of money by selling them the blueprints to what are little more than surplus copper pipes bundled together with cardboard and duct tape, like prop Gatling guns from a primary school Civil War play.

Now, New Age conspiracy theorists and alternative science advocates tend to erroneously conflate Reich and Tesla in a way that would have annoyed Tesla to no end, considering that what he was doing actually was "science" and not "making shit up." The elevation of Reich to Tesla's level of genius isn't so much a compliment to Reich as it is an insult to Tesla. We hear stories now about Tesla's experiments with orgone energy (which never happened, because it's not a thing) and in many cases people simply take true stories about Tesla and shoehorn orgone in there somehow to give Reich's magical nonsense force an air of credibility. Like the amusing story about the time Tesla made Mark Twain poop himself through application of alternating current. Substitute the term "orgone field" and New Agers make a hilarious tale about 1000% more nonsensical.

One of Tesla's most frequently claimed forgotten achievements is that of "free energy." Those fans of Tesla whose understanding of science is considerably weaker than his own (all of them) badly misinterpret Tesla's experiments, and through a combination of scientific illiteracy and wishful thinking, they believe that Tesla discovered how to create free, unlimited, clean energy, and we'd all be free from slavery to the coal industry if not for the fact that those corporate fat cats burned Tesla's notes and covered up his discovery. Old photographs exist of the "Wardenclyffe tower," which Tesla was about to fire up and bathe the world in free wireless electricity before his sudden death and the demolition of the tower, probably by Edison, that bastard.

"Free energy" is an interesting subgenre of cargo cult science. Throughout history, hundreds of crackpots have come out of the woodwork to declare that they've solved the mystery of how to produce infinite clean energy. For the most part, what they claim to have produced are "perpetual motion machines," devices which output more energy than you put into them to operate. As much as Al Gore would applaud a working prototype, this is unfortunately forbidden by the laws of the universe – the laws of thermodynamics command that any machine we build is going to produce, at the very least, a little less energy than you put into it. This doesn't stop people from trying, or from claiming to have succeeded.

In 1872, an eccentric inventor named John Keeley declared that he'd invented a working perpetual motion machine powered by water.

His claim was that he could power a steamship from New York to Liverpool on one gallon of water, which was obviously more efficiency than he required for a vehicle traveling on the ocean.

Despite the scientific impossibility of this feat, Keeley managed to attract enough excitement in his revolutionary project to get people to invest in it. He set up demonstrations of his machine in his lab, demonstrating in front of an amazed media and some rich people with more money than sense how he could pour a cup full of water into the thing and make it run for hours. To avoid too much scientific scrutiny, he cloaked his mechanism behind technobabble, calling it a "hydro-pneumatic-pulsating-vacu-engine" and suggesting that it ran via "quadruple-negative-harmonics."

Keeley made enough money off his outrageous claims that he was able to live off the profit from excited investors for the rest of his life, even though he was never actually able to build that steamship or anything else but his lone prototype. After he died, enthusiastic scientists were finally able to analyse the machine to find out how precisely it worked. What they discovered was that he was running it off a generator in his basement – it was an elaborate hoax that should have been easily detected.

The history of perpetual motion, though, stretches back centuries. All the way back to Leonardo da Vinci, who, before the age of modern physics, wouldn't have known better. A working prototype for perpetual motion is the Holy Grail of engineering. And, although it's technically possible that our understanding of physics is wrong and there may be a loophole that allows for perpetual motion, it's unlikely that the person who finally cracks it has a 1800 number.

Tesla may have been in the echelon of physicists who might have been able to work it out. But the fact is that Tesla was a little nuts, and got a little more nuts as his life went on. Brilliant, to be sure, but the extent of his crackpottery is a little hard to determine. He was crazy smart, to be sure, but what exactly was the *ratio* of crazy to smart? Tesla made a lot of claims that he didn't back up with proof, and he shouldn't be given a pass from having to substantiate his claims just because Tesla coils look really cool and he could rock a moustache like nobody else.

The Wardenclyffe tower wasn't actually a free energy machine. It was an attempt to distribute energy for long distances without the use of wires – essentially by pumping it into the atmosphere. But it didn't create energy – that would still have to be generated, presumably through the use of coal-based power plants, keeping the fossil fuel industry rolling in cash. Would Wardenclyffe actually have even worked? We can't be sure. Certainly nobody else thought so, because Tesla couldn't find anyone who actually wanted to fund the thing. Tesla wasn't defeated by a conspiracy of science, but by mundane capitalism and the unwillingness of rich people to drown crackpots in money.

Much to the chagrin of Tesla cultists, the man was just another scientist. To be sure, he was a wicked-cool, handsome, steampunk electro-scientist from the future, but he was still a man. Even Einstein made his fair share of mistakes, and his name is a *synonym* for genius. Tesla had plenty of ideas that didn't work out, made lots of claims he couldn't back up, and definitely didn't build a free, perpetual-motion energy machine.

That doesn't stop scam artists from trying to sell them to you. Google "Tesla free energy" and you'll discover about a thousand websites by a thousand different con artists each promising to sell you the blueprints to Tesla's forgotten free energy technology for only $49.95 plus shipping.

**Pictured: Bullshit**

The legacy of Tesla as a kind of superhero character to balance the pure evil that was Thomas Edison is unfortunately a product of our tendency to make a Saturday morning cartoon out of the world. Sure, Tesla groupies repeat endlessly that Edison electrocuted animals to death to prove the risks of alternating current technology. So what? Tesla was a fervent supporter of eugenics. *Everybody* was an asshole back then. It's just that some assholes were easier to base a genre of science fiction on than others.

## The Imaginarium of Doctor Pertussis

When I was a child, I contracted whooping cough, known in the medical community as pertussis, a very painful bacterial disease. For those who haven't had the privilege, whooping cough feels mostly like a very bad cold or flu except for the cough that the disease is named after – imagine that you have a coughing fit, one of those really bad hacking ones, except that your lungs are set up like a reverse bike tire in that they'll let air out but not back in again, so you feel like an astronaut who left the shuttle without a space suit. Eventually you're completely deflated, but your diaphragm continues to do the Heimlich maneuver on you even though your face is turning blue and all that's coming out is blood-spittle and little bits of sick. As you begin to suffocate, your body goes into a kind of drowning reflex and you try to inhale so hard that you just about rip your own respiratory system from its awnings and turn your lungs inside out. The struggle to breathe is extremely painful and produces that characteristic "whoooooooop" sound, which is actually the sound of you suddenly realising you're about to die. You go through this about once every ten minutes for around a week.

One of my most vivid memories from my youth concerns my week or so struggling with what is commonly referred to as a harmless childhood disease. It's just one of those rite of passage things that you're supposed to go through, like chicken pox. Most of my friends got the chicken pox. I never did, I got whooping cough, and children shouldn't need to go through the experience of feeling the uncontrollable need to cough but knowing you may die if you do. It's like holding an activated grenade out at arm's length. If I could go back and choose, I'd roll the dice with chicken pox.

At the time of writing this, the United States is in the grip of a whooping cough epidemic, the worst since 1950, which is unexpected because we have a vaccine for that now. Getting whooping cough nowerdays is almost like getting smallpox. But, unlike smallpox, whooping cough is breaking through the vaccination firewall, as more and more parents decide against vaccinating their kids. In the hotbed of the epidemic, the state of California, there has been a steady drop in routine vaccinations over the past ten years, from around 93% in 2002 to 90% in 2010.[53] That doesn't sound like much, but every percentage point serves to break down what's known as "herd immunity," which is the immunity effect that non-vaccinated kids get from their entire class having had their shots. When another kid in your class, or two, or three, or four, hasn't been immunised, then the chance that one of them is going to bring the pertussis bacteria in for show-and-tell one morning increases dramatically. But why aren't these kids getting their shots?

When I did my writing degree, a good percentage of my peers (the ones who weren't hipster poets) were 30-something mothers looking to learn a side-hobby. I remember one class in particular in which we were asked to present an open writing project, and a classmate presented a proposal for a vaccination promotion brochure. When the presentation was done, I noticed a lot of crossed arms and frowning faces among that crowd of what I'd come to jokingly refer to as the "supermums." Immediately, hands started raising, and over the next few minutes of question time, the supermums made it explicitly clear that they weren't going to take any of this snotty kid's pro-vaccine propaganda. At the time, I hadn't realised that the "anti-vax" campaign was a thing. I had a lot to learn.

The United States isn't the only place the whooping cough legions are breaking through the vaccination phalanx. Australia is currently going through the worst pertussis epidemic since records began. Ground zero for this epidemic is the north coast of New South Wales, where cases have risen 25% above the five year average.[54] I don't know about you, but I strongly suspect it's no coincidence that this region is currently the most under-vaccinated area in the nation. In Byron Bay, nearly half of children are denied shots by their parents.[55]

Byron Bay is also the home of Meryl Dorey, Australia's most outspoken anti-vaccination activist. Dorey is the president of the Australian Vaccination Network, one of the world's most notorious and outspoken mainstream anti-vax organisations. Since its formation in 1994 as the Vaccination Awareness Network, the AVN has lobbied against vaccination programs and fought to ban the needle or at least stop most parents opting for it, although that's not quite the spin that Dorey puts on it.

---

[53] http://www.healthycal.org/archives/8001

[54] http://tinyurl.com/8qbsbwh

[55] http://tinyurl.com/9zcs85l

Perhaps the reason the AVN has seen such mainstream success is that it categorically denies being an anti-vaccination group. The stated goal of the AVN is to fairly lay the risks and benefits of vaccination on the table and allow parents to make up their own minds on the matter. Of course, the AVN claims impartiality in the same way that Fox News uses the slogan "fair and balanced" while delivering all of its news with a hard conservative spin. Although the AVN only speaks *against* vaccines, it defends this with the argument that the scientific community is overwhelmingly *for* vaccines, so it needs to tip the scales massively on the anti-vax side just to provide balance. In this way, it can claim to be impartial even while being obviously and demonstrably an anti-vaccination lobby.

This kind of thing is an example of the balance fallacy and the golden mean fallacy working together like two idiot henchmen, like Beebop and Rocksteady. An extremely common misconception that underpins most of the anti-science and alternative-science positions is that science is putting forward a "side." The positions that science holds can't be called "sides" because proper science is already balanced. Meryl Dorey's effort to find the other "side" of the vaccination debate is an excavation at the bottom of the scientific barrel, cherry-picking the occasional study that reveals a possible risk, many of them since discredited or withdrawn. The "other side of the debate" that Dorey and the AVN put forward is a precarious structure built from antiquated, discredited or downright fraudulent science, misrepresentations and misinterpretations of current science, loads of anecdotal evidence, the speculation of conspiracy theorists, all mortared together by a bunch of shit she just made up. It's like building a castle out of mud, twigs, and chewing gum, and claiming it's as mighty as the stone fortress across the lake just because it's roughly the same height, provided the wind doesn't blow too hard.

The illusion is that, just because Meryl Dorey may be able to write *as many words* against vaccination as a scientist could for it, both sides are as strong as the other. But although Dorey claims wherever possible that her views come from "20 years of research," her sources (conspiracy theorists, housewives and con artists) cannot compete on the same level with the thousands of scientists who have dedicated their lives to this research over the past century. And the golden-mean myth that there are "two sides" to this issue and that the truth lies somewhere between the extremes is precisely like arguing that, while science believes the world is round, the Flat Earth Society provides the other side of the story, so therefore the Earth is probably some kind of cube with rounded edges. The fact is that Meryl Dorey's ignorance can't compete with science's research even though there's a *really really huge amount* of it.

So why does Dorey want so badly for vaccines to be evil? By and large, the anti-vaccination movement tends to be closely tied with conspiracy culture – the vast majority of conspiracy theorists are also anti-vaccination, for readily apparent reasons (if you believe that the government and its scientists are lying to you, that they may be Satanists and they may be readying humanity for a multi-billion strong genocide event, then you're going to be nervous when they start lining everyone up for an injection, no matter what they say is in it). Not every anti-vaxer is a conspiracy theorist, however, because there is a strong culture of "motherly intuition" entwined in this as well. Many parents, particularly mothers, really get their backs up when some kind of authority figure tries to tell them what is good for their child. No matter what the science is behind it, a lot of parents hear "we need to put all of these chemicals inside your baby so that she won't get sick" and just tune out there and then. It doesn't sound natural, and no amount of lecturing by an impersonal scientist who has never met your baby is going to shake that feeling that this just doesn't *sound* right.

However, most of the ringleaders of the anti-vaccination movement do appear to be either deeply embedded within, or at least flirting with the idea, of New World Order style conspiracy theory. In this sense, it's another kind of gateway conspiracy, a fairly intuitive narrative, warm and shallow waters that you can ease your feet into before you get more comfortable with the harder stuff, like the Illuminati and the Queen being a reptile. Conspiracy leaders validate your doubts about doctors sticking needles into your children, and that's how they earn your trust. The shrewdest conspiracy leaders, those who know something about PR, are conscious about how much of their true beliefs they reveal to the public, as too much too soon can see you dismissed as a nut. Once a concerned parent trusts that you know something about the *real* risks of vaccines and the *real* motives of pharmaceutical companies, then perhaps it's time to take their hand and teach them a little something about discrepancies in the official story of 9/11, or some interesting things that you spotted in the moon landing photographs, or some questions you have about Obama's birth certificate.

The AVN is a fairly shrewd organisation when it comes to dealing with media attention, and Dorey herself is careful not to explicitly reveal the extent to which she might be a conspiracy theorist.

Unlike other popular anti-vaxers who go on the Alex Jones show and complain that the swine flu threat was staged by the government, Dorey doesn't openly mention government plots or suspicions about an Illuminati-controlled medical industry. She carefully tries to control who is allowed to quote her and what they are allowed to quote, often by suing people or threatening legal action under the pretense that she has some kind of copyright ownership over her own quotes and beliefs, or something.

But there are clues that Dorey doesn't simply believe that the medical establishment is incompetent, and that she actually believes there is an organised evil, a secret agenda, and a world-spanning conspiracy. At the very least, she believes that vaccines were invented by "big pharma" to make a profit, perhaps even to deliberately make kids sicker so that they can make even more money. Generally, you can spot a closet conspiracy theorist by the amount of power they perceive the villains in their narrative to have over the population. Dorey doesn't go around warning about the Illuminati, at least not publically and not by that name, but who is the "big pharma" she often mentions, and how powerful does she think they are? Do they have the media in their back pocket? Do they control the scientific community? Do they control governments? Do they permeate society with "disinfo agents" in order to keep the sheeple in line?

Dorey certainly believes that "big pharma" has a significant cross section of the population on their payroll, because she suspects anyone who has claimed their child died of a vaccine-preventable disease to be under the employ of the Illuminat- sorry, big pharma. Because conspiracy theorists can't simply stop at believing that powerful people bend the truth, and they have to actually believe that the truth is 180 degrees from everything the authorities say it is, one of Dorey's more outrageous claims is that diseases like whooping cough, chicken pox, measles and other vaccine-treatable conditions are actually harmless. Not only can't they kill you, but they're not even that bad, in fact they might be fun! If your kids don't get a case of the old chicken pox, then they're being deprived of some kind of rite of passage. At least one case has been picked up by the media of an AVN supporter deliberately giving her healthy child chicken pox due to this mentality.[56] Believing in the inefficacy of vaccines is one thing, but to run with that ball to the extent that you don't believe disease is harmful, and that you in fact believe *it is necessary*, is just absurd. It's like first being skeptical that seatbelts save lives, and then from that coming to the conclusion that car crashes can't hurt you. Then you force your child into the passenger seat and repeatedly drive into a tree for some reason.

One of the most notorious episodes in the AVN's chequered history was the death of Dana McCaffery, a 4-week-old baby girl, from whooping cough, and the harassment of the McCaffery family by the AVN and its associates. Understandably, the McCafferys began a campaign against whooping cough, as many don't realise just what a horrible disease it is, or that it can be fatal. This is no thanks to Dorey's organisation, which contends that pertussis is a harmless childhood disease and that its negative consequences are a product of the pharmaceutical industry's imagination. But Dorey wasn't about to let a grieving family make her look bad – after seeing an article about McCaffery's death, Dorey went on a campaign to prove that the baby had not died of whooping cough. Hint: When your campaign against the health industry reaches such an extreme that you become vehemently pro-whooping cough, it's time to take a hard look at your ideology.

After contacting the baby's doctors and attempting to get them to release McCaffery's private health records to her (as though doctors have an obligation to consult her as an expert on pertussis – 20 years of

---

[56] Cohen, David. Chickenpox response 'inadequate.' *Perth Post*, 21 January, 2012.

internet research under her belt, after all) Dorey managed to drag the parents of a recently-dead infant into a media storm in which they were, horribly, put on the spot to publically prove that their daughter had died of the disease that they claim she died of. In the meantime, the AVN set upon the McCaffery parents like rabid dogs, with one associate, Judy Wilyman, accusing the McCafferys of having been paid by somebody to promote the lie that whooping cough had killed their daughter. Some kind of powerful group, acting behind the scenes, with full ownership of the entire scientific establishment, its tentacles extending throughout the media, paying shills to pose as ordinary people in order to protect science's lies? This narrative sounds familiar. It would at this point be more surprising if Meryl Dorey *didn't* believe in the Illuminati, the New World Order and the coming global genocide. If you believe that the pharmaceutical industry is so powerful that they own the entirety of the media, the entirety of the scientific establishment, and entire governments, and that they have paid agents disguised as ordinary families whose job is to perpetuate the myth that certain diseases kill, then what exactly is it about the Illuminati or the reptilians that you find implausible?

We can't blame Meryl Dorey or any one organisation for the public's difficulty sorting bad science from good. Much of that blame can probably be attributed to the media. The media doesn't get science very well. That really hit home with me earlier in 2012 when scientists finally discovered the Higgs boson (or *probably* discovered it – it should be clarified that what they've discovered is a new particle that fits most of the description). The media has had a passing interest in the "God particle" for quite a while because they understand that it's a big deal to science, but when it comes to actually reporting on the discovery, journalists are held back by their own inability to understand it. Most tended to report something that amounted to the Higgs being "the most fundamental" particle in physics which, while not true, is probably close enough for rock and roll, at least in terms of what the public needs to know.

But the Higgs discovery is real, a real result of real science that was done right. At the time when the discovery hit the media, it could have gone either way. Maybe CERN researchers actually thought they'd discovered the Higgs boson, or maybe some guy was claiming the Higgs boson flew out of a pie after he hit it with a mallet. We wouldn't know until the scientific community weighed in on it, and even then, only those of us who were listening closely. The problem with science in the media is that, after the initial story comes out, the media doesn't wait around to see whether science is going to tell them they're wrong.

You might remember, for example, that in 2011 the media reported that a particle called a "neutrino" had been found to be capable of breaking the speed of light, thus throwing everything that physicists believe into question. The story was huge, though the media only knew enough about the topic to communicate that breaking the speed of light was a big deal (though it's probably a bigger deal than they realised). What you may not have heard was that, after the noisy media shut up about it, the scientists calmly explained that the discovery was the result of some malfunctioning equipment and that the faster-than-light neutrino had never actually happened.

This poor ability for the media to judge scientific merit is partly to blame for the anti-vaccination movement (or at least the mainstream, non-Illuminati version) having blundered into setting off what many consider to be one of the most damaging misreportings of science by the media in history – the accusation by the media that vaccinations somehow play a causative role in the development of autism.

It should be noted that anti-vaccination movements are not a new thing, and haven't been a new thing since vaccines were invented. As Ben Goldacre points out in his book *Bad Science*, every vaccination program since 1888 has had major resistance from paranoid opponents. In fact, that we were ever able to eradicate smallpox is a miracle precisely because of the virus' allies among the anti-vaccination movement. An attempt was made to eradicate polio through the same means by 2005, but this plan was foiled by the actions of conspiracy theorists who successfully lobbied to ban the inoculation in Nigeria, purely on the basis of fears that it was an Illuminati plot. Polio snuck back through this chink in the armour and devastated Nigeria again as well as several surrounding countries, and although Nigerians are warming up to the idea of vaccinating again, the kids who caught the disease in the name of fighting the imaginary NWO probably aren't smiling.

In the western world, attempts to eliminate or reduce diseases like polio, measles and whooping cough are constantly foiled by large numbers of people who organise campaigns to stop the immunisation program usually based on threats that exist in their imaginations. One attempt to relegate whooping cough to the dusty archives of archaic diseases was thwarted in 1982 when a television documentary called "Vaccine Roulette" sparked panic that the pertussis vaccination may be causing brain damage in children. After a massive backlash against inoculation, several governments withdrew the pertussis vaccine and whooping cough came back with a furious vengeance, 10 to 100 times worse in those countries which had banned the needle.[57]

But the most recent and probably most well-known backlash against vaccination came after a 1998 study by one Andrew Wakefield published in the journal *The Lancet*, which purported to reveal a connection between the measles, mumps and rubella triple-jab and the childhood onset of autism. The obscure study, which was far from compelling in the first place, should have been relegated to the thousand-ton slush pile of research that flatly disagreed with its findings, but the media picked up the ball and pushed a fearmongering campaign that probably seemed very exciting to the world of journalism but did enormous damage to the public image of vaccination, leading to boycotts and the return and rise of the three diseases that the program was attempting to shield our children from.

The study, it turned out, was baseless. The *Lancet*, in fact, later fully retracted the article and apologised for running it, after it came to light that Wakefield had probably manipulated the data, having been granted a large amount of money to conduct the study by a group of people who were trying to put a case together against the medical industry and needed a scientific study that proved the MMR vaccine was evil somehow. Science doesn't work too well when someone is paying it to come to a specific conclusion, especially when the scientists fail to come to that conclusion, panic, and decide to make a bunch of stuff up. Wakefield, disgraced by the finding that he'd manufactured the entire vaccine-autism connection, was struck off the medical register for the fraud.

That didn't stop the anti-vaccination movement, including Meryl Dorey, who to this day assert that vaccinations cause autism in children, and that Wakefield is the innocent victim of a conspiracy to squash his findings. In Britain, the panic exploded when then Prime Minister Tony Blair was asked whether his newborn son had been given the scheduled MMR injection, and he refused to answer the question. There are many reasons why politicians might refuse to answer certain questions about their private lives, but the one the media assumed was that the Prime Minister knew more than he was letting on about the hidden dangers of vaccines, and unwittingly he triggered a media firestorm.

---

[57] Poland, G.A. and Jacobson, R.M. (2011) The Age-Old Struggle against the Antivaccinationists. *New England Journal of Medicine*, 364:2.

In the United States, the public face of the MMR scare was Playboy centerfold Jenny McCarthy and her then boyfriend, rubber-faced man-child Jim Carrey. In 2005, McCarthy's son was diagnosed with autism. Later on, it emerged that he probably didn't have autism at all, but something called "Landau-Kleffner Syndrome." Nevertheless, one of the worst things to ever happen to misguided American celebrity causes was that someone handed McCarthy some literature about the Wakefield paper that explained to her in small words that were easy for her to understand about how autism is caused by vaccinations. What followed was that McCarthy spent the rest of her public life putting the full weight of her celebrity against getting people to stop having vaccinations (and Ace Ventura the Pet Detective leant his own celebrity to the cause for the rest of the time that McCarthy was letting him see her naked.) She took it to the daytime television circuit, getting Oprah on board, Oprah being the human being who has probably done the single most tragic amount of damage to the public understanding of science since the Pope sent Galileo to prison.

To reiterate, there is no connection between autism and vaccinations. You can say that I can't know that for sure, and we can keep doing tests until the sun goes supernova looking for this elusive correlation, but no published study except the fraudulent Wakefield paper has ever been able to find any connection. And the thing about the Wakefield paper was that it wasn't even a very good fraud – scientists didn't find his study compelling in the first place, being that his sample size was way too small and his science was as clunky as a robot in a 1950s science fiction classic. Only the media took Wakefield's science seriously, because the media didn't know what the hell it was doing.

That all said, the number of kids who die of measles reaches into the hundreds of thousands every year, though this has thankfully fallen from the scale of millions since—you guessed it—we started vaccinating. On the other hand, you know how many kids die of autism every year? That's a trick question. Autism is an abnormality of neurological development that isn't very well understood, but it's not the kind of thing that can be considered "a disease," let alone a potentially fatal one. There are some statistics out there about autistic kids who tragically wander, for example, into traffic, but you can't compare autism with measles, mumps or rubella. Autistic people, in fact, are sometimes offended by the vaccination controversy – God forbid there's a very small chance according to celebrities that your child might become socially awkward and good at video games, right?

180

Better that we roll the dice with the much higher chance of him having a normal social life but dying horribly from a crippling disease before he hits puberty. Autism is just about the worst thing that Jenny McCarthy could manufacture a panic about, because she's unwittingly created a view of autism that having an autistic child is worse than having one with goddamn polio.

But it's a false dilemma. The good news is that you don't have to choose because, I'll say it again, there's no connection. But Jenny McCarthy's anti-vaccine organisation, Generation Rescue, has since set about spreading the word about vaccine dangers, implicating them as the source of not only autism but every disease known to mankind, even some truly bizarre ones.

In 2009, the organisation's attention came to the case of one Desiree Jennings, a 25 year old former cheerleader who had been struck down with a bizarre condition which rendered her unable to walk or speak properly. Through what was no doubt some top-notch internet self-diagnosis, Jennings believed that her condition was dystonia, a neurological disorder, and that she had developed it from a seasonal flu vaccine. Her evidence for this was that she had received a seasonal flu vaccine. True to form, the hysterical media began to report that she had dystonia, and she had gotten it from a seasonal flu vaccine.

There were of course some problems with that assessment. Firstly, what Jennings had didn't remotely resemble dystonia, and had the media decided to ask any neurologists about it, they could have known this. Science was actually pretty baffled by her behaviour – she could run normally, and even walk backward without any problems, but she couldn't walk forward. Sometimes she could speak, sometimes she couldn't, and sometimes she spoke with an Australian accent, or at least a bad American approximation of an Australian accent. Sometimes when she was distracted, she seemed to lose her symptoms as though she forgot she was supposed to be crippled. The only thing that her condition resembled was what's known as a psychogenic disorder – it was all in her head.

That's not to say that Jennings was making it up. She may not have been consciously aware that her disorder wasn't real, but the subconscious mind is a powerful thing, especially when Jenny McCarthy's anti-vax hysteria brigade comes screaming in and surrounds you with people who tell you not to listen to those neurologists, you totally have a muscle disorder and it definitely came from a flu vaccine.

Because western medicine kept stubbornly trying to treat Jennings' condition as though it was anything that wasn't dystonia brought on by an evil flu vaccination, Generation Rescue convinced Jennings to put her health and money into the hands of their wide selection of alternative medicine quacks. An osteopath named Rashid Buttar was brought onto the case, and after about five seconds of thinking about it, he diagnosed Jennings with "acute viral post immunisation encephalopathy and mercury toxicity," which isn't a thing, except it's a technobabble sentence that basically says "you got screwed by a flu shot, yo," which is pretty much Buttar's diagnosis to every human medical condition.

Now, if you're ready for it, here's the fabulous irony behind Generation Rescue and the anti-vaccine movement – feeling that regular western science has betrayed them by constantly insisting that vaccines don't kill people or give them autism or wobble disorders, people frequently turn to alternative medicine practitioners like Rashid Buttar to cure them of the nasty side effects they developed from having western chemicals injected into them. So what's Buttar's amazing cure for vaccine injury? Something called chelation, which is… well, it's injecting chemicals into your body. But they're *alternative* chemicals, which means that they bypass all those poisonous scientific principles such as proof of efficacy and some kind of theory about how they work, and just go straight to pumping random heavy metals into your bloodstream until you stop being autistic anymore (or die. Sometimes you die.)

Desiree Jennings made a miraculous recovery after Buttar injected her with his best-guess chemical cocktail, which doesn't really speak to the efficacy of the treatment. More than anything, it adds weight to the idea that she could have cured herself whenever she wanted to. Chemical chelation was just as good a treatment as any alternative "cure" would have been, up to and including chanting over the entrails of a blessed goat.

Immunisation is a very tricky issue. Many of the political issues that we argue over from day to day deal with the sovereignty of the human body. There are debates about the extent to which we can violate the liberty of the individual "for their own good." No matter which side of the spectrum you're on, most people agree that politicians need to get their laws and their ethics "off my body." But immunisation is one place where the moral waters become murkier. Vaccination programs ask you to undergo a medical procedure so that *other people's children* don't die. It's more than just you deciding whether or not you're personally going to skip the shot and risk getting some disease. It's you deciding whether you're going to skip it and risk your neighbour getting the disease. Even then, people are fairly willing to oblige most of the time – the problem is when we ask people to put *our children* through a medical procedure so that someone else's children don't get sick.

Our attachment to our own offspring is pretty damn powerful. Just ask any woman with a very unwanted pregnancy who nevertheless goes through psychological hell deciding whether to get an abortion. Biologically, save for some abnormal circumstances, we're programmed to care for our kids and not to stab them with things. Other people's kids, not so much. Maybe that accounts, at least in part, for society's reluctance to embrace vaccination even given its remarkable track record and absolute lack of evidence for any kind of remotely comparable risk, not for lack of trying.

What's fascinating is the way we rationalise it. Rational consideration often conflicts with the "gut feeling" that we get about such things as sticking yourself with a needle. It's hard to decide that you're going to act *against* everything you know of science and opt instead to go with what your id is telling you to do, whether that be immunising your children or having sex with a fence. In such circumstances, your brain just throws up a runtime error. In conflicts between rationality and intuition, some people solve the problem by throwing out intuition, while others… well…

## After All, It's Just a Theory

In line with the adage that there is no idea so absurd that there isn't someone out there who believes it, there is a thriving community of people who deny that germs are the cause of infectious disease. While people might argue with me that flat-earth theorists and believers in Icke's reptoids are so fringe that they're hardly worth talking about, germ theory denial is worryingly prevalent – almost all of what we call "alternative medicine" either tacitly or expressly hinges upon it. I suspect that the popularity of alternative medicine is due in part to the fact that the purveyors of these treatments don't go on about the fact that they don't believe in germs – that it's central to the theory of their profession just doesn't come up that often. But if you think about it, treatments that focus on the management of germs almost always fit under the banner of conventional medicine. It's when they declare disease to be caused by something else—bad qi or a misalignment of the spine, for example—that the treatment becomes "alternative."

These days, alternative medicine has been trying to counter its reputation for pseudoscience by relabeling itself "complementary" or "integrated" medicine, as though it's something you can try in addition to whatever conventional western treatments you're using. But that doesn't make a lot of sense – either you believe in germs or you don't, so a treatment that denies the existence of germs isn't going to do much of anything to "complement" a treatment in which germ theory is paramount.

So how silly is it to deny germ theory? Skeptics wring their hands over people denying evolution and global warming but germ theory denial is more extreme than that. The germ theory is one of the most well established—and easily verifiable—principles in all of science. When you introduce a virus to a healthy person, they get sick. You just can't get any more cut-and-dried than that. Denying germ theory is like denying the existence of gravity and suggesting, for example, that things only fly toward the earth because it's in a band and everyone wants to be its friend. In a very real way, subscribing to an alternative to germ theory is like subscribing to the stork theory of pregnancy.

People don't deny germ theory because there are problems with the science. Much like people who deny other major scientific theories, evolution for example, because of the way it conflicts with their religion or ideology, germ theory deniers have a major motivation not to believe. After all, if disease is caused by tiny organisms like bacteria and viruses, that takes a lot of the *personal* responsibility out of staying healthy. Fighting disease becomes a *social* responsibility. You have to trust other people to wash their hands, get vaccinated, and not take public transport when they're shitting out their internal organs. You have to trust that the kitchen is clean and that the chef didn't spit in your food due to some racial prejudice. That's a lot of pressure for your average hypochondriac. It's no coincidence that all of the "alternative" theories that people propose as the cause of disease are all focused on personal responsibility. If you're sick, it's because something is wrong with *your* body. Your forces are out of balance, or your spine is crooked, or you're not eating right, or you're not thinking positively. And the outright lunacy of all of these theories is that none of them allow room to explain one of the most readily apparent phenomena in all of medicine – contagion. No alternative to germ theory can attempt to explain why it is that you can catch a disease from somebody else just by being in their vicinity. In fact, you'll often find people trying to *ridicule* the concept of contagion by pointing out that, sometimes, you *don't* catch the disease. Again, that's like refusing to believe in gravity because, if it were real, birds wouldn't be able to fly.

So if you don't believe in germs, then what? In alternative science circles, the two main competitors to the germ theory (if we can humour them by suggesting it actually has competition) are what is known as the "terrain theory" and, I would argue, the theory which is the theoretical basis for homeopathy, and, in all likelihood, history's greatest scam.

Firstly, the terrain theory. It's convenient because it's a well-established scientific theory that was once proposed and developed alongside germ theory at a time when germ theory really was open to debate and competition. In fact, support for this theory has its roots in another "underdog scientist" feud that mirrors Tesla worship. If Louis Pasteur, the father of germ theory, can be thought of as the Thomas Edison of medicine (and he is, with denialists constantly referring to him as a plagiarist, a corporate shill and a sociopath) then his contemporary, Antoine Béchamp, is certainly the Nikola Tesla.

Before the mid-1800s feud between Pasteur and Béchamp, there were many competing theories about what caused disease. The most prevalent was "miasma theory" which argued that disease was caused by miasma or "bad air." Now, as medieval as it sounds, this made a hell of a lot of sense. People knew for millennia that certain kinds of disease were transmissible, in that people living in the same community or in the same home were likely to come down with the same diseases. They also knew that disease was in some way associated with filth. They didn't know how, exactly, but they knew there was a correlation between, for example, smelly meat and spending a day with your head in the toilet. There also seemed to be some connection between getting sick and having a lot of poop lying around everywhere. It was this observation that led to the invention of sanitation systems long before people knew what disease was, and so it's surprising for most people to discover that we didn't know about germs until the 1850s, even though we've been putting the toilet at the opposite end of the house from the kitchen since Roman times.

The miasma theory settled upon the idea that disease was caused by proximity to rotting organic matter, and that the smell of rot was associated with the transmission of the disease. It wasn't a theory of contagion, not as such – scientists didn't have a working theory as to how disease could pass from one human to another, but they were trying to explain why people in close proximity get the same diseases, and why these diseases often originate from poor sanitation. It was pretty sound as far as theories go. What it didn't really have was a proper mechanism. *How* did bad smells translate into disease when they got into the body?

In the meantime, the existence of microorganisms had been known to science since the 1700s, but they weren't really known to be associated with disease. It wasn't until the middle of the 19th century that people noticed that certain kinds of bacteria seemed to show up in tandem with certain kinds of disease that people decided there was a connection. They didn't know what it was, just that it was a connection.

This leads us to Pasteur and his rival Béchamp. Pasteur solidified the germ theory (which had been proposed before but not taken any more seriously than any other as a rival to miasma theory) by showing that he could stop wine from spoiling if it was heated and sealed. This is why milk today is "pasteurised" – Pasteur showed that, if you heat something to the point where you kill all of the bacteria in it, then you don't get sick when you eat it. If you boil lake water before you drink it, you don't get cholera. If you cook sausage before you eat it, you don't get E. coli. If you incinerate zombies, they can't make more zombies. This was a huge step toward the acceptance of the idea that microorganisms cause disease – if you murder the bugs, you don't get sick.

Béchamp's terrain theory was sort of the upside-down version

of this. Rather than germs causing disease, Béchamp proposed that disease caused germs. The way that it's sometimes described, if we imagine that cockroaches are like germs, we can observe that keeping a messy kitchen is a good way to attract a roach infestation, but killing all the roaches does not improve the hygiene of your kitchen. According to Béchamp, germs are attracted to disease and feed off it, but they are not its cause. As significant and well-regarded a scientist as he was, he simply couldn't fully let go of the long-established idea that disease was caused *directly* by unsanitary conditions, rather than Pasteur's model, which suggested that unsanitary conditions were simply one of the contributing factors, but only because germs are attracted to rotting foodstuffs. Unfortunately for us, Pasteur's theory implies that you can't avoid all disease for your entire life just by keeping the kitchen clean and keeping an eye on use-by dates.

But just because Béchamp's theory provides a much simpler solution to curing disease, alternative medicine gurus absolutely vilify Louis Pasteur as history's greatest monster. This whole germ nonsense is, after all, what led to the development of the useless vaccines which are giving us all autism, and the growth of Big Pharma which sells us useless antibiotics in order to make trillions of dollars. According to those who find germ theory decidedly inconvenient to their ideology, some of them as high profile as Bill Maher, Antoine Béchamp was unfairly censored by the evil Louis Pasteur who not only pushed the germ theory scam through with the power of, I dunno, black magic, but also knew secretly that Béchamp was right all along. A popular and often-repeated anecdote is that Pasteur recanted germ theory on his deathbed. Suspiciously, Darwin is also said to have recanted evolution on his deathbed. (Not only is this not true, for either Pasteur or Darwin, but it wouldn't even matter if it was. A scientific theory is not like a photograph of Bigfoot – you can't just "take it back.")

Now, Bill Maher's rejection of germ theory is a touchy subject in the skeptic community, mainly because he's an outspoken atheist and builds his schtick on ridiculing religion, which many skeptics think is more important. As such, many skeptic websites tend to skirt far around Maher's anti-science views while heaping praise on him for making the film *Religulous* – in essence, the enemy of my enemy is my friend. Ironically, Maher's atheism is so much more important than his rejection of science that he was, in 2009, granted the Richard Dawkins Award for *promotion* of science. This is despite his repeated assertions that vaccines are useless, that they cause disease rather than prevent it, that western medicine is a scam, and that old canard that Pasteur admitted on his deathbed that Béchamp was right. This award-winning crusader for science is the same man who, in interviews, has advised Larry King to stop getting flu shots (they cause Alzheimer's, apparently) and told David Letterman to stop taking his heart medication.[58]

So if germs aren't the cause of disease so much as symptoms of it, then what actually does cause disease? Maher and other alternative health cranks will usually tell you that it's something they call "toxins." You've heard this before, even if it's in the context of something as mainstream as "detox" diets. Although the word "toxin" does refer to a real kind of thing that exists (informally, poison), in the context of alternative health, they are referring to something a little different and much less well defined. In most cases, the advocates themselves don't even know what they're talking about. It's generally a bunch of hippy-dippy nonsense that people like because something something corporations. In keeping with Béchamp's terrain theory of disease, illness is caused by a kind of aggregate toxicity from an environment full of fast food, fluoridated water, pesticides, second-hand smoke, exhaust fumes, heavy metals, and of course, pharmaceuticals.[59] The cure for disease, therefore, is detoxification, and avoidance of "toxins." The question that you have to ask is how disease could possibly have existed before fast food, fluoridated water, pesticides, second-hand smoke, exhaust fumes, heavy metals, and pharmaceuticals. Often (but not always) when you see the word "detox," you're swallowing health advice from someone who thinks the existence of germs is a money-making scam by Big Pharma and subscribes to the long, thoroughly discredited "toxicity" theory championed by Antoine Béchamp.

Now, there's another popular alternative to germ theory, as I mentioned, and that is the one that proponents think can be treated homeopathically. It's difficult to explain what homeopaths actually believe is the cause of disease, because it's quite... let's say,

---

[58] http://tinyurl.com/cfkxu for the Larry King transcript. Also in this interview, King questions Maher about the elimination of polio due to vaccines, to which Maher replies "A lot of diseases that have been they say, whoa, this was eliminated because of a vaccine, they find out well no actually the country got toilets and that's what happened." Clearly, Maher is here arguing that disease is caused by piles of poop and not by the microbes in the poop. He gives no explanation for how smallpox was eliminated in countries that already have toilets.

[59] Just don't say a bad word in alternative health circles about marijuana smoke, that shit is healthier than carrots.

"complicated." In fact, I'm going to let homeopath Dr Charlene Werner explain the physics of homeopathy in her own words:

I'm going to explain to you exactly actually how it works.

Now, has everybody had chemistry, like, in school, way back when? But you do know what $H_2O$ is? And have all of you heard of Einstein? Well, you know that light is energy, right? And he gave us the theory that energy equals mass times the speed of light. $E = mc^2$. Now, if you take that formula, and, we think there's a lot of mass, right? OK, if you collapsed all the mass down into the universe, so there's no space between the mass, do you know how much mass there is in the entire universe? You think you're a lot of mass right? Well, the whole universal mass can be consolidated down into the size of a bowling ball. That's all there is in the whole world, and the universe! So how much mass are you? That's right - an infinitesimal amount. So if you take that formula, $E = mc^2$, you can almost cross out mass! The formula ends up being energy equals the speed of light. And that's why the vision system is so important, because we have lots of photoreceptors that receive light.

But when Hahnemann died, the scientists didn't fall in his camp, and the pieces of the puzzle didn't fit well together. So God in his infinite wisdom sent another Einstein called Stephen Hawkings[sic]. And Stephen Hawkings gave us the string theory. And what he discovered is that there are other energetic particles in the universe, and they're shaped like little youies, and what they do is they work by vibration. So our body is so wonderfully designed, we have light receivers, and ears, string, vibratory, they pick up vibration. So if you add that to that theory, Einstein's theory of relativity, we have $E = mc^2$ (but mass is crossed out, almost) and strings - vibration.

But that still doesn't tell us the whole picture, because, what is a cell? A cell has cell walls, cell membranes, cytoplasm. Is that mass? Not very much really, so what is that? You can break down the cells into tiny pieces of energy called electrons, protons, neutrons. So the whole body has an infinitesimal amount of mass, but what is the remainder? Energy. So I am energy, you are energy. Now, if you go to study physics, energy cannot be created: we do not know how to create energy. But we don't know how to destroy it either - that is not humanly possible. So what we do is take energy and we transform it from one state to another. That's all we do. So if that's all we do, guess what the definition of disease is? It's not mass. We have transformed our energy state into something different. That's what the definition of disease is. So we should be able to re-transform our energy into a previous better state. Right? And, what we do is we use light, we can use sound, we can use homeopathy.

So what is homeopathy? Well, if nothing is really mass (or an infinitesimal amount of it) and everything is energy, that means everything has a vibration to it. So what if I could, encase some sort of energy for later use? So if I wanted to make a bomb, and I took all these chemicals, and I encased it in a, you know, a bomb, and tonight, my neighbour lets his dog poop in my yard, literally, and I'm mad at that dog and my neighbour. So I'm going to take this bomb and get back at him. So what if I threw that bomb at his house. Would he be happy with me? Because what happens now when that energy is released? It destroys something, or changes it. It makes the building now not in structure form. It changes its energetic state. Well that's what we do with homeopathy. We take substances, and we pulverise them, we and we put them in solution, and we succuss it just like the bomb, to release its energy into this liquid. Then we take these little white pellets, and sprinkle them with that solution. Then guess what we have just made. An energetic substance - to be used when we choose to use it.

So, how homeopathy works is, whatever your disease process is, it's an energetic change, and if I can find the remedy that matches your state and give it to you when we so choose, what can we do with your energy system? Transform it to a previous better state. And that's how it works.

This comes from a 2007 lecture that Werner gave at some kind of "wellness" conference in Montana, USA.[60] It's about the best summary I've seen of the homeopath's general grasp of science. The density of nonsense in this speech is so great that it's practically a neutron star of stupid. But just like David Wilcock assumed my ignorance when he tried to scam me with technobabble, Werner *sounds* legit to the layman because she's using genuine scientific terminology. Well, except for the stuff about "youies." There really were scientists named Einstein and,

---

[60] At the time of writing this, a video of this speech is still available on YouTube, although Werner's lawyers keep trying to have it taken down. http://tinyurl.com/ya355xd

though she butchers his name, Hawking. The amount of true solidity in the universe is surprisingly small (though I don't know where she gets the "bowling ball" equivalence), there is something called "string theory" that postulates the universe is constructed by tiny vibrating "strings." Her understanding of the composition of an atom is more or less correct. These are all real science words. But everything in between these words is absolute *gibberish*.

There's a popular phrase among scientists and skeptics when faced with an argument like the one Werner has put forward here – "not only is it not right, it's not even wrong." That is, not only does it fail to meet the basic criteria it needs to be considered correct, it's *not even coherent enough to be considered incorrect*. Just because both string theory and the hearing sense involve kinds of "vibration" doesn't mean that string theory has something to do with hearing. Even if you can compress the true mass of the universe down to the size of a bowling ball, that bowling ball is still going to weigh *as much as the entire universe* (that number in kilograms has around 53 zeroes after it) so you really can't "cross it out." If Einstein thought that the "m" in $E = mc^2$ was negligible, he *wouldn't have freaking put it there*. Dr Werner (and I doubt she's a doctor of anything) is so far from right that she's not even wrong. She *wishes* she was wrong. If she was wrong, it would indicate that she at least knows what science is.

So there's your technical explanation about where homeopaths believe disease comes from – it's because there's no mass in the universe and string theory says there's a bunch of youies out there and that's why you can hear things, so we're all just energy and if you're mad at your neighbour's dog then you can throw a bomb at it, and *pow*, that's what disease is. Here's the layman's version:

In the late 1700s, before Pasteur, when any one theory was as good as any other about what causes disease, a German doctor named Samuel Hahnemann came up with the theory that disease was caused by kind of overdosing ourselves on the substances around us. Or something like that. What Hahnemann thought was the cause of disease isn't as clear or important as what he figured the cure was. Here's where homeopathy starts getting really strange.

Hahnemann decided, in essence, that a disease can be cured by giving you more of the same stuff that might have given you the disease in the first place. For example, if you have a rash, Hahnemann would prescribe poison ivy to cure it. If you have insomnia, he'd try to cure you with coffee.

Here, Hahnemann achieved something truly remarkable – in an age where nobody really knew how we get sick, he was the only one who came up with an idea that was literally the opposite of what a reasonable person would think. It was the equivalent of hitting someone in the face with an iron to fix their broken nose. But as though Hahnemann hadn't drifted far enough from the rational world, he came up with a way to make his cure even less intuitive. Obviously he realised immediately that rubbing poison ivy on someone to cure their rash didn't work very well, but rather than abandon the idea, he decided to dilute the substance in water so that it was less powerful. In accordance with what you'd expect, the more he diluted the mixture, the less of a negative effect it had. So he continued diluting it – taking one drop of mixture, putting it in a vial of water, shaking it, and then taking one drop of *that* mixture, putting it in another vial, shaking it, and repeating that until the solution was so weak that it had no effect on the person who drank it whatsoever.

By this time, the patient's rash had probably cleared up on its own and he was cursing whoever it was who referred him to this particular doctor. But Hahnemann declared that he had actually cured it… by taking the substance that caused the disease in the first place and then diluting it until it barely existed anymore. This is what homeopathy is, and it hasn't changed since Hahnemann, through whatever mental disorder he had, came up with the idea.

Though that's not *entirely* true – homeopathy resisted the germ theory and other discoveries that discredited it, but they did need to take Dan Brown's hammer to it at least once. Later that century, science discovered a new principle that they named *Avogadro's number*, named after the Italian scientist Amedeo Avogadro, and it works like this: When you dilute one substance into another, there is a point at which the original substance literally does not exist anymore. In other words, you cannot just dilute something forever. We'll get back to that in a moment.

When you fix yourself, for example, a glass of scotch and cola, you might mix a third of a glass of scotch to two thirds cola. If you're not much of a drinker or you're liable to start dancing the Macarena with a lampshade on your head if you mix too strong a drink, you might prefer to pour one fifth of scotch to four parts of cola. If you're *really* worried about it, because you remember the last time you took a shot of tequila and wound up with your pants around your ankles, then maybe you'll pour *one tenth* of scotch to nine parts of cola, at which point you're not drinking so much as pretending to.

A homeopathic scotch and cola, using the strongest dose that homeopaths are willing to risk, would be a cocktail of one part scotch to 100,000,000,000,000,000,000 parts cola. That's one with 20 zeros – for reference, this is approximately the amount of water on Earth, measured in litres. You would need to pour a bottle of scotch into a vat of cola larger than the ocean, and (assuming you can mix it all up into a homogenous solution) dip your glass into that. According to a homeopath, this will get you nicely toasted.

And generally this is less than the homeopath is willing to dilute a substance. They prefer to go up to 30, 40 or 50 zeroes. We don't have any reference for how much cola that would be, unless you imagine pouring your bottle of Johnny Walker into a vat the size of the solar system.

Here's where we go back to Avogadro's number – roughly, what you need to know is that it has 23 zeroes, and that is the limit at which you can dilute something and be sure that there is even a single molecule of that substance remaining in the mixture. Once you get past that, to a mixture of one part scotch to (one with 24 zeroes) parts cola, that, my friend, is a glass of cola. There is literally no scotch in it, not one molecule.

This is obviously a problem for homeopathy, because most of their remedies are much, much more dilute than that. So it doesn't matter that they're treating you with a substance that, by definition, will make your condition worse, because there's nothing of it left anyway. A homeopathic remedy is water. What they call a "24c" solution (1 with 24 zeroes of water to one part medicine) is water, and after that it doesn't matter *what* they do with it. A 25c solution is water, a 26c solution is water, and a 1500c solution (the most powerful solution homeopaths are willing to mix for fear of giving you superpowers) is water.

Homeopaths *don't deny this*, but that's where they bring the hammer in. Since Avogadro, homeopaths have had to adjust their theory to claim that water has "memory." Even though it's true that they dilute it beyond (far beyond) the point at which the original substance doesn't exist anymore, they claim that the water "remembers" the fact that it once had something in it. That's how they get around Avogadro's limit – your glass of cola will still get you drunk because it remembers it had scotch in it at one point in the past, many dilutions ago.

To be clear, what we're talking about here is magic. Homeopaths are unable to couch in scientific terms any mechanism through which water has a memory of the substances that have been dissolved in it, how that memory gets more powerful as you continue to dilute or how a memory of a substance that gives you a specific symptom can paradoxically take that symptom away. Without a scientific mechanism (or even the pretext of a scientific mechanism) to explain these principles, homeopathy can only be described as a magic potion. They take a vial of water and, in essence, cast a spell on it. The ritualistic process of adding dilute quantities of several ingredients, shaking the mixture, then removing those ingredients is basically the same as messing around with eye of newt and dragon's breath. It's not enough to say that these remedies don't work, but it's actually impossible by the known laws of science for them to work.

Homeopathy is a good example of a tradition that exists today through the sheer force of inertia. It was so widely held among cargo cult scientists at the time that homeopathy is an effective treatment for disease that medical scientists and governments are hesitant to dismiss it. If it's been around for hundreds of years, there must be something to it, right? Like the imperial measurement system, we're only sticking with it at this point out of habit.

You might rightly wonder why it is that alternative medicines remain entrenched in society, often funded by governments, and, in fact, have a powerful industry behind them, if they are ineffectual and even in some cases (like with homeopathy and many eastern therapies like acupuncture and Reiki) actually based on magic. One reason is that most people don't actually realise this, or understand the implications of this.

The media tends to give more or less equal time to alternative medicine in the interest of being "open minded" or balanced, and we don't really have doctors in pop culture to tell people the truth about these things. We have celebrity icons in so many fields who for the most part relay accurate advice in their area of expertise – celebrity chefs don't try to convince us that sand is tastier than ravioli. But probably the closest thing we have to a celebrity medical professional is Dr Mehmet Oz, and although he provides a lot of good advice, he also tries to give equal time to homeopathy on his show and give it his official stamp of approval as a medical doctor. This is deeply disappointing because, while people may be skeptical when someone dressed like a hippie tells them that homeopathy is a valid remedy, they're much less skeptical when a professional surgeon like Oz tells them this. Here, Dr Oz is operating under the same principles as the History Channel when they give equal airtime to shows like *Ancient Aliens* – sure, it may not be true in any stretch of the imagination, but it's *entertaining!* Dr Oz is kind of boring when he's telling you that you should eat more vegetables and exercise regularly, but you're going to tune in when he says he's discovered an exciting new cure based on alternative medicines your doctor doesn't want you to know about.

I seem to recall a movie about another man named Oz who fraudulently claimed to work miracles in exchange for the respect and popularity of those who worshiped him. It turned out there was a charlatan behind the curtain.

As I discussed regarding the vaccine hysteria, the media does a pretty bad job sorting good science from poor science and even outright quackery, because people don't want to hear about the monotony of real science. They want to hear something exciting, amazing or terrifying. In that way it is sometimes said that we have the media we deserve.

That said, there are a few reasons why people, by and large, might become convinced that a particular therapy (be it acupuncture, homeopathy, goat sacrifice, or wishful thinking) is responsible for curing some particular condition, or a range of conditions, when it might not really be the case. For example, many common diseases are what's known as "self-limiting." This means that you will eventually recover from them whether you treat them or not. Most people who come down with the flu, for example, just take a couple of days off work and wait it out. In a few days, and without the interference of some other chronic condition, the flu "cures" itself.

Homeopathy sells a cure for the flu. It's called "oscillococcinum." What they do is they take a duck's liver, blend it up, mix it in water and then dilute the mixture to the point where, mathematically, it's one part liver to more parts water than there are atoms in the known universe. They then take one droplet of this and drip it onto a sugar pill no bigger than a tab of Splenda. You swallow this, and in a few days, your flu is gone.

Can you see the problem here? We call it the "regression to the mean" fallacy. It's the illusion that comes with confusing "normal" and "abnormal" states of being. What does that mean? I'll give you a personal example: Earlier this year I had an ear infection that rendered me essentially deaf for the best part of the month. And I do mean deaf – people's attempts to communicate with me sounded like they were warbling through a foot of water. When I did have to buy food, I had to guess what the cashier was saying to me from context. Interacting with colleagues and answering phones wasn't fun. It didn't take long to fall into a depression, but I found ways of dealing with it. If I was going to continue to operate in society, I needed to learn a few tricks. My left ear was slightly better than the right, so I would keep people on my left. I had a better chance of understanding people if I watched their mouths as they spoke. If I had a choice, I'd approach the bank cashier who looked like she had a loud, clear voice, and not the young skinny thing who looked like she was afraid of birds.

Then, one day, weeks later, my ears came back with a painful crackle, and my hearing returned immediately to normal. It was shocking – for the rest of the day, I seemed to be sensing a depth of sound that I'd never had. I could hear cars zipping past and distant barking dogs that I'd never noticed before. It took days before I stopped staring at people's mouths in an effort to understand what they were saying to me. After just a few weeks, I had begun to "normalise" my deafness in an attempt to cope with it, so the return of my hearing suddenly became an abnormal state. Normal hearing became super-hearing.

When you recover from a disease, sometimes you think you feel much better than you did before, because you quickly forget what normal feels like. And if you've been taking a remedy, even if it's just water dripped on a sugar pill, you'd be inclined to make the association between the remedy and this great feeling you're experiencing. You were told that this was some great stuff, and lo and behold, you feel incredible!

The answer to the efficacy illusion that a lot of skeptics might be surprised to hear, however, is that some alternative therapies actually kind of work, in a way. By that I mean that they do something small to contribute to the effect you're looking for. It's just never working the way that people think it's working. Acupuncture is a little like this – researchers have found that sticking little needles into people triggers a natural local anaesthetic called adenosine, which is released by the body because, frankly, you're injuring it with needles. The adenosine works to provide minor relief for minor pain close to the site of the acupuncture.[61] It is not, as acupuncturists insist, because they are

[61] Ferber, D. (2010). How Acupuncture Pierces Chronic Pain. *ScienceNOW*. 30 May. http://tinyurl.com/39tyfo7

manipulating the path of a magical life force called qi that is circulating improperly through your body and only needles can fix it.

Similarly, pleasant smells can have a small effect on chronic pain, but the effects of aromatherapy aren't because your body is absorbing the volatile healing energy of nature. Chiropractic, the discipline of curing disease by fixing misalignments in the spine, has some beneficial effects on diseases that are caused by misalignments of the spine. The idea that it fixes all diseases is just a flight of fancy. The point is, a lot of alternative treatments originated from a real observation that some effect was occurring. People went wrong in figuring out why it was happening, its physical mechanism. Even Hahnemann probably derived his homeopathic theory after finding one remedy that caused a similar complaint in overdose to what it cured in smaller quantities. He just took that one observation and declared it universal across the board, refusing to investigate why it actually happened.

We tend to believe in alternative medicine for a number of intertwined, fallacious reasons. One, I think, is the paradoxical notion that, the older a remedy is, the "purer" it is, or the closer it is to the truth, because it's been practiced for thousands of years and is, as such, pristine. This doesn't work for any other kind of science, but for some reason we apply it to the fields of health, developing such things as the "paleo diet" because the way that cavemen naturally ate must surely be the optimal diet for human health. You know, back when the human life expectancy was around 25. The argument that "acupuncture has been working for thousands of years, why change it?" should really be "acupuncture has been working poorly for thousands of years, what we should be doing is figuring out why it works so that it can work better."

Then again, we just don't really trust corporations, and the same thing applies to Big Pharma as it does to McDonald's. These bastards just want to kill us. How do we know? Because they're rich. Rupert Murdoch wants to kill you, how can you look in his eyes and doubt that? So we wind up believing things that don't make sense, like homeopathy. Sometimes, we believe things on a wide scale that contradict things you don't realise you already knew.

## McBullshit

Karen Hanrahan carries a McDonald's hamburger around in her purse. She doesn't do it because she wants to eat it – she would never, ever put such a thing near her face. For you see, Karen Hanrahan is a wellness educator ("wellness" being the term that you use for what you're not legally allowed to call "health," usually for lack of credentials.) She carries the burger because it's 12 years old... and it still looks like she bought it yesterday. She's part of the cult phenomenon that is leaving McDonald's food out and watching in amazement as it doesn't decompose. Not even after *twelve years!*

Nobody has ever suggested that McDonald's food is healthy. Interestingly, not even McDonald's claims this. Nevertheless, to this day, it will still make headlines whenever someone "discovers" that McDonald's food is bad for you. And I'm always baffled by the point that people are trying to make, or think they're making. As the problem of obesity grows worse, activists will go to ever increasing lengths to wake the public up to the fact that *McDonald's is bad for you.* As if the problem is that everyone thinks it's good for you. The problem is that it tastes really good, and people have low self-control. I actually had to leave the house while I was writing this chapter because I couldn't stand the hankering for a Big Mac meal.

Morgan Spurlock's hit 2004 documentary *Super Size Me* absolutely skewered McDonald's and led to a PR nightmare for the company. In order to valiantly prove that McDonald's food is bad for you, Spurlock actually *risked his life* – eating only McDonald's food for an entire month. He couldn't complete the task, having become dangerously malnourished, a testament to the fact that *even if you eat everything on the menu*, McDonald's still does not provide absolutely everything a human being needs for a balanced diet. Moreso, what they do provide tends to be high in cholesterol.

Despite the hysteria that emerged, did anyone really sit down and ask what *exactly* the point was of Spurlock's experiment? If I had eaten only carrots for an entire month, there would probably not be a resulting scandal when I wound up in the hospital. *Super Size Me* did provide some genuinely interesting insight into America's obesity epidemic and fast food culture, but it also contained some scenes that were baffling in their pointlessness. The most confusing, oddly, is also the one that most people seem to remember and be under the impression that it was making some kind of argument.

This was the part where Spurlock put a variety of McDonald's burgers and a pack of fries in a series of sealed jars and left them out for some weeks. In other jars, he put another burger and fries from a non-franchise restaurant as if to serve as a comparison, and then proceeded to not show what happened to them, captioning simply that they were thrown out. For the whole five minute scene, he shows the decomposition of McDonald's food over the ten week period that the experiment ran for. It's pretty gross.[62]

Internet comments are pretty united in their hysterical response. "I can't believe people actually put this stuff in their body!" But actually, we don't put ten-week-decomposed, liquefied and mold-covered burgers inside our bodies. The goal of the experiment, as Spurlock explains at the beginning, is to show how McDonald's breaks down so that we can see how it breaks down in our bodies. But first, that doesn't make sense because digestion is a different process to decomposition, as evidenced by the fact that the burgers grew mold over ten weeks instead of turning into turds in 12 hours. Second, having conveniently not shown what a regular burger does in that time, we don't know what we're supposed to believe normal decomposing food looks like. Presumably, it explodes into butterflies and rainbows. For the length of this scene, we would assume the point he was making was important enough not to leave on the cutting room floor.

Perhaps it has something to do with the fries. Over the weeks, he keeps cutting back to those fries – and they're not decomposing. They just stay exactly as they were when he bought them. And he's *blown away* by this.

"This, I can't explain," he says, "but this is what you're eating, every time you get these fries." And later, "Why are these not breaking down? That's a really good question. And you have to ask yourself, wow, *what's that doing in my stomach then?*"

Instead of asking himself, maybe he should have asked a scientist.

Nevertheless, the decomposition of McDonald's food is a fascination of the internet, and it's been a creepy fascination with people, apparently, for a long time, considering the number of people who have been carrying burgers around for decades. More strangely, they seem more impressed for every year that the burgers fail to decompose – as if something that hasn't broken down after 20 years might begin to break down in the 21st year.

But what point are they making?

Many people seem to believe that it has something to do with shelf life. They think that burgers and fries that don't break down have a freakishly long shelf life due to the preservatives that McDonald's

---

[62] http://tinyurl.com/3kwy92s

pumps into them, as though they could possibly have any motive for giving their burgers a shelf life of three decades. But I would dare anyone who has been saving a burger on their mantelpiece since Reagan was president to take a bite of it and tell me that it's still within its shelf life. Whatever motive McDonald's has for not letting its burgers decompose, it's not so they can survive a nuclear war.

We can ask Karen Hanrahan, wellness expert, what she thinks is going on here. According to her website: "Do you find this horrifying? McDonalds fills an empty space in your belly. It does nothing to nourish the cell, it is not a nutritious food. It is not a treat. I marvel at how McDonalds has infiltrated our entire world. A hamburger here tastes exactly the same in China or some around the world place. It's cloned. Makes you wonder doesn't it?"

What makes *me* wonder is why people who openly wonder about things don't just go and find the answer. It's probably because the real answers aren't nearly as terrifying as the ones that pop into our head when we're told "you really have to ask yourself," or "it really makes you wonder."

In today's world of high processed foods, we're increasingly panicky about "chemicals" being in the things we eat. The thing is, like people who go on about "toxins," people don't really have a clear idea of what the "chemicals" are that we're afraid of. There's a dichotomy between "food" and "things that are not food." The things that are not food are the chemicals. And McDonald's, Hanrahan asserts, is made of chemicals. That's why it doesn't break down. If you actually look at the ingredients of a McDonald's hamburger, however, you find rather astonishingly that it's made of things like beef (from actual cows) and lettuce (that actually came out of the ground) and bread (yes, real bread.) Where are the chemicals? *What* are the chemicals?

In March of 2012, ABC News ran a hysterical story[63] about a whistleblower from the meat industry who revealed that up to 70% of the ground beef that winds up on your plate is not beef at all, but a chemical filler that was nicknamed "pink slime." The article, in which the term "pink slime" appears seven times, weaves a terrifying story about how scientists who are desperate to get pink slime off the shelves are thwarted at every turn by money-grubbing corporate overlords and government bureaucrats who insist beyond all logic upon calling this

---

[63] Avila, J. (2012). 70 Percent of Ground Beef at Supermarkets Contains 'Pink Slime.' *ABC News*. http://tinyurl.com/7bez7yo

concoction "meat." After this expose, many consumers went off buying ground beef and some supermarkets vowed not to carry this hideous slime byproduct. But what really is "pink slime?" Right there in the original article, it explains:

> The "pink slime" is made by gathering waste trimmings, simmering them at low heat so the fat separates easily from the muscle, and spinning the trimmings using a centrifuge to complete the separation. Next, the mixture is sent through pipes where it is sprayed with ammonia gas to kill bacteria. The process is completed by packaging the meat into bricks. Then, it is frozen and shipped to grocery stores and meat packers, where it is added to most ground beef.

So wait, it's beef? The article seems variously to disagree with itself on this point, at first describing it as "beef trimmings" but explaining that it's usually only found in dog food. Then they quote their whistleblower, Gerald Zirnstein, who states that it's "economic fraud" that pink slime is being labelled as beef. Then the article author actually uses the word "meat" to describe the substance, then backtracks by warning that you won't find it on a label because unscrupulous bureaucrats are classifying it as "meat."

It turns out, of course, that pink slime is indeed meat. It's not prime rump that's been pushed through a mincer, but the smaller bits that are trimmed off whole cuts to give them their shape. The media likes to use buzz terms like "mechanical separation" to dispel the idea that butchers are lovingly slicing bits of meat apart by hand, and the term "pink slime" is pushed to inspire an icky feeling that this is not the most appetising-looking food product before it lands on your plate. The fact is that the slimy appearance comes from the process to remove the fat from the product, making it much leaner than a fatty prime slice of chuck.

In a similar scene[64] from Jamie Oliver's *Food Revolution* program, in which he tutors school children on healthy eating, Jamie decides to show the kids exactly what's in their "fucking nuggets." With a dark tone to his voice, he introduces the kids to the horrors of "mechanically reclaimed meat."

"Once they've taken the breasts off and the legs off," he explains, they're left with the carcass. The carcass, he shows as he stuffs the chicken torso into a blender, is liquefied and mixed with

---

[64] http://tinyurl.com/38gkedg

breadcrumbs to make "fake food." It's the meat that they dare to not throw straight into the dumpster where it belongs even though it's not the 30% or so of a chicken that looks like a succulent piece of thigh.

Of course, Jamie is right in so far as the point that he's making: we shouldn't be feeding chicken nuggets to kids like it's a meal. But where people go wrong is in judging food as "real" or "fake" based on how easily it is to stomach watching the manufacture of the raw product in the factory. We're reminded that only the prime cuts sliced whole from the meatiest parts of an animal are edible, and the less pretty parts are garbage "fake food" byproducts that will kill you, which is an interesting position to take in a world where we're having trouble feeding everyone.

The meat industry, as of the time I write this, have filed a lawsuit against ABC for the hysteria they generated by calling their meat "pink slime," arguing (reasonably, I believe) that the term is a deliberately misleading one intended to inspire a reader's gross-out reaction. ABC's lawyers argue that the term is a constitutionally protected piece of "rhetorical hyperbole," being that the meat product is indeed both pink and slimy, so they weren't lying.[65] The result of the suit is pending.

Morgan Spurlock isn't playing a slight of hand when he's almost killed by eating nothing but McDonald's hamburgers. The food, nutritionally speaking, is crap. But let's not fool ourselves by misunderstanding *why* it's crap. People who campaign against fast food and other junk food items fall easily for terrifying myths about what goes on behind the curtain. I hear them all the time from liberal-minded friends and colleagues. Many of the more enduring and science-fiction-dystopia-style tales concern KFC. A pervasive myth is that KFC was forced to change its name from "Kentucky Fried Chicken" because they legally weren't allowed to call it "chicken" anymore – the story being variously that it's a chemical substitute or that the "chickens" are genetically modified beyond recognition, missing beaks and feet and kept alive by feeding tubes. The mundane truth is that KFC changed their name to "KFC" because that's what lots of companies are doing nowerdays in an effort to become more hip, like the National Australia Bank somewhat obnoxiously becoming "the nab" complete with hipsterish full lower case. KFC don't raise their own chickens in

---

[65] Eaton, K. (2012) ABC News Asks Judge to Toss 'Pink Slime' Lawsuit. *ABC News*. http://tinyurl.com/d3zvudy

spooky chicken factories, they get them from the same farms that everyone else gets them from.

You've probably heard that Hostess stopped making Twinkies back in the '70s, and what they're selling are the backlog of immortal Twinkies that have no shelf life due to, once again, their chemical composition. The truth is that Twinkies have a use-by date of about four weeks, and that may hit home soon now that Hostess is going belly-up. You've probably also heard that Coca-Cola is so dangerously acidic that you can clean with it and it'll dissolve a steak or a nail overnight. In actual fact, you have little to worry about from Coke, because much more acidic substances include orange juice and the acids that are already in your stomach.

One particular bit of food chemical hysteria that I find amusing is the pervasive claim that margarine is "one molecule away from plastic." This can sound kind of scary, but true or false, it's a meaningless statement. The tiniest differences in the atomic structure of a substance can completely change the nature of that substance. Water is, after all, one atom away from being hydrogen. A similar misunderstanding of chemistry is the basis of the alternative health practice of "ozone therapy," which relies on the idea that, since oxygen ($O_2$) is good for you, then ozone ($O_3$) must be some kind of *super* oxygen that's even better for you. What people fail to understand is that one extra oxygen atom makes ozone a completely different (and actually toxic) substance. So while people might tell you that margarine is chemically similar to plastic or something else, that doesn't mean that it shares any of the properties of that other substance. The issue is exacerbated by the fact that many people can't say offhand what margarine actually is, and assume it's "chemicals." So let's clear the air right now – margarine and butter are essentially the same thing, which is solidified fat, salted and dyed yellow. Butter fat comes from milk, while margarine fat comes from vegetable oils, and apart from that, there's almost no difference.

So what's the deal with McDonald's hamburgers not decomposing? We should ask Len Foley, the world's foremost collector of non-decomposed McDonald's burgers. Foley inherited his collection from one Matt Malmgren who has been collecting burgers for 20 years and patiently waiting for any of them to decompose. Deciding that this was the scoop of the century, Foley continued the tradition, creating an internet sensation known as the "Bionic Burger Museum." Now he takes his museum on the road to educate people about how McDonald's is not food, but in fact, a "chemical" product.

The reason that none of his burgers will decompose, in his professional opinion, is this:

> McDonald's has over 33,000 restaurants worldwide. The only way they can make their hamburgers and fries taste virtually the same at every restaurant is by taking the 'uncertain variables' out of the food service equation: namely, they replace food (which has a tendency to taste different depending on the season, environmental conditions, and quality) with chemicals, which always look, smell, and taste the same.
>
> That's why McDonald's is so profitable in this slow economy. They are not selling food, which is expensive; they are selling chemical concoctions, which are very cheap.[66]

Of course, anyone who knows a little something about scientific investigation into a phenomena has probably noticed something a little strange about people who obsessively collect McDonald's burgers to see if they decompose. Well, besides the fact that these people are strange to begin with. What you may have figured out is that throughout this entire phenomenon, nobody has *ever* decided to use a control group. By which I mean, nobody has ever bought a non-McDonald's hamburger to see if it decomposes.

Len Foley would probably be insulted by the idea, because as he knows, it's just common sense that *real* food decomposes. So he won't try it, so maybe you should, if you're taken in by the "Bionic Burger." See, I can just about promise you that your home-grown, organic, family business hamburger from your parents' home town won't decompose either. Given a little common sense, you'll see why.

Cast your mind back to your student days when you lived like an absolute pig. (If you currently live like an absolute pig, then we'll go with that.) If you've ever taken too long to eat the loaf of bread in your pantry, you'll know that it starts to get a little green inside its plastic. If, however, you left a half-eaten sandwich under the bed and then found it again a few months later, you probably found that, while it could now be used in a pinch to hammer a nail back into the wall, it still looked exactly the same. Why is that? Is it a dangerous chemical Bionic Sandwich?

Another example that's very easy to use here is uncooked pasta. You'll probably notice that pasta doesn't decompose before

---

[66] Media release from *PRWeb*: http://tinyurl.com/d4cmkh

you've cooked it. You can keep pasta, noodles, and rice pretty much forever until your student loans are due and you need endless food that doesn't cost anything. Why doesn't it decompose? Stop! Don't touch that Bionic Ramen!

The fact is, noodles, sandwiches and McDonald's burgers won't decompose because only wet things decompose. That's the beginning and the end of it. You might counter me by buying a nice, juicy, fat burger with the lot from your fish and chips shop and watch as it decomposes over the next few weeks, but that's a different story. If McDonald's is guilty of food crimes, it's not that their burgers are made of "chemicals," but that they're dry, flat, and half the size of your fist. They won't break down because they dry out faster than they can attract the various moulds and bacteria which are responsible for what we call "decomposition." If you don't understand what role moisture plays in the decomposition process, just think about mummies drying out in the desert sun. Mummies aren't there because Egyptians were "made of chemicals."

It's true that we need to educate people better about good nutrition. There are a hell of a lot of fatties walking around. But it doesn't help anyone if the information we're disseminating is nonsense, even if the advice is sound, like "don't eat so much Maccas." If we're going to explain that burgers are unhealthy because they're made of chemicals, it's exactly as useful as explaining that they're unhealthy because a coven of druids put a curse on them. If you want to stop people from eating fast food, don't pump your funding into burger museums, put it toward research into how to make carrots taste good.

## The Oprahfication of Science

On an episode of her show, Oprah Winfrey tried to explain the principles behind "The Secret," a new-age idea espoused by a small-time Australian TV writer named Rhonda Byrne. Oprah explains that one day she did a show that featured some guy who blew giant soap bubbles as an art form. While watching the spectacle, she decided that she wanted to blow some bubbles too, but she didn't have the technology on hand. When she went back to her dressing room, though, she found that there was a silver Tiffany bubble blower right there on her desk, an item which Google informs me costs about $300. She called her assistant to ask if she'd run out and bought the extravagant item to feed her need for bubbles, but the assistant replied that it had been there all along – she'd bought it for Oprah's birthday earlier in the year.[67]

The universe, Oprah explained, had given her bubbles, because she wanted them and she focused her thoughts on getting them. That's the secret of *The Secret*, otherwise known as the "law of attraction," probably the most iconically middle-class brand of pseudoscience ever dreamed up, which grew in popularity in the second half of the 21st century's inaugural decade.

There are multiple ways of explaining this story depending on your perspective, either being Oprah or being someone who definitely is not Oprah. Not Oprah, my interpretation would be something along the lines of Oprah being an insulated monarch so out of touch with humanity that she interprets a birthday gift not as an example of the altruism of others, but of the universe conspiring to give her things that she wants, when she wants them – the real forehead-slapper of this story is that she didn't even notice she'd been given a gift until her me-me-me complex kicked in.

According to Oprah, however, and according to the nobody who was launched to billion-dollar stardom after writing this nonsense, there is an actual scientific, physical law that dictates that if you really, really want something, you will get it. They're not talking about the power of positive thinking or keeping your mind on a goal or any of that general self-motivation stuff. Rhonda Byrne really does mean that your brainwaves interact with vibrations in the universe to actually manifest objects and events that you desire, in a worldview that closer resembles Neo's world-altering mind powers in *The Matrix* than anything else. And now Byrne has made (probably) millions of dollars selling this nonsense because Oprah came to the astonishing realisation one day that she got everything that she asked for. But like her invisible assistant whose ridiculously expensive gift she never noticed, Oprah is under the impression that all these presents are just falling out of space, getting spat out of the universe into her lap, because she doesn't notice her minions scurrying about to get things for her. The law of attraction works better when your net worth is more than the GDP of a third world country.

Despite how patently ridiculous the concept is, Byrne sells it in her documentary on the subject by bringing out a bunch of quantum

---

[67] Though I tried to find a copy of this story as told by Oprah herself, I have to make do to trust the accuracy of this Newsweek article that recalled it: http://tinyurl.com/3cw9bl7

physicists, putting them in lab coats, and explaining how the universe operates on a subatomic level. Like our homeopath friend "Dr" Werner pointed out, the whole universe is energy and vibration (no mention of youies here) and so the law of attraction has a sound scientific basis because your brain vibrations interact with the vibrations of the universe somehow. It's quantum, dummy!

The evolution of modern quantum physics (the science of atoms and their constituents) is the greatest thing to ever happen to the snake oil industry. From homeopathy to *The Secret*, people can suddenly get away with making claims about anything that seems like magic by suggesting that its mechanism lies somewhere in the murky mysteries of quantum physics. The problem is that even scientists aren't quite sure how everything works down there – Einstein was famously baffled with it, and he was Einstein. Don't get me wrong, science isn't absolutely clueless, but there's a lot of work to do, and where science has unknown territory, that's where people shove the explanations for their woo. How does water have a memory? Well, it has something to do with quantum physics! That'll do!

There's a term for this kind of marriage between quantum physics and metaphysical weirdness – quantum mysticism. And it's not necessarily total garbage. How could I say that when we don't know enough about quantum physics? But hold your horses, Dr Werner. Just because science doesn't fully understand something, it doesn't mean that *you* do. In fact, I'd venture a guess that you're *less* likely to understand it if the scientists don't.

Quantum mysticism has skyrocketed in popularity over the past few years, because it's so easy to manipulate it to give your crazy some sciency-sounding credibility. It's the foundation of Deepak Chopra's entire philosophy, and in 2004 a somewhat popular documentary called *What the Bleep Do We Know?* used it to attempt to prove that reality was consciousness or something. Quantum physics provides appropriately scientific-sounding terms like *superposition* and *quantum entanglement* and *wave mechanics* and *half-integer spin* and the *uncertainty principle* and *quantum teleportation*, which, when put in a sentence in any given random order, can seem to lend scientific legitimacy to absolutely anything at all. The fact is, Deepak Chopra doesn't understand quantum physics. The creators of *What the Bleep?* don't understand it either, and you can sure as hell bet that Rhonda Byrne doesn't understand it. They know some words that are used sometimes in that field of science, and while they don't know what those words mean, they only need to use some words that you can Google to prove that they are, in fact, science words.

That is, at least, all they need to convince Oprah. You don't need much to convince Oprah of anything, which is unfortunate because Oprah is one of the most influential people on Earth. Her power to influence people's beliefs and wallets is perhaps unrivalled. In 1996, she single-handedly crippled the meat industry when she announced a personal choice to stop eating beef. And that wasn't some small, obscure industry – it was the *meat* industry. Oprah could convince the world that Earth is flat if she really wanted to, and certainly she can sway the public perception of science in any direction that she wishes. Unfortunately, to this point, she's decided to sink it.

Oprah's attitude toward science really illustrates the mindset I've been exploring here, that what scientists conclude about the nature of reality is just one opinion. Oprah claims that she doesn't endorse any one point of view, whether it's the scientific or the alternative version of reality, but that she wants to give a voice to both sides and let people make up their own mind. This is a very strange way to go about education. It's kind of like if you hold an anatomy lesson by inviting one guy in to explain how the eardrums convert air vibrations into sound, and another guy to argue that their real purpose is as plugs to keep your soul from dribbling out, and the teacher telling the class to make up their own minds. Setting up every educational forum as a debate between two sides is frequently not conducive to actual insight, especially when only one side understands the issue. It's just confusing to people.

That said, Oprah doesn't *really* give voice to both sides, and neither do any of the other hosts who sprouted spin-off shows like Dr Phil and Dr Oz. What they usually do when they're hosting a debate about some controversial alternative science concept is they invite the woomeister onto the show, invite a skeptic to sit beside them, and then the woomeister and the host start tag-teaming the skeptic about why they are so stuck up and closed-minded. It's not even a debate in the sense that one guest is allowed to do any better than the other – that would at least be something. Usually, if the skeptic starts cleaning the floor with the other guest, the host will come in and silence the proceedings.

A favourite example of mine is an episode of Dr Oz, where he invited prominent skeptic Dr Steven Novella to debate the merits of alternative medicine with him and an "integrated medicine" practitioner.[68] You can get some prediction as to the mood of the rest of the segment when Oz, straight off the bat, where he firmly plants himself on the side of alternative medicine by saying "There are a lot of doctors, *including me*, who are putting our reputations on the line because we're using alternative therapies in our traditional practices." Right off the bat, he puts Dr Novella in the negative corner by saying that there are some doctors who are *afraid* of alternative medicine and don't want people like Oz talking about it. "Your doctor could be one of them," he warns.

The medical establishment may be the "biggest hold-outs," he explains, when it comes to harnessing the potential power of alternative medicine. He softly paints a picture of himself as medicine's lone Galileo figure who has been criticised for "exploring new territory." His audience, he says, has shown that they're not afraid to try out alternative therapies, so *why is your doctor?*

It's a common tactic among proponents of alternative science to paint their opposition as being "afraid," which is why they walk their narrow line of evidence-based science instead of waving crystals around. This is pretty absurd – I've never paid an acupuncturist a hundred bucks to stick needles into my arms, not because I'm afraid of it but because I don't want to waste my time and my money. Before I spend time and money on anything I want to be able to do some research to find out whether it's actually going to do anything. Dr Oz isn't going to help me sort through twenty therapies and tell me which ones work and which ones don't – he wants me to try homeopathy and Reiki and acupuncture and naturopathy and osteopathy and chiropractic and aroma therapy and Rolfing and qi gong and chromium chelation and mineral supplements and reflexology and pranic healing and craniosacral healing and ozone therapy and goddamn bloodletting on my own time and dollar and "make up my own mind." Luckily, I have some scientists who can lay out for me all the evidence for the efficacy of all these treatments, which can best be represented by a tumbleweed blowing softly across the plains of Death Valley at dusk.

"Why do you not want me talking about these therapies on the show?" Oz asks Novella at the beginning of the interview.

Dr Novella replies that "alternative medicine" isn't a real category. And this is true – when people talk about "alternative

[68] Available on the Dr Oz website: http://tinyurl.com/azkalxu

medicine," they're talking about everything that doesn't fall into the category of scientific medicine. This is literally everything from acupuncture to prayer. Novella explains that doctors like himself would prefer there to be a single standard of scientifically studied treatments that we can understand as either having some merit or being a total waste of time.

Next, Dr Oz asks his other guest, alternative health practitioner Dr Mimi Guarneri, why she puts her faith in alternative medicine. Her total non-answer to the question is:

"As a cardiologist, I've always been faced with what can I do to prevent heart disease? So because of my patients, I reached out and I said 'If you have pain, let's look for another solution.' Maybe that solution is acupuncture. If you're stressed out, maybe your solution is prayer. The rosary. Meditation. And certainly, I don't think today we can call nutrition alternative medicine. Or call exercise alternative medicine. Other things that I teach my patients every day to prevent heart disease." She looks at Dr Novella accusingly as though he just dismissed exercise and nutrition as quack treatments.

"That's a pretty compelling argument," Dr Oz replies. The only problem is no it isn't, it wasn't an argument at all, she simply stated that she likes to actually help her patients, therefore acupuncture. The old "Big Pharma" ruse is in full swing here, the implication being that western doctors don't have an interest in actually helping people. And all too often (as Novella also points out) proponents of alternative medicine include things like "nutrition" and "exercise" under the umbrella of "alternative" therapy, the perception being that western science based medicine is entirely composed of pharmaceutical prescriptions. You can tell that this interview isn't going to go well for Dr Novella when Dr Guarneri answers a query by simply rewording the question, and Oz describes her response as a compelling argument. It was, in fact, only what he wanted to hear.

Dr Oz then lumps alternative medicines into a few different categories and begins a blow-by-blow debate with Dr Novella about what his infernal problem is with all of these treatments. First up is herbs, and Novella repeats that herbs are not, in and of themselves, "alternative" treatments, but since the alternative health crowd hijacked them, they no longer have to be held to any standard about which herbs work and which ones don't, or have their dosage controlled in any strict way.

"I'm- I'm- I- I totally disagree," is Dr Oz's incredibly insightful rebuttal, and he moves to acupuncture. Asking Dr Guarneri why she uses this, she essentially replies that she needed a way to relieve her patients' pain, which again doesn't speak to the efficacy of the particular treatment. Dr Novella explains that, having carefully reviewed the literature, he hasn't found any evidence that acupuncture does anything at all.

Dr Oz is gobsmacked. "There are *billions* of people around the world who use acupuncture as the foundation of their healthcare! It's the basis of ancient Chinese medicine! I just think it's very dismissive of you to say because we couldn't take this idea that exists with a different mindset and squeeze it into the way we think about it in the west, that it can't be possibly effective."

Dr Novella reiterates that he wasn't dismissing it at all, that he reviewed the studies very carefully, and that it's a fallacy, specifically the argument from popularity, to suggest that just because a lot of people do it we have to accept that it works the way that it's supposed to. He brings up bloodletting, the idea that diseases can be cured simply by bleeding out the patient, which was used for hundreds of years before the germ theory came into vogue, and surely we should agree that this isn't effective even though it was once the consensus standard.

Dr Oz nods dismissively and begins to mansplain to Dr Novella why he doesn't think acupuncture works: "There's two reasons you might not be able to show that it doesn't work, and one of them is that you don't understand it well enough to study it the way it has to be studied, and there are many examples of that where we have struggled to understand things that we now know to be true, but because we couldn't put our arms around them, and couldn't study them in an insightful way, that we failed."

What the hell are you talking about, Dr Oz? How exactly are we not able to understand acupuncture in the way that it needs to be studied? This strikes me as one of those arguments that you could say is "not even wrong." From what I can gather, Oz is trying to apply a supernatural cop-out here by suggesting that the methodology of acupuncture exists outside of and beyond science. Certainly, that is the way that it's supposed to work according to Chinese mysticism – it's the manipulation of a supernatural life force called *qi*. I didn't expect Dr Oz to bring this to the table, though. Novella begins to retort, but Oz puts his hand up and speaks over him to change the subject again, to "mind-body" medicine, a category in which he puts such things as meditation.

He cuts to a pre-recorded interview from one of his dismissive physicians who is afraid of alternative therapies. The anonymous doctor explains that meditation might be helpful, but we have other remedies that we *know* work, so why not use those? A clip is shown of someone very ominously tapping a bottle of pills into their hand. He turns to Novella again – what could his problem possibly be with *meditation?*

Dr Novella replies that he's absolutely fine with meditation. It relaxes the body, it reduces blood pressure, and there are potentially a lot of things that it's good for, just don't wrap it up in mysticism and suggest that it can cure cancer.

Dr Oz is done on this point. It's time to mansplain meditation as well – calling it "mysticism" is again dismissive, he argues. Who are we to say? Maybe we can train our immune cells to battle cancer. "Neither you or I know that," he argues, and then cuts straight to his closing argument as the arbiter of the debate. Surprise surprise, alternative therapy wins: "My advice to everybody is customise therapy for yourself. Figure out what makes sense to you." Alternative medicine, he explains (without saying which one, exactly, whether it be chiropractic or animal sacrifice) is a targeted approach, like a bow and arrow, as opposed to the "ballistic missile" that is science-based western medicine. While we're talking about dismissive, this seems like an oddly dismissive opinion for someone who is, by all accounts, one of the top surgeons in the world. The mind boggles.

In conclusion, Dr Oz explains that there are a lot of studies that prove alternative medicine works, and a lot of schools in the nation offer classes in it, so who are we to judge? Alternative medicine is at the "grass roots level, and because of that, nobody owns it." His final judgment, kind of bafflingly, is "don't let anyone take it away from you." Like any alternative science guru or conspiracy theorist, the message is clear: Don't let any of these killjoy scientists persuade you with their "evidence." Reality is what you hope and believe is true.

I have some more advice in the same vein as Dr Oz's advice about alternative medicine: If you prefer the simplicity of Newtonian mechanics, don't let Einstein take it away from you with relativity. If the "plum pudding model" sounds like a tastier version of the atom, then don't fall for any of this junk about probability clouds. Go ahead and embrace geocentrism if you're more comfortable with it. Just like Samuel Rowbotham insisted with his simplistic arguments for the flatness of Earth: If it *makes sense to you*, to use Dr Oz's words, if you can measure the surface of a puddle as level, then don't let anyone take it away from you.

The hostile treatment of skeptics and scientists by the media is, I think, a significant hurdle for the public understanding of science and the public's ability to differentiate good science from bad. The skeptic-as-object of ridicule position actively promoted and presented by media powerhouses such as Oprah and her various padawan apprentices sees skeptics frequently cast as the antagonists, even the villains, of whatever the media's idea of a debate may look like. Often, they are used as kindling to throw onto the fire, and treated as such. James Randi, the stage magician and professional skeptic, learned the hard way how Oprah plays this game – he maintains that he was misled about the topic of discussion before his one and only appearance on the Oprah show in a deliberate effort to ensure that the debate was spun against his favour. And of course, these are not debates in the formal sense – the host, outside of his or her capacity as a debate moderator, wields inordinate control over the discussion, and the outcome is always in favour of the "alternative" practice being discussed. The format of the Oprah show or the Dr Oz show is set up so that the host can reinforce the truth (or, at the very least, the equal viability) of alternative practices after silencing and dismissing the skeptic guest, often taking the time to condescendingly explain to the captive skeptic how the alternative practice works (and it's usually described as being something beyond science or beyond the skeptic's possible understanding.)

Why would skeptics be painted arbitrarily as the villains in so many cases? I suspect it has something to do with the reason the state of documentary television is so abysmal, with *Ancient Aliens* and *Conspiracy Theory with Jesse Ventura* passing for science somehow. We have the media we deserve. Still, it feels as though it wasn't always like this. I grew up in the days of Carl Sagan and Stephen Hawking, when it seemed like people were looking at science with more open-minded wonder and less ridicule and scorn. You don't get many people saying that they hate Carl Sagan or Stephen Hawking. I would only be speculating if I wondered whether people are turned off by a public perception of today's skeptics and the inheritors of Sagan's throne— like Richard Dawkins and the late Christopher Hitchens, among others—as angry, elitist, hateful and arrogant. Certainly I've thought at times that the skeptic community can be an uncomfortable group to be around, such is the degree of scorn. I don't intend to point the finger back at skeptics, here, but just to open the possibility of a little self-reflection. It is not, in any case, the result of any dropping of the guard.

If we may continue the onslaught upon Dr Oz, it's clear that he or his producers don't want to alienate any of their potential audience by dismissing any kind of alternative therapy out of hand. But the problem with this is, by accepting all treatments inside or outside of scientific medicine as viable and effective, Dr Oz has, in effect, undermined his entire purpose for existing. "America's Doctor" endorses various diets and then goes back and endorses contradictory ones, depending on who the producers have decided to endorse this week. He not only teams up with Deepak Chopra and his quantum mysticism, but endorses Joe Mercola, a conspiracy theorist who has been ordered by the FDA to stop making illegal claims about the efficacy of his treatments, and who has believed in just about every magical cure you can imagine, just as long as it is not one that is accepted by science. More recently, Oz has put his stamp of approval on not only faith healing, but even *talking to the dead through a psychic medium* as a form of therapy. Although I always imagined the art of cold reading was fairly well known at this point, Oz claims that he can't explain how John Edward does what he does.

Now, Mehmet Oz is, no doubt, an intelligent man. If his reputation is remotely accurate, he's one of the most accomplished heart surgeons in the world. This makes it very difficult to determine how much of Dr Oz's opinion is, indeed, Dr Oz's opinion. After all, when it really comes to the crunch and somebody's ribcage is splayed inside-out across his operating table like a Lovecraftian barn door, he seems to rely on traditional medicine rather than waving a crystal pendant overhead and dripping a homeopathic dilution of cholesterol onto his patient's arrested heart muscle, although his own advice would seem to indicate that either of those would be just as efficacious as a triple bypass. I do suspect that the pressure on Dr Oz to promote wealthy quacks on his show might be such that he's stretching his personal principles of integrity to accommodate them (for clues, watch the anguish and conflict written on Oz's face when Dr Mercola brings anti-vaccine views onto the show.[69] Unlike Oprah, Oz seems to know what he's talking about, and seems genuinely torn between the Hippocratic oath and not being allowed to disagree with his guest. To his credit, he does not end this segment endorsing anti-vaccination views.)

---

[69] http://tinyurl.com/d9ocvd7

But endorsing every possible treatment from sound nutrition to homeopathy to the curing ability of prayer confuses and effectively eliminates the point of Dr Oz and renders his education and intelligence completely irrelevant. He's supposed to be using his knowledge and experience as a medical professional to advise his viewers on nutrition and health, but instead he arbitrates between sound advice and patent absurdity, declaring his approval of all of it, and asking viewers to make up their own minds. I don't *want* to make up my own mind, Dr Oz, that's what I go to a goddamn doctor for. I don't go to a chemistry class to decide for myself whether the table of elements begins with hydrogen and helium, or fire and earth. An educator isn't supposed to arbitrate between those two views, he's supposed to tell me which one is right so that I actually learn something. If Dr Oz is going to give equal billing to homeopathy, faith healing, psychic surgery and genuine science-based medicine, and tell me it's all good, then it doesn't matter whether I'm asking the world's top cardiac surgeon or the homeless person I keep in my basement.

What I'm calling the "Oprahfication of Science" is, I think, as good a place as any to finish up on our journey through the modern history of pseudoscience. Because what Oprah and her orbiting moons represent is truly a kind of a postmodern end-point. When we accept, as Oprah and Dr Oz do, all ideas of alternative medicine being on equal footing in terms of their effectiveness as treatments—even when they directly contradict each other, as many do—or when we accept any mystical interpretation of quantum physics as equally valid, or start replacing science with sciency-sounding gobbeldigook that doesn't mean anything, then we've gone beyond Occam's worst nightmare and entered a world where logic and meaning aren't even relevant anymore. Stick a fork in the history of rational progress – it's done.

# Q&A WITH DAVILD WILCOCK

I don't know whether David Wilcock is crazy, a charlatan, or whether he's simply mistaken. For reasons of protecting myself from litigation, I refuse to make that call here. I am however going to make the call that he's *wrong*. If only because the predictions he made for the end of 2012

– that humanity would ascend, that the Illuminati would be arrested, etc. – never happened.

Wilcock's biography on his website, *Divine Cosmos*, states that he was overweight as a child and was bullied for it. One would imagine that his self-esteem recovered upon discovering that he was not only the reincarnation of the world's most renowned psychic, but that he would be almost single-handedly responsible for bringing down the Illuminati, the eternal enemy of conspiracy culture throughout its history. I remain unconvinced, but then, I'm not Edgar Cayce or any of his reincarnated progeny.

AGE 15          AGE 17

**One assumes he must have figured out that a McDonald's hamburger is "made of chemicals."**

Wilcock's lecture seems to fall apart in the closing hours, as I notice that nothing he says seems to feed into any kind of central thesis anymore. He just starts throwing out random garbage as though he knows he's running out of time but he has a lot more snake oil to sell.

Science has proven, he says, that if you drop a bowling ball on a hard surface, it loses mass. But you shouldn't use this as a weight loss method (he laughs hysterically here, and the audience with him) because the mass will return in twenty minutes.

One time, a bunch of hippies camped out in Stonehenge, but when the police came to arrest them, they were met with a blinding light, and suddenly the hippies were gone. "They were teleported through time," Wilcock explains, because Stonehenge is a time machine, like the Bermuda Triangle, except it's probably less accurate now that many of the stones have fallen away. Who knows where those hippies ended up? He then recounts one time a dinosaur was spotted by an explorer, clearly an ancient victim of one of these natural portals.

This is the most momentous time in all of human history, he tells us. The 2012 ascension is coming soon, and the extraterrestrials are making preparations for us. Apparently, war doesn't even work anymore – according to Wilcock's unnamed sources, America recently tried to invade Syria, but when they approached the border, they found that their guns didn't work anymore, their tanks wouldn't move, their bombs wouldn't explode. Likewise, Israel recently tried to nuke Iran, but they found that their nuclear weapons had been deactivated, as have all nuclear weapons in the entire world (this is, he explains, why the Cold War ended). I don't remember seeing any of this on the news.

Most importantly, the Dragon Family are, in the next few weeks, going to destroy the Illuminati. There will be mass arrests, and David Wilcock himself will be held to account in the international news for single-handedly exposing the information that will bring them down. In the coming weeks, he says, "I won't be able to walk down the street, in any country, without everybody recognising me." He isn't looking forward to the fame, but he'll accept it, as his dreams have told him to. And over the coming year, he tells us, we'll be seeing him on prime time television – he's working on a television project "starring alongside an A-list star" that's definitely moving forward.

"Don't put that on the internet, though," he warns again.

In the closing minutes, Wilcock invites us all to meditate. Still not wanting to appear conspicuous, I close my eyes and spend the time trying to process what the hell I just listened to. It's not like I'm going to be able to make a spiritual experience of it in my current state of discomfort, and with Wilcock playing what sounds like a kind of passable Native American sounding tune through some kind of wooden flute at his pulpit. After what feels like two months, Wilcock asks us all to stand and hug each other. As I'm hugging my neighbours I try to figure out which one had been doing all the farting, but I'm still not sure.

This wasn't over. I'd bought VIP tickets, and as such I was eligible to stay behind and participate in a Q and A session with our esteemed guest. The cheap tickets file out, and we are asked to fill out the DAVILD WILCOCK SURVEY, which I pretend to do. Then the man returns, and we finally get to move about the arena and choose our seats. I pick somewhere to sit that's relatively close to the exits, just in case everyone strips off their skin suits and reveal themselves as reptilian pod people.

This has been a true account, to this point. But I feel like I need to add another disclaimer right here, before you read on: Friends, I swear to God, this is something that happened:

David Wilcock, identifying primarily as a spiritualist, wanted to talk about the ascension, and thanked anyone who asked him a spiritual question. For the most part, however, everybody wanted to talk about the Illuminati and the aliens. So the first question leveled at him was whether all the aliens in the universe were humanoid.

He laughs. "No," he says, "that's just something I tell people to put them at ease." As VIPs, we were entitled to the real story, not unlike those who climb the ranks of Scientology and finally get to learn about Xenu.

There are lots of non-human aliens in the universe, Wilcock explains. "For one, there are the Mantis People. They evolved from insects." Apparently, they don't like to laugh in human company, because when they laugh, all of their mandibles open up and it's a horrifying sight, so when you tell them a joke, they bury their heads in their pedipalps and chuckle to themselves.

"There are the Fish People, too, and ones who have giant alligator tails that they use to lean back on." Furthermore, he tells us about a race of diminutive aliens who speak with cultured British accents, and wear Renaissance style clothing, complete with a hat with a giant feather on it. "The people of the Renaissance," he explains, "were actually copying the style of clothing that these guys wear. It came from them."

Somebody else asks Wilcock about the Hollow Earth theory. He shrugs it off. "I don't believe that the planet is actually fully hollow," he explains, "But I have heard that it contains a kind of honeycomb structure, and there are beings living within." The story of Admiral Byrd, whose flight over the Arctic (that never happened) bolstered the theory when he claimed to have seen through a hole into the Inner Earth, is a misconception, Wilcock tells us. What he was actually flying over was a time portal, and he was seeing back into the past. The questioner nods approvingly, and scribbles notes.

"Can any of the alien species actually shape shift?" someone asks.

"Yes," Wilcock replies, "but they are actually robots." He says that the White House has been having trouble with these beings, who are very similar to the T-1000 from *Terminator* fame, and can become carpets and furniture in order to spy on us.

At the end of the day, Wilcock, the former esteem-challenged fat kid, went on a diet and found his esteem in the art of bullshit, and earns his career separating people from their money for a few hours of charismatic science fiction. I lined up to get my book signed, and thought about what I would say to him when I shook his hand. I considered messing with him, telling him I was an Illuminati spy, or an alien in disguise, to see whether I could bring out the lie in his eyes. The guy in front of me nearly burst into tears when he met the guy. "Sorry, I'm a little star-struck," he explained.

Then I stood in front of him, and Wilcock's weird, spaced-out expression fell upon me. He was tall, lanky, his eyes wide and his smile compelling.

"Hi," I said. "How are you enjoying the country?"

"It's great!" he replied, and signed my book over his standing waist.

"You'll cramp your hand, writing like that," I told him.

He laughed.

Then it was over. I didn't mess with him. In the end, I don't think it would have mattered. Maybe in five years, when he returns to tell us about the impending alien return, Illuminati collapse and ascension of mankind set for sometime over the next decade, totes, for sure, I'll tell him then. It probably won't mean anything more.

# BIBLIOGRAPHY

I'm not a scientist, or a psychologist, or an academic, or a philosopher. At best, I'm an obsessive trivia aggregator. These are some of the best resources, both online and in dead tree format, that I devoured in order to put this book together, organised by author. They all provide a much more in-depth analysis of their individual topics.

**David Aaronovitch**

*Voodoo Histories: The role of the conspiracy theory in shaping modern history* (2009)
From the anti-Semitic paranoia that emerged in response to the *Protocols of the Elders of Zion* forgery, to the popular speculation surrounding "dead deities" such as JFK and Princess Diana, to the internet sensation that is 9/11 conspiracism. An intricate analysis of the modern phenomenon of secular conspiracy theories and their place in history.

**Michael Barkun**

*A Culture of Conspiracy: Apocalyptic visions in contemporary America* (2006)
The best academic work on conspiracy culture that I've read. Michael Barkun is professor emeritus of political science at the Maxwell School of Citizenship and Public Affairs, Syracuse University, New York. I nearly went crazy wading through the work of conspiracy theorists and crackpots over the past year, and I didn't go nearly as far into it as Barkun has. I applaud him for doing it so that others don't have to.

**Jason Colavito**

*The Cult of Alien Gods: H.P. Lovecraft and extraterrestrial pop culture* (2005)
An excellent and most comprehensive analysis of the history of pseudoarchaeology and the ancient astronauts hypothesis. Colavito makes the convincing argument that the fictional work of H.P. Lovecraft is the spiritual father and originator of the theories that authors like Erich von Däniken repackaged as science in the 20th century.

## Ben Goldacre

*Bad Science* (2008)
A highly entertaining foray into the world of alternative health and the quacks who push it. Goldacre is a British physician who has been attacked, sued, and defamed for his (incredibly patient and polite) arguments that things like homeopathy don't work. He stubbornly refuses to change his opinion.

## Phil Plait

*Bad Astronomy* (http://www.badastronomy.com)
Popular science blogger Phil Plait focuses his beam of skepticism on astronomical nonsense like Nibiru. According to Plait, "the universe is cool enough without making up crap about it."

## Jon Ronson

*Them: Adventures with extremists* (2002)
A very entertaining, gonzo-style adventure with conspiracy theorists such as David Icke, Alex Jones, and others. Ronson didn't know much about conspiracy theory beforehand, and so he provides a very unbiased, journalistic account of the phenomenon. The way that Ronson comes away from it half-convinced gives some insight into how professional conspiracy theorists can actually sound pretty convincing to the layperson.

## Carl Sagan

*The Demon-Haunted World: Science as a candle in the dark* (1995)
Probably the best known book on skepticism by the world's most beloved popular scientist. One of the best basic introductions to how science works and how we can sort rational ideas from nonsense.

## Michael Shermer

*Why People Believe Weird Things* (1997)
*The Believing Brain* (2011)
Psychologist and founder of *Skeptic* magazine, Michael Shermer, looks at years of study into the human brain in an attempt to unlock the mystery of why people become such dedicated, unwavering believers in pseudoscience, conspiracy theories and religion.

## Mick West

*Contrail Science* (http://contrailscience.com)
A great resource for anyone who is curious about how contrails work.
West is a pilot, and extremely patient with conspiracy theorists who
regard him to be public enemy #1 for spreading the lie that clouds are a
natural phenomenon.

## Chris White

*Ancient Aliens Debunked* (http://ancientaliensdebunked.com)
*David Icke Debunked* (http://davidickedebunked.com)
Chris White is a conspiracy theorist who does believe in the Illuminati
or the New World Order in general. I cite him as a resource because
these two films are nevertheless very well put together. While we may
disagree about whether David Icke is really in contact with spirit
beings, White's documentary nevertheless gives a very good analysis
of the genealogy of New Age beliefs from theosophy to Icke. The
Ancient Aliens documentary is a very valuable and thorough debunking
of the ancient astronauts theory and its proponents. Regardless of his
stance on other conspiracies, the information he presents is mostly well
sourced.

# ACKNOWLEDGEMENTS

I never would have believed that my first book would be non-fiction, or about science, or a comedy. With a drawer full of half-finished novels, I wasn't even sure there would be a first book. My mind has a very strange way of latching onto an obsession and refusing to think about anything else until a new obsession comes along and pushes the old one out of my ears. There can only be one obsession at a time, and it rarely lasts long enough to get a whole book out of it. This is the first one I've powered all the way through. Hopefully I'll continue to do so, as the next obsession is biting at my frontal lobe.

They tell you that you need a back door into the writing community if you're ever going to make money doing it. I found my back door without ever knowing that I had, around the year 2000 or thereabouts, when I became acquainted with an internet comedian named David Wong (the pseudonym of author Jason Pargin) and took a volunteer job helping to moderate his forums. Pargin is now the senior editor of Cracked, and my boss, having given me my first job as a writer. Editing for Cracked over the past few years has also taught me how to sort fact from fiction, how to spot inaccuracy in media, and how to write a book like this. This is, ultimately, their fault. So I'd like to thank them – Jason, Jack O'Brien, Dan O'Brien (no relation) and the rest of the team, some of whom I've had the pleasure of meeting and some I haven't. I'm not the only author who has found success purely because these folks believed in us.

Randall Maynard, who does the graphic design for Cracked, enthusiastically agreed to help me out with the cover art even though he absolutely did not have the time to do so. The result is phenomenal, so a giant kudos to him. Thanks also to the talented Mariusz Popieluch, who also did not have time to draw the character portraits in this book while focusing on his Ph.D., but managed anyway.

Generally, I want to thank all of my friends who listened to me ramble about conspiracy theories over the past year even though they didn't necessarily care. And thank you for reading it to this point.